Leon-Joseph Car

THE HIDDEN HAND OF GOD

The Life of Veronica O'Brien
and our Common Apostolate

Translated by Elena French

VERITAS

Published 1994 by
Veritas Publications
7-8 Lower Abbey Street
Dublin 1

Copyright © Fiat-Rozenkrans-VZW 1994

First published 1993 by
Librairie Arthème Fayard
Paris
France

ISBN 1 85390 227 6

British Library Cataloguing
in Publication Data.
A catalogue record for
this book is available
from the British Library.

Cover design by creative a.d., Dublin
Cover photograph by The Slide File, Dublin
Printed in the Republic of Ireland by Colour Books Ltd, Dublin

Contents

Part IV   **In Apostolic Communion**

PREFACE

This book is a sequel to *Memories and Hopes;* it is, in some ways, Volume II of my memoirs. It is about the hidden hand of the God of surprises, at work in my life as bishop. It begins with the years 1947-48, when I first encountered an evangelical movement known as the Legion of Mary, and met two very extraordinary people: Frank Duff, founder of the movement, and Veronica O'Brien, his envoy to France, Belgium, Greece, Turkey and Yugoslavia.

This second volume no longer deals with Peter's Church — the Church gathered in council — but rather with Paul's Church, the Church reaching out in its evangelising mission. The story begins, for me, in 1948, when I first met Veronica O'Brien. As I have said in *Memories and Hopes,* this fortuitous encounter marked a turning point in my life. It determined our joint apostolic initiatives for evangelical renewal.

I will begin with the story of Veronica's life — from her birth, in 1905, to the time of our decisive encounter, in 1948. These early years provide an introduction to, and shed light on, our fifty years of collaboration. This major surprise was to bring in its wake a stream of unexpected events. It is the key which will allow the reader to unlock certain episodes from the past and some of my dreams for the year 2000 — and beyond!

The reader will find in these pages much that is unexpected, picturesque, and humorous; above all, he will discover a living faith which dares to move mountains, and an active hope which belongs to the realm of the courage of the impossible.

Thus my *Memories and Hopes* become a Magnificat of thanksgiving to God and to the hidden hand of his love, always attentive, always faithful, always startling, concealed both in the *fioretti* and in the profound surprises of my life.

L.J. Cardinal Suenens
February 11, 1993
Feast of Our Lady of Lourdes

7

PART I

PRELUDE TO A MEETING
THE LIFE OF VERONICA O'BRIEN
FROM 1905 TO 1945

1

FIRST STEPS IN LIFE
1905–1923

I have called you by your name — you are mine.

Isaiah 43:1

At a meeting in Dublin after the International Eucharistic Congress of 1938, Cardinal Verdier, Archbishop of Paris, shared some of his reactions with members of the clergy. "In the Scriptures," he said, "the Lord asks an astonishing question: 'When the Son of Man comes, will he find any faith on earth?' Now I know what my answer will be: 'Yes, Lord — in Ireland.'"

These words come to mind as I set out to make known the role and the work of an Irish woman, now eighty-seven years of age, whose life belongs to her people's great tradition of faith.

In writing these first few chapters, which cover the period preceding our meeting, I have relied on memories gleaned from Veronica and from members of her family. I have also made use of an unpublished manuscript by Canon Cordier of Nevers, whose role in her life will be explained in chapter 5.

Birth

Louise-Mary O'Brien was born in Midleton, County Cork, in the south of Ireland, on August 16, 1905. She was the eleventh of thirteen children. She was baptised the following day; her aunt Louise was her godmother.

Some time later, the same aunt Louise decided to enter religious life – as a result of an incident involving her horse! One day, she was roaming about the countryside on horseback, as she often did, when she had to stop at a blacksmith's to have a missing horseshoe replaced. While the smith took care of the horse, she decided to pray for a few moments in the village church.

As it turned out, the church was crowded. Suddenly, from the pulpit, the preacher pointed at the congregation and cried out: "The Master is here, and he is calling you!" These words, she felt, were addressed to her, and challenged her personally. Deep in thought, she left the church, and went back to find her horse. Eventually, she decided to consecrate her life to the Lord, by joining the community of the Sisters of the Presentation of Mary, in Limerick.

Veronica's aunt Louise deserves an honourable mention in the opening pages of this book. On the back of an old and yellowed photograph – in which we can still see little Lulu, at the age of three, playing with her sister Joe – Louise copied out a few verses of the Song of Songs:

> So I will rise and go through the City;
> ....I will seek him whom my heart loves.
> .... The watchmen came upon me....
> Scarcely had I passed them
> than I found him whom my heart loves.
> I held him fast, nor would I let him go.

Beside this quote, she wrote the following words: "May this be a prophecy for my little Lulu." As we shall see, this prophecy has become an astonishing reality.

The name "Louise", which Lulu received from her godmother, appears only on her birth certificate: the family adopted the nickname "Lulu", which they still use today. Later, as we shall see, it was replaced by the name "Veronica", which she chose for herself, and which is the only one used outside the family.

Family and home

Lulu's father, Dr O'Brien, was a surgeon in Midleton, a small town in County Cork. The large family home, known as Midleton House, stood on a bend in the main street, beside a river. It was surrounded by a large garden, which separated the O'Brien property from that of the adjoining church. This garden was the doctor's favourite hobby, and his main source of relaxation; here, he had acclimatised exotic fruits and vegetables, built beautiful greenhouses, and planted vines. During the summer, three gardeners took care of the garden and arranged for the sale of seasonal produce on the market.

Lulu's mother, Kathleen Leahy, was originally from Cork. She came from a large, well-to-do family; she was distinguished and profoundly devout, and was careful to teach everyone in her household — young and old alike — to respond to the three tolls of the Angelus, which were heard, at noon and at dusk, from the nearby church. She also made sure that everyone was present, in the evening, to recite the Rosary. This was done kneeling in the drawing-room, or, when the weather was good, walking through the garden.

Prayers ended with a hymn, which Lulu always sang at the top of her voice — in her own unique way. Not everyone appreciated her enthusiasm. One evening, she invited her younger brother Kevin to accompany her to church for the Benediction — he accepted, on condition that she would promise not to sing!

Her reputation as a singer is confirmed by another musical anecdote from the same period. One day, at school, the students were all singing a hymn; Lulu sang with such gusto that the teacher signalled all the other girls to stop and listen to Lulu's solo. When she realised that she was singing by herself, and that all her schoolmates were laughing, she was so upset that she developed an inferiority complex and never dared to sing again — until one day, half a century later, at a Charismatic Renewal meeting in the United States, she found the courage to sing and to express her contagious love of God in loud and joyful tones.

13

Among her childhood memories, there is also the image of a priest whom she met every morning on her way to school, after mass, outside the parish church. As he passed, he never failed to place his hand on her head, smile, and say "God bless you, my child." This moment was a daily ray of sunshine which left its mark on the child's mind.

At home, the atmosphere was that of a happy united family. A few details provide an insight into the style in which they lived: meals were served by maids wearing white aprons and bonnets, and as soon as the children reached a certain age, they were addressed as "Miss Lulu", "Master Kevin", and so on.

The family were on friendly terms with a few neighbouring families of similar social standing. There were frequent gatherings — dances, musical evenings, games — for the young people, and Lulu always joined in enthusiastically.

First encounter with the Lord

Against this background of quiet family life, one episode stands out: Lulu's first communion, which left a lasting mark on her childhood.

Pope Pius X had just authorised children to receive communion as soon as they reached the age of reason. As a result of this pastoral revolution, as Lulu's seventh birthday drew near, she prepared for her first communion. This was a time of intense expectation for Lulu; more than ever, her family surrounded her with love and affection. At last the great day arrived. She and her classmates, all dressed in white, filed towards the communion rail. Suddenly, overwhelmed with emotion, she lost consciousness, "crushed by the weight of the love of God, who was coming to her, in person".

They carried her to the sacristy, where she gradually regained consciousness. It was decided, however, to postpone her first communion. She received it a few weeks later — not in the parish church, but in the church in Ballycotton, a seaside resort where the O'Brien family rented a house every summer.

To avoid an excess of emotion, the ceremony took place in private, and she received the Holy Eucharist in the sacristy; this time all went well.

The child's loss of consciousness was due to a supernatural cause, and one of rare depth. At the moment when she went forward to receive her first communion, she experienced a spiritual grace which was to mark her entire life. It is not easy to describe such an experience of being seized by God, and even more difficult to label it; God's ways are different for each one of us.

Half a century later, as we talked together about this experience, I asked Veronica how she remembers it now. She told me, "I received, all at once, without any verbal expression, something like a global intuition which opened my soul to the mysteries of God, of the Trinity, of Jesus, of Our Lady. In a way, I have never learned anything new, since then, about the life with God to which he was calling me almost irresistibly. I was in his power."

Seeking words in which to write about this experience, I asked her if such a global intuition could be compared, for example, to a seed which contains the germ of the fruit that is to come. "No," she answered; "it is more than a seed, because in a seed, you cannot see what is to come. If you want an image, I would say that it is more like a tiny apple, early in spring, just emerging from the flower on the apple tree. It already contains all that will grow and develop into the ripe fruit."

This initial grace was to mark her spiritual life for ever. Gradually, as we shall see, she went on to explore all its vital riches.

An impossible vocation

Veronica must have been seven or eight years old when she innocently informed her mother that she wanted to become a Jesuit. Her mother explained, very gently, that only men can be Jesuits. In that case, Lulu announced, she would marry a Jesuit. Her mother explained that this would not be possible either. Not to be deterred, Lulu insisted: "Well, if I cannot marry a Jesuit, I shall marry a priest." When her mother tried to explain that this too was impossible, Lulu burst into desperate tears.

A stained-glass window

In the church in Ballycotton, there was a stained-glass window which fascinated Lulu; it represented the miraculous catch of the apostles. To her, this was a call to become, one day, a "fisher of men," in the service of the Master. Jesus' promise "I shall make you fishers of men!" – was permanently engraved on her heart.

For Veronica, the Ballycotton stained-glass window has remained a source of fascination. One day, she thought she heard the Lord say to her: "Do not weep because you cannot become a priest; I shall give you a vocation to be a fisher of men." Recalling those early childhood days, Veronica once concluded with these words: "The Lord must have been quite distracted when he made me a woman; I wanted so very much to be a priest! "

The sacrament of confirmation – which she received from the Bishop of Cloyne, Bishop Brown, on May 4, 1918 – further increased her desire to become a witness to the Lord among people. On this occasion, in accordance with the Irish custom, she chose an additional name for herself: Thérèse, after St Thérèse of the Child Jesus.

A fierce independence

Lulu was always independent and impulsive, rebelling against the logic of grown-ups. "I could never understand," she said, "why loving my mother should keep me from displeasing her by stealing chocolates or apples or jam. I loved my mother with all my heart, but as for obeying her – that was another matter altogether. I could see no connection between love and obedience to rules. I could not enter into this grown-up logic."

It was much the same at school. Lulu refused to conform; there, too, she was impetuous, and rebelled against any constraint. She cherished her independence, protecting it fiercely, ready to pay the price when necessary. Faced with Lulu's consistent lack of discipline, combined with her ability to learn very fast, her teacher eventually gave up, and Lulu was free to read fairy tales quietly during classes, keeping her book discretely hidden on her lap.

16

Since she cheerfully disobeyed everyone in sight, she thought, quite logically, that she did not have the right to say that she "loved God". "In class, when we had to recite the Act of Charity — 'My God, I love you with all my heart, with all my soul, with all my strength' — I would keep my mouth shut, my lips tightly closed. I was afraid that saying it would be hypocritical, because I was so disobedient; I did not want to lie to God."

In a letter to one of her sisters, she gives a humorous account of one of her childhood "crimes". She describes how she involved all the saints in heaven whenever she stole a few juicy apples. "On Sundays, I sometimes stole apples from the garden," she wrote, "and I would pray to all the saints in paradise that I would not be caught. To be honest, it must be said that the saints took their responsibilities very seriously, for I was very seldom caught red-handed!"

Worse was to come, however: her determined refusal to obey grown-ups almost cost her her life.

It happened in Ballycotton, by the sea. Dr O'Brien had strictly forbidden his children to swim in the vicinity of a little island, where the tide sometimes rose very suddenly, and where the underwater currents were treacherous.

Lulu, who was then fourteen, was unable to resist the temptation to break this rule. To make things worse, she convinced another girl of the same age to join her in the escapade.

Sure enough, while the girls were playing in the water, the tide rose and covered the island, endangering their lives. Despite their desperate efforts, they came close to drowning, especially as Lulu's friend, who was not as strong a swimmer, clung to Lulu with all her might. Just in time, Kevin, Lulu's brother, spotted them from the shore; he had the initiative and the courage to jump into a little boat and rescue the stranded swimmers.

The next morning, the front page of the local newspaper carried the story in full; no detail was omitted, save for the names of the foolhardy swimmers. Lulu's father read the story aloud at the breakfast table, pointing out how wise he had been to warn his children of the dangers of swimming at that particular spot, and congratulating himself on his foresight. Lulu and her rescuer listened in silence, punctuating Papa's wise pronouncements with approving nods, their eyes fixed on their plates. It remained a well-kept secret — one which their father will no doubt discover in heaven!

Lulu's childhood held other crimes. I remember hearing about the clever way in which she avoided practising the piano — a daily chore which she reluctantly endured. Seated on the piano stool, she would keep her hands on the keys, playing a few notes now and then; hidden on her lap would be a book of fairy tales, which she read avidly, never taking her eyes off the page.

None of this prevented her from loving both God and her mother most tenderly; outwardly, however, her devotion was not obvious.

Given Lulu's resistance to all forms of discipline, her admission to the Children of Mary naturally presented some difficulties. The school chaplain had to intercede personally with the superior before Lulu was admitted. A compromise was reached: she was admitted, but the ceremony took place in private, during the holidays.

Conversion

Having completed her primary education in Midleton, with the Sisters of the Presentation of Mary, Lulu was sent to England to continue her schooling with the Sisters of St Clotilde, in Eltham, near London.

In one of his sermons, the school chaplain told the story of Fr Doyle, an Irish Jesuit famous for his self-mortification and his apostolic courage. Lulu was overcome with emotion.

On the day after the sermon, she was in bed with a cold in the school infirmary, and the nurse gave her a biography of Fr Doyle to read. Tears streamed down Lulu's cheeks as she read. The nurse found her crying and questioned her. Lulu did not dare to reveal the true reason for her tears, which was her own conversion, her desire to consecrate her life to God with a zeal equal to that of Fr

Doyle; instead, she told the nurse that she had terrible cramps in her stomach. The nurse gave her a sedative, and the patient immediately declared herself vastly improved!

Once the nurse had gone, Lulu was plunged into remorse for her terrible lies – for having refused to admit that the true cause of her tears was her love for God. Later, she went to confession, to confess that she had "betrayed and denied the Lord".

She once told me that from that moment on, as a result of reading that book, she "surrendered" to Jesus, saying to him: "I can no longer resist you, nor refuse your love; I choose for ever more to love you and to do your will, not mine."

For Lulu, the decisive turning-point did not take the form of a wilful resolution, but rather of a surrender to God's love, which relentlessly continued to overpower her. "It was," she said, "a total abandonment of myself to his overpowering love, which triumphed over every obstacle. I felt myself cornered into saying 'yes' to God. It was like the end of a duel: vanquished, I had to bow down before God's victorious love." Since that time, her love of God has never stopped growing.

During that same period, at a retreat in the boarding house in Eltham, she heard the famous Fr Mattheo speak of the love of the Sacred Heart. His sermon overwhelmed her. She ran to him and said: "Father, I want to love Jesus!" Fr Mattheo asked her: "What will you do for him?"

These words guided and enlightened her whole life.

Dance, music, tennis and apostolate

Lulu lived at once fully in the world and a thousand miles from it. She once explained to Canon Guynot, the first Legionary priest in France, how she lived out this paradox; he recorded it in his memoirs:

"I danced a lot, after I turned fifteen. I was quite young still, but since I was the eleventh of thirteen children, my older sisters could not very well leave me at home, and so they took me along to parties in the homes of our 'high-society' friends, as we said in those days. I danced with great enthusiasm, but I never missed a chance to speak of God to my dancing partners.

"As we waltzed, I told them of the joy I derived from my weekly confession; and, with a smile, I suggested that they should try for themselves and taste the same delights! I complied easily with the demands of social life; I danced well, but in spirit I was very distant both from the dance and from my dancing partner. I paid no attention to the man; I was always thinking of Our Lord and, in a way, dancing with him.

"I played tennis with other young people; but as soon as we sat down between games, racquets still in hand, I would speak to them about spiritual matters and engage in apostolic work. This was, in fact, my only reason for playing.

"I enjoyed singing love songs, but the love I sang of was not of this world; my songs were addressed to Our Lord. I wanted, instinctively, to be attractive – as every woman does; but my motive was only to lead my admirers higher up, to God.

"Once, during a retreat in the boarding house in Eltham, I even told my confessor, Fr Benedict, that I hoped to become an actress, so that men would be attracted to me, and I would be able to lead them to God. My confessor tried very hard not to smile; he calmly suggested that I should give up this dangerous vocation and serve the Lord in more traditional ways. No doubt, this was wise counsel; but the Lord in his mercy blessed my innocent zeal."

A letter to Mr Ogino

Lulu decided to write a letter to Mr Ogino. This was, to say the least, unexpected and daring, coming as it did from a young girl of fifteen. Lulu often heard her older sisters criticising the Church's position on birth control; they often mentioned in these conversations that the Ogino method was not really a satisfactory solution. Lulu listened; she only half understood, but she was anxious to defend the Church and to be of service. And so, without a word to anyone, she wrote a letter, addressing it simply to Mr Ogino, Tokyo. In this letter, she simply asked him to be so kind as to describe his method and send detailed information.

Years later, she told this story to a group of friends. Among them was Pierre Goursat, founder of the Emmanuel Community; he asked her, with a mischievous grin, whether she had ever received a reply from Mr Ogino. "No," she said, laughing; to which Pierre Goursat responded: "How cheeky of him!"

This little anecdote is not irrelevant: it was the first of Veronica's many high-level initiatives in this area. Half a century later, she was still attempting to find a way out of this impasse!

Stormy seas off the coast of Ireland

During her years in London, Lulu regularly came home to Midleton to spend the school holidays with her family. She travelled by sea; and one of her crossings almost ended in tragedy.

She was returning home for her Christmas holidays when a fierce storm broke out – apparently caused by an underwater earthquake. Many of the passengers were seasick; they lay on the deck, tossed from side to side by the rolling waves, which shook the boat violently, threatening to capsize it. The passengers' relatives waited anxiously on the quay. Several other boats were destroyed that night, and theirs too was given up for lost. They had left the south of Wales at about 11.00 p.m.; instead of arriving in Cork around 9.00 a.m., as scheduled, they finally docked at seven the following evening. As they were finally landing, Lulu overheard one of the passengers say: "There must have been a soul favoured by God among us on board, or we would not have been spared."

Years later, describing the event, Lulu told me that never for one moment was her inner peace troubled, or her union with God disturbed; for her, the whole experience was "like a honeymoon with him". Still deeply moved by these memories, she added: "Throughout the storm, I intuitively knew that the Lord would save us, and that he destined me for some mission in the service of the Church."

21

A stay in Paris

When she finished school in Eltham, Lulu secretly decided to enter religious life in the Congregation of St Clotilde. The Congregation's mother-house was in Paris, so she wanted to improve her knowledge of French. One day, one of her schoolmates showed her a classified ad in a newspaper: a family in Clichy, near Paris, were looking for a young girl who would be willing to take care of a child and teach her some English. Lulu jumped at the chance, and informed her mother that she was going to accept this offer and go to Paris.

Her mother was panic-stricken, fearing that her daughter would be lost, alone in Paris, with all the dangers that this implied. However, she was unable to talk Lulu out of her plan; so she wrote a desperate letter, addressed simply to the parish priest in Clichy, entrusting Lulu to his care!

Lulu calmly arrived in Paris, where she was met by a young man − all of her mother's worst fears were being confirmed! The young man, however, turned out to be a friend of the family she was to stay with; he took her to Clichy, to the very respectable home of the Müller family.

Introductions were made all around, and Lulu was shown to the maid's room − a small garret which made her shiver. Then she was asked to peel the vegetables in the kitchen; it was a disaster!

But worse was yet to come. When the time came for dinner − which she was expected to share with the servants in the kitchen − Lulu innocently showed up in the family dining-room, wearing an elegant evening gown. Mr and Mrs Müller glanced at each other in surprise, but they had the presence of mind and the courtesy to react by inviting the newcomer to join them at the dinner table for the rest of her stay, and by offering her a room in their own apartment. The tone was set. Lulu innocently showed them a photograph, taken recently from an aeroplane, of the beautiful family house in Midleton.

Then her duties were explained to her. She was to take care of Gisèle, who was about four or five years old; take her out for walks;

and teach her a little English. The days went by uneventfully. There was, however, a slight problem with Lulu's walks with Gisèle: curiously, they seemed to take more and more time. Finally, a relative who lived nearby was asked to clear up the mystery by following them discreetly. He soon discovered the secret: some of the time was spent in the Passionists' church on the Avenue Hoche, where Lulu would do the stations of the Cross every day, dragging Gisèle along to all fourteen stations!

At first, the Müllers found this excessive piety a little strange. In time, however, Lulu became a close friend of the family, and was able to tell them – much to their surprise – that she planned to join a convent in the near future.

Thanks to Lulu's influence, Mrs Müller began once again to practise her faith, which she had not done for some time. It was not long before the whole family found its way back to Sunday Mass.

Avenue Hoche

Lulu's stay in Paris with the Müller family was marked by a religious experience which left a deep impression on her. Today she can still point out the precise spot where it happened: on the Avenue Hoche, not far from the Arc de Triomphe.

She was about to cross the street when suddenly she stopped, as though struck by lightning, overwhelmed by a powerful spiritual certainty, which expressed itself inwardly in the words "God loves me, and he is all-mighty".

In some ways, this was a repetition of the experience she had had at the time of her first communion, and a renewed invitation to consecrate her life to God. The feeling of being loved by God was accompanied by an intense desire to make him known and loved by others around her. Now she had only to find a concrete way to consecrate her whole life to this task.

This experience on the Avenue Hoche merely served to strengthen Lulu's determination to present herself, as soon as possible, at the door of the mother-house of St Clotilde. She had confided her secret intention to a friend, Suzanne Benoit, who tried to dissuade her, saying, "How can you think of locking yourself up in there? You hate studying!" Lulu had replied: "The only thing I am interested in is the tabernacle; I couldn't care less about the rest."

Approaching St Clotilde

It was now time for Lulu to take the decisive step of presenting herself at the mother house in Reuilly. Her sister Joe was in Paris at the time, and met with her on the very day when she intended to do this. She told Lulu, "All French women have spiritual directors. The superior general of the convent is sure to ask who your spiritual director is, and what he thinks of your vocation."

Lulu decided that she had to find herself a spiritual director that very moment, make herself known to him, and obtain his approval. She had no idea what a spiritual director was, but she ran to the nearby Passionist monastery and asked to see the superior. "What can I do for you, young lady?" he asked her. "Father", she replied, "I would like to know whether I have a good vocation." He answered: "I'm sure you have an excellent vocation!"

They chatted about this and that for a few minutes. Only much later did Lulu understand that the priest had not taken her question very seriously. She knew so little about spiritual direction that she concluded, from this brief conversation, that the necessary decision had been reached. Years later, she told me that she thought a meeting with a spiritual director was something like an eye test at the optician's.

And off she went to see the mother superior. The mistress of novices was called in, and Lulu was questioned about her intentions, her qualifications, her skills, and so on.

The conversation went much as expected:
"And who is your spiritual director?"
"The superior of the Passionist fathers."
"What does he think of your vocation?"
"He says it is excellent."

These opening questions were followed by all the usual ones:
"Do you have a degree?"
"No."
"Do you enjoy studying?"
"No."
"Can you sing?"
"No."
"Can you sew?"
"No."
"Can you at least obey?"
"No, but I might be able to learn to do that."

No less surprising than her answers was the outfit which the future postulant wore to this interview. The time set for the meeting with the mother superior overlapped with an afternoon tea-party and dance at a friend's house, to which Lulu had gone appropriately dressed. She left before the end of the party; so as not to be late, she jumped into a taxi and went straight to her appointment with the superior general, who had certainly not expected this young woman, who aspired to enter religious life, to appear before her in a red and black cocktail dress!

Despite her outfit, and despite her answers, the overall impression which Lulu gave was a good one; this rather unusual postulant was accepted on a trial basis.

Her stay with the Müller family ended on a very friendly note; they understood her startling decision. On the eve of her departure, they kindly invited her to a goodbye dinner in an elegant and fashionable restaurant in Montmartre — a rather unexpected place, given the circumstances!

2

A VOCATION IN SEARCH
OF EXPRESSION
1924–1935

One thing I ask of Yahweh, one thing I seek:
to live in the house of Yahweh all the days of my life.

Psalm 27

PARIS

Postulant and novice —1924-26

On May 31, 1924, Lulu entered the Congregation of St Clotilde, in rue de Reuilly, to begin her formation in the novitiate.

From the very start, contrary to all expectations, she was seized by anxieties and doubts about her vocation. She spoke of these to the mistress of novices and to the confessor of the community, a priest of the Fathers of St John Eudes; they both reassured her and encouraged her to persevere. The young postulant decided to trust them in the darkness of faith. Outwardly, she radiated such joy that no one could have suspected how troubled she was.

She effortlessly accepted obedience to the rule. She threw herself wholeheartedly into routine housekeeping chores; indeed, she had to be reprimanded for an excess of zeal. On one occasion, one of the sisters discovered her awkwardly sweeping a long corridor, step by step, on her knees!

The period of her postulancy ended on December 8. It was followed by two years of novitiate, which began with the ceremony of taking the habit. It was on this occasion that the new novice chose the name of Veronica, which she has kept to this day.

This period may have seemed uncomplicated; but for Veronica, it was a time of anguish and doubts. Yet she overcame her hesitations, and took her first vows.

LONDON

Back to the books

At the end of her novitiate, Veronica was sent to Eltham Park, south of London, where the sisters of St Clotilde ran a boarding-school — the very same one she had attended. At the time, there were twelve nuns in the community which ran the school: six "choir sisters" and six "lay sisters", as they were called in those days. The student body comprised fifteen boarders and about fifty day students.

A major change had just occurred in the laws regulating English schools: according to the new law, schools were only eligible for government subsidies if their teachers had proper qualifications. The school in Eltham was in a difficult position with respect to this law, so Veronica was asked to undertake the studies necessary to ensure that the school would be in line with the regulations.

Sister Veronica immediately began studying, under particularly difficult conditions: Latin was the only subject in which she had some help — from a priest who gave her a few private lessons. She tackled the entire humanities curriculum by correspondence; she had no professor and hardly any books.

"It was very hard," she said later. "There were times when I would pray on my knees, crucifix in hand, to untangle some algebra problem or some abstruse Latin construction."

Moreover, she had very little time for private study; she had to use whatever time was left after school hours. This meant she had to give up the evening period of recreation with her community. As a result, her health began to fail, and she suffered from constant insomnia.

In spite of these difficulties, she obtained all the necessary degrees, one by one: first, the matric, then the bachelor's degree. She chose Latin, French, history and geography as her options. After another year of study, she received the Cambridge Teaching Diploma, specialising in psychology – which accounts for her interest in Freud, Adler and Jung.

Whilst pursuing her studies, she actively participated in the life of the school. She convinced the superior to make a number of innovations in various aspects of school life: with the generous help of her brother-in-law, she provided a tennis court and a stage for theatrical productions, and introduced dance classes. Enrolment at the school gradually increased to one hundred students.

During this period, Veronica's father died. She was unable to attend his funeral in Ireland; in those days, the rules of religious communities did not allow it.

An unresolved problem

Each year, for three consecutive years, Veronica renewed her temporary vows. Each renewal was an agonising experience. Once, as she was standing at the altar, candle in hand, about to pronounce her vows, she found herself unable to say the words of consecration; her throat was as tight as if held in a vice. Once she even had to repeat the entire ceremony in private, in the superior's office; even then, her voice was broken by sobs, but she did not reveal their cause.

No one was aware of her anguish, such was the joy she radiated outwardly – a joy that came from her unfaltering, trustful, filial abandonment to the love of God.

One day, Fr Benedict, the Assumptionist chaplain of the house, told her that he was struck by how deeply she had been influenced by Fr de Caussade's book, *Abandonment to Divine Provi-*

dence (which will be mentioned again later). She told him th...
she had never read the book, nor even heard of Fr de Caussade;
her harmony with him was innate.

Also among her favourite books was a popular work by Fr
Faber, the well-known Oratorian: *At the foot of the Cross*. Her
great love for Francis Thompson's famous poem, "The Hound of
Heaven", also dates back to this period; she knew it by heart, and
every line was a personal challenge to her.

"I suffered a great deal," she once told Canon Guynot. "This did
not keep me from being happy, but it was the happiness of suffering. I knew very well that I was destined to suffer greatly, and I
was terrified at the thought. But my fear disappeared when I
began to pray for the grace of loving my suffering." She obtained
permission from her confessor to trace a cross in the flesh of her
chest, as a welcome to all the sufferings she anticipated. As a further sign of her acceptance of suffering, in union with Our Lady
of the Seven Sorrows, she also inscribed the letter "M" — for
"Mary" — on her arm.

It was in this spirit that, year after year, she renewed her vows:
with "death in her soul and joy in her heart," as she said.

In the same spirit of total and irrevocable self-surrender, she
obtained permission from her confessor, Fr Benedict, to make an
additional private vow of stability. She promised, before God, that
she would never leave the Congregation of her own initiative, or
even voluntarily consider such a possibility — no matter what
happened. She did this in order to put an end to her anguished
doubts about her vocation; to burn her bridges behind her.

Her disposition was still the same when, on August 11, 1930,
she made her perpetual vows, in the presence of her family. Much
later, she was to say, "I felt like a consenting prisoner, enclosed in
a coffin which I myself had sealed, hammering in the nails from
the inside, in order to die more completely to my own will."

During the ceremony, Fr Benedict, who knew the price of this
spiritual self-immolation, could not hide his tears. No one guessed
why he was weeping.

An unsympathetic local superior

The headmistress of the school was Swiss; when new legislation required that all school principals be English citizens, she had to be replaced. There were only two English sisters in the community who could have replaced her. The superior general privately asked Veronica's advice before making her choice. Without the slightest hesitation, Veronica answered, "Choose the older sister." The superior general said, "If I appoint her, you will have much to suffer." Veronica was well aware of this; but for the good of the school, she stood by her first suggestion.

The appointment of the new English headmistress did, in fact, mark the beginning of a time of pain and suffering for Veronica. The new headmistress interpreted the health problems which Veronica was experiencing by that time as signs of mental instability. She therefore set out to persuade Veronica to leave the convent for health reasons.

Due to the fact that Sister Veronica was taking university courses as well as doing her regular full-time work, she was suffering from the effects of overwork, and her health was seriously impaired. She slept very badly and frequently fainted; in addition, she suffered from chronic tonsillitis and from mysterious toothaches. It was the chaplain, who celebrated the Eucharist each morning for the community, who finally discovered the cause of the toothaches: while distributing communion, he noticed a strange infection on Sister Veronica's tongue, and mentioned this to the superior. A doctor was consulted, and X-rays revealed the cause of the infection: during earlier dental work, a small fragment of an instrument had accidentally been left embedded in her gums! This was immediately removed. The doctors prescribed a month in hospital because Veronica's general condition was so poor.

In spite of these objective factors, which more than accounted for the state of Sister Veronica's health, the superior, still set against her, resolutely held to her own diagnosis: "You are mentally unbalanced," she told her, "and very close to insanity; sooner or later, you will certainly become completely insane. You have been a heavy burden to the community, and this is only likely to get worse. Leave with a good grace, before you are asked to go."

She once told Sister Veronica: "You pretend to be humble, but it is only because of your pride. The devil makes you ape humility, while pride devours you. You have no more vocation than this door." To the community confessor, she said, "Sister Veronica is very obedient, but her obedience is sheer pride."

In talking to the schoolgirls, she went so far as to insinuate that Sister Veronica was an unbalanced person; to Sister Veronica's family, she announced it in so many words. She twisted everything. When, after a brief visit to Ireland, Veronica brought back three postulants whom she had recruited there, the superior insisted that this was "unhealthy seduction". It became obvious that her diagnosis was as inalterable as it was inaccurate.

Eventually, the superior brought in a specialist from London to examine Sister Veronica's mental health. The doctor was unfamiliar with religious life, and had been influenced by the superior; he discovered signs of spiritual pride, and concluded that the physical symptoms were all imaginary.

Finally, faced with Veronica's persistent refusal to leave of her own accord, the superior called Veronica's sister, Kitty — who was a doctor — and asked her to take Veronica back to the family. She said to her, in these very words, "Your sister is mental".

Kitty found this hard to believe, but she decided to resolve the issue once and for all: she demanded a second opinion from a psychiatrist. She personally chose a reputable doctor, and the superior took Veronica to see him. The psychiatrist examined Veronica and concluded that his client was remarkably well-balanced; he severely and angrily condemned what he described as the unspeakable attitude of the superior.

The situation remained tense: due to her secret vow of stability, Sister Veronica continued to refuse to leave of her own accord.

Later, when the ecclesial superior of the community was informed of this, he declared the vow null and void. Inwardly, Sis-

ter Veronica felt relieved and liberated; but she decided to persevere in her fidelity to her religious commitment, until such time
as she might have an exterior sign that would free her. Smiling
and playful as always, she continued to hide her suffering; she
never complained or spoke of the tense situation.

Since the doctor had prescribed a full month's rest, Sister
Veronica's mother came to fetch her and took her to the seaside.
One night, Mrs O'Brien — who slept in the room next to Veronica's — was woken up by a terrible scream. Veronica was having a
nightmare. Later, she told her mother that she had dreamed that
a murderer stabbed her in the back with a dagger. Her mother
suspected that Veronica, tortured morally by her superior, was
under great stress. But question her as she might, she was unable
to elicit any information that might have set her on the right
trail. Not in vain had she once taught her daughter a little poem
about the courage of silence in the face of life's trials and tribulations:

> To play through life a perfect part,
> unnoticed and unknown...
> To write no secret on the face
> for men to read it there.

SWITZERLAND

A transfer

The interpersonal situation in London had become quite unten-
able; a radical change was essential. The superior general, who
respected and loved Sister Veronica, decided to transfer her to
Switzerland. Henceforth, she would belong to the community of
St Clotilde which ran the boarding-school in Aigle, near Lau-
sanne. The local superior was friendly and understanding, even
though she and Sister Veronica were not really on the same wave-

length when it came to the implications of the students' religious education.

Earlier, Sister Veronica had taken part, as a delegate, in an internal conference of the Congregation, where she had the opportunity to plead for a better Christian formation of the students. Her suggestions, which were worded carefully and with great tact (I have read the notebook which contains a draft of her speech), seemed far too revolutionary at the time, and were rejected.

At one point, the Congregation developed a questionnaire in preparation for the general chapter, which was to be held some time later. When the superior at l'Aigle received the questionnaire, she insisted — despite her own somewhat more traditional views — that Sister Veronica should answer it and freely express her own ideas.

In a spirit of obedience, Sister Veronica set to work. She submitted her result to a Jesuit father from Lyons, who was acting chaplain of the community during the holidays. He encouraged her, congratulated her on her apostolic courage, and told her "You must send this off just as it is. I imagine that you will have to suffer as a result, but 'it is fitting for one man to die for the people' (John 18:14)." These words remained engraved on her heart.

She was very much aware that she was fighting an uphill battle: in right-thinking circles of society, the time was not yet ripe for the changes she advocated. The negative response she received only served to hasten the new orientation of her life.

A mystical experience

On the night between September 14 and 15, 1935, in Aigle, Sister Veronica had a prophetic mystical experience which both prefigured the future and determined its course. This is the tale that sheds light on the astonishing events of the rest of her life; as it is pivotal to all that followed, I have asked Veronica to tell it in her own words.

"On the night between September 14 and 15 — feast of Our Lady of Sorrows — I quietly fell asleep in the common dormitory. At about two o'clock in the morning, I awoke with a start: an image, far more vivid than a dream, impressed itself on my mind.

"I could see myself, dressed in lay clothing, a flaming torch in my outstretched hand; I was walking this way and that, passing the flame from my torch to others. There were people of all kinds there, but mostly priests and religious. I could almost see their faces.

"I burst into tears. So as not to disturb my sisters, who were still asleep in the dormitory, I hid in the bathroom until it was time to get up. I prayed and wept, and the conviction grew steadily within me that I must leave St Clotilde to follow my own personal vocation of direct apostolate."

To understand Sister Veronica's reaction, it is important to remember that she had bound herself with a vow never to leave the Congregation *motu proprio* — of her own volition — unless she received an outward sign.

On the day after her prophetic vision, Sister Veronica received a letter from the superior general. In a state of intense emotion, she went to the chapel to open the letter in front of the tabernacle, asking the Lord to make his will manifest through this letter.

The first words to spring to her eye were "leave the Congregation".

The sentence was in the conditional; the superior went on to say "...if you are not prepared to change your attitude and your views concerning the instruction of the pupils...". But for her, the key word — "LEAVE" — shone as brightly as a star in the night, pointing to a new path. This one word gave her the inner freedom she needed; it brought about her decision to set out on a new path.

Departure

Faithful to her habit of placing the important decisions and turning points of her life under Mary's protection, Veronica chose to leave on December 8, the feast of the Immaculate Conception — a day consecrated to Mary.

Although she left Aigle and her past behind, she has always retained a special and faithful affection for consecrated souls. She deliberately chose to continue to use the name "Veronica". Throughout her life, she has kept the cross of her religious profession on her bedside-table; she kisses it fervently each morning and evening.

It is significant that, thirty-five years later, when Veronica wanted to give away a large building in rue Boileau in Paris, her first thought was to offer it to the Congregation of St Clotilde. Due to their declining numbers, however, the sisters were unable to accept the gift.

Although Veronica was moving to a different way of life, the call to a life of apostolic commitment remained unchanged in her heart; her apostolic life was to grow and spread in mysterious ways, following the pattern of the astonishing vision glimpsed on the night of September 14.

3

IN SEARCH OF A FULL-TIME APOSTOLATE
1936 -1938

God always prepares his greatest works in the dusk of faith.

Cardinal Danneels

LONDON

Waiting with Kitty

Veronica's ideals remained luminous and unchanged, but they seemed to entail an insoluble conundrum: how was she to devote her life totally to God, in some active service of evangelisation, while supporting herself without working for pay?

While she searched for a solution, Veronica went to stay with her sister Kitty, in her home near London. Kitty had been, in her time, the youngest woman doctor in the world: she had obtained all the necessary degrees and qualifications by the age of twenty-one. She was married to a Dr Frazer, who was also a physician. In this intensely medical environment, Veronica and her sister talked at length about the problem of birth control. Gradually, Veronica was able to temper her sister's strong criticism of the Church's attitude on this delicate and crucial matter; she persuaded her to promote the Ogino method with her patients.

Because of her concern with preserving a strong and vital Christianity within young Christian households, Veronica has been haunted by this pastoral problem ever since, at the age of fifteen, she wrote her famous letter to Mr Ogino. Her various initiatives in this area will be mentioned later in this book.

A penny pamphlet

Veronica was still in London when she received the rescript from Rome which released her from her vows and gave her back her freedom. On the day the document arrived, she went to the Brompton Oratory for the Blessing of the Holy Sacrament.

At the end of the ceremony, she paused at the back of the church to glance at a small display of booklets and leaflets; she picked up a pamphlet, written by a Passionist priest, about the Legion of Mary. She read it on the spot, from cover to cover, and copied down the address of their London office. A few days later, she went to the office and met one of the Legion's leaders, a distinguished young woman by the name of Mme de la Mare, to whom she expressed her desire to dedicate her life to full-time apostolic work. Much to her regret, however, she learned that the Legion of Mary makes no provision for full-time service; it expects members to offer a few hours of apostolic work each week. So nothing came of this encounter.

Messengers of the faith

In 1937 Veronica discovered a small association called the Messengers of the Faith. A brochure, published by the Catholic Truth Society, explained their goal, which was nothing less than to convert all of England to the Roman Catholic faith. In its early days, the group, which was very small, enjoyed the support and patronage of Fr Martindale, a well-known Jesuit.

Veronica contacted them, explained her apostolic ideals, and asked to be admitted, provided that they could guarantee that she would be involved in full-time apostolic service. They promised that she would. Very soon, however, she felt ill at ease in this pious association; its ideal of religious life did not correspond to her own. In any case, the ecclesial authorities dissolved the association soon thereafter.

Veronica returned to Kitty's house and continued her studies at the university; she had decided to obtain an MA in education, which would require two more years of study. She was, in fact, particularly interested in all that had to do with education; she wrote a paper on schools in Portugal, after spending some time there for research purposes. In later years, all of this was to prove very useful in her pastoral ministry.

Reminiscing about those days, Veronica said:

"As part of our practical training, we were expected to take turns giving public lectures on subjects of our own choice. I chose to speak on 'The historical role of the Jesuits in the education of the ruling class'.

"With some difficulty, I was able to obtain from a London library the Jesuit Constitutions, which were not intended for public consumption. I felt comfortable with the subject. I knew that in England, at the time, the prevailing attitude towards the Jesuits was an unfavourable one, and one supported by myths. But I had an idea which I hoped would surprise and amuse my audience, while at the same time shaking some of their prejudices. I had asked a well-known Jesuit, Fr Martindale, to attend my lecture in the university hall (incognito!) and – if all went well – to speak after me. We agreed that he should hide on the stage, behind the curtains, and surprise everyone. Fr Martindale had a good sense of humour, and he was willing to run a few risks; so he accepted.

"When I reached the end of my presentation, I asked my audience: 'Have you ever seen a real live Jesuit?' They answered, 'No, never.' 'Would you like to see one?' I asked. They laughed and called out, 'Yes, yes, yes!' I drew the curtains and said, 'Well, here you are! Allow me to present an authentic Jesuit, Fr Martindale!' The timing was perfect, and the surprise was a great success. The brilliant Jesuit improvised an excellent speech, which was very well received."

This was Veronica's original way of rooting out deep-seated prejudices; it was a worthwhile attempt to promote ecumenism, in those prehistoric days!

The *Handbook* of the Legion of Mary

A few months later, in early March 1938, Veronica attended a religious ceremony in her sister's parish, in the church of the Sacred Heart. The church was surprisingly crowded, and at the end of the celebration, she commented on this to the priest. He explained that this was due to the praiseworthy efforts of the legionaries of Mary. When he realised that Veronica knew very little about this movement, he gently remonstrated: "How can it be that you, an Irishwoman, know nothing about the Legion of Mary?"

The priest lent her his own copy of the *Handbook* of the Legion of Mary. It was about four hundred pages long; it was dog-eared, crumpled with use, and covered with handwritten annotations — "as unappetising as could be, in other words!" Veronica was to say later.

Despite all of this, Veronica began reading it that same evening. One of the first sentences went straight to her heart: "The Legion of Mary is an organisation which, thanks to Mary, has the power to communicate life, gentleness and hope to all nations, through faithfulness to its statutes and unfailing energy."

Later in life, Veronica was to say that these words had a profound effect on her; they determined the very course of her life. "I fell to my knees, and in this position continued to read the book until I finished it, in the early hours of the morning. But my problem was still unsolved: how could I be a legionary? Nowhere in the *Handbook* is there any mention of living this ideal full-time; no one is provided for financially, and members must earn their own living."

On the practical level, therefore, the problem of her vocation remained unsolved.

ROME

On St Peter's Tomb

Veronica continued her studies; but her future was still uncertain, and she continued to be haunted by her desire for a full-time apostolate. Her thoughts returned, again and again, to the evocative stained-glass window in Ballycotton; there, as a child, she had been fascinated by the image of the apostles who threw their nets out into the open sea in response to the Master's command.

Finally, she decided to go on a pilgrimage to Rome: she would pray on St Peter's tomb, and ask him how she too could become a "fisher of men". She did not have enough money for the trip, so she decided to drop out of the Masters' programme at the university and ask for her tuition fees to be refunded. University rules were very clear on this point: once the money had been paid, it could not be refunded. Nevertheless, she decided to try her luck; she wrote to the rector, asking him to make an exception and explaining the reasons for her request.

I have no idea how she argued her case; all I know is that the rector responded, with great courtesy and elegance, that (a) no exceptions could be made to the regulations; and (b) he would be happy to let her have the sum in question, as a personal gift. He wished her the best of luck!

And so Veronica was able to travel to Rome. Here, in the convent of St Sabine, she received an answer from the Lord – through her cousin, Fr Garde, who was, at the time, assistant general of the Dominicans. (Some years later, having been appointed professor of theology at the Angelicum, he supervised the doctoral thesis of a student by the name of Karol Wojtyla, the future John Paul II.*) Veronica went to Fr Garde for advice concerning her spiritual aspirations. He told her, "You must speak to Frank Duff, in Dublin. He is a genius of the apostolate. Tell him about your dream of life in a small community in full-time service to the Lord." He promised to

---

* Curious readers might like to know that the future pope got full marks for that paper – I have seen a photocopy of it!

write to Frank Duff personally, to introduce Veronica and set up a meeting. She took his advice; and this determined her future.

During her brief stay in Rome, Veronica heard of a religious association called Our Lady of Work, whose members wore lay clothes. She went to see Fr Creusen — a highly respected Jesuit who promoted this association — and took down the association's Paris address, in the hope that in future they would support the apostolate which was still her dream.

LONDON

A meeting with Frank Duff

Veronica's next step was to meet the founder of the Legion of Mary. Back in London, she contacted the spiritual director of the Legion in England, Fr Heenan of Mill Hill, the future Cardinal Archbishop of Westminster. She explained her dream of forming a Marian team: two or three young women, who would live together, and whose specific purpose would be an apostolate through the Legion of Mary.

Fr Heenan replied: "The ideal is magnificent, but you will find it difficult to win Frank Duff's support. Are you prepared to suffer?"

Veronica wrote to Frank Duff, asking to meet him. By return post, he set an appointment — not in Dublin, but in London, where he was about to arrive.

He was indeed opposed to the idea of a small team engaged in full-time apostolate through the Legion; in fact, he rejected it immediately. Between the two, however, a profound harmony emerged: they shared the same Marian spirituality, fully open to the Holy Spirit; the same desire to pray and to act out of prayer; the same yearning to witness to the Lord to the furthest corners of the earth.

At the end of the interview, they knelt together in prayer, renewing their act of consecration to Mary in the words of St Louis-Marie Grignion de Montfort. It was agreed that Veronica would go to Dublin to study the Legion.

4

GOODBYE TO IRELAND AND FIRST STEPS IN FRANCE

1939

Yahweh said to Abraham, "Leave your country, your family and your father's house, for the land I will show you."

Genesis 12:1

Goodbye to Ireland

Veronica returned to her motherland in November 1938, to make contact with the Legion of Mary; at Christmas, she would say goodbye to her family.

Her stay in Dublin was brief: she attended only one meeting of the praesidium*, where she was able to observe the principles of the *Handbook* in action. She was immediately aware of the energy and apostolic courage of the women in the group.

Next, she said goodbye to her family. Most of them felt that in view of the prevailing political circumstances, her departure was most unwise; but their attempts to stop her went unheeded. Only her mother accepted nobly the sacrifice which this departure entailed; coming as it did on the very eve of the War, it was a true adventure in faith, a walking on water. Concerned for the material well-being of her "missionary" daughter, she added a special clause to her will, giving Veronica the right to live in the family house should she ever need to. She left everything else in God's hands!

---

* The praesidium is the central unit of the Legion; at its weekly meetings, decisions are made concerning work for the following week

From then on, as far as Veronica was concerned, "her parish was the world". She was never to see her country again, except on brief visits. But in her heart, she has always kept her deep love for Ireland; and wherever she happens to be, she celebrates St Patrick's Day, March 17, with a contagious enthusiasm. We once asked her to put in writing, off the top of her head, her feelings about her country; this is what she wrote:

"First of all I want to tell you how touched I am that you should ask me to share with you my feelings about 'my home'. There's no place like home. And yet, to be honest and truthful, home is really here, right here where the Lord wants me to be. And the definition which I coined with Fr Guynot is just as beautiful and real today as the first instant we found it. He asked me: 'Where is your home?' And I replied: 'Wherever I am, I am with my Father, in the arms of my Mother.'

"So it will be a strange feeling of belonging and not belonging, but the first sentiment will dominate. I gave up Ireland with joy. For you, I gave up these windswept, strong, fairy skies, the silver lakes, the green meadows, the thatched cottages, the lazy cows, the bearded sheep and above all the old stock of peasants with their weathered wrinkled faces and their 'God bless you' ever on their lips. And Ballycotton, and that church high up on the hill, with its stained-glass window of the miraculous catch, where my vocation of 'fisher of men' was revealed to me."

Henceforth, Veronica's life would be spent in the service of the Kingdom of God, crossing all geographical boundaries.

First steps in France

Veronica deliberately chose to land in France on the Feast of the Holy Family, January 7, 1939. As we shall see in the following chapters, the welfare of the Christian family has never ceased to be one of Veronica's constant preoccupations.

Frank Duff had personally met with Cardinal Verdier, Archbishop of Paris, and obtained his authorisation to bring the

Legion to the Diocese of Paris. However, there had been no immediate follow-up to this visit. The council in Dublin had entrusted the task of introducing the Legion to France to an Irish legionary, Miss Denisson, who had done some excellent pioneer work in Africa. Since Miss Denisson spoke no French, Frank Duff asked Veronica to help her. He gave her enough money to live on for two or three weeks; beyond that, everything was left to the unpredictable hand of Providence.

At the last minute, Miss Denisson was unable to travel to France, due to health reasons. So it happened that, as a result of circumstances, Veronica was left on her own in French territory — although, at this initial stage, she had not been formally delegated.

She hoped to discover some community where she could live a religious life while at the same time devoting herself fully to the apostolate. She went to the association of Our Lady of Work in Paris, hoping to find both support and a framework for her life. Mlle Charrat, who was in charge of this secular institute, welcomed her wholeheartedly, and sent her to Normandy on probation.

Veronica did not yet attempt to establish the Legion of Mary. However, with the authorisation of the local bishop, she attempted to fill the gap left by some of the priests who had been mobilised because of the impending war. In one village, she brought together a few young girls and organised prayer meetings in the church. In another, she gathered together about fifty people and improvised a liturgy. She personally rang the church bell to announce this service — and learned at her own expense that you have to let go of the rope very fast, if you don't want to be swept off your feet!

During a sermon in a village church, the priest, who was responsible for several parishes, thanked Veronica publicly for the courage with which she had undertaken initiatives which went well beyond anything he could have hoped for. His words were so lavish in praise, and so full of enthusiasm, that Veronica was quite upset.

"I knew right away," she said later, "that my death warrant had just been signed as regarded membership in the community of Our Lady of Work, whose purpose was essentially social reform."

Sure enough, word of her activities, which were essentially and primarily of a religious nature, reached the community; and Veronica was asked to leave, for reasons of "incompatibility of orientation". Her final meeting with Mlle Charrat took place on October 7, 1939, the Feast of the Rosary. With tears in her eyes, Mlle Charrat told her, "You must leave us. Your vocation is not a social vocation, it is an apostolic vocation."

They parted ways in a spirit of friendship and mutual respect. Veronica's goodbye letter to Mlle Charrat ended with the following words: "Allow me to sign, just this once, the name I would have taken had I had the joy of making my profession: Marie de la Reconnaissance — Mary of Gratitude."

In the darkness of faith

This parting threw Veronica's entire future into question once again. As far as this was concerned, she was plunged into total darkness. In a letter from Angers — where circumstances had brought her — she shared her feelings with her sister Kitty. In this letter, dated November 4, 1939, she described her last meeting with Mlle Charrat, and invited Kitty to join her in silent acceptance of the mystery of God's plans for her future.

Her sister kept the letter preciously; it is reproduced here in full, including those parts which deal with family matters, since they too are significant and revealing.

November 4, 1939

Kitten Darling,

At long last a delightful letter from Ruth [her youngest sister] giving me news of each one of you and of her darling little Bernard. It was pages long, and I did so love even seeing your names written down on paper. One of the inconveniences of advancing in the love of God is that one loves those already dear a thousand times more. It is a wee bit disturbing in this life but, oh! what will it be like in the next, when perfect union will be the result!

Bernard and Anthony have now come along to rival the place Felicity held in my heart. I owe all three of them such a lot, but especially Anthony, for he teaches me so many lessons every day. I think of Joe and Chris, so ready to give their "all" to cure those little arms, and often I see her bending over them, trying with all her mother's love to straighten them out, with the least possible hurt. Poor little Anthony must think it all so very unnecessary, and so very trying at times; if he could speak, he would plead so to be left alone, for he cannot see into the future, nor can he yet understand that Joe's love for him is the cause of her longing to see him perfect in every way, and therefore the source of her courage to hurt him day after day.*

Kitten darling, I, too, am on the operating table, happily watching the great Surgeon's knife digging out and cutting away all in me that makes me unfit for the love of his Divine Son. In other words, I have to leave Our Lady of Work.

Since about August, I noticed that Mlle Charrat was a bit strained with me, and could not make out why, for she assured me that she was very pleased with my conduct. She seemed so sincerely fond of me, that it made it all the harder to understand what I felt was in the air. Finally, she told me on the October 7, the Feast of the Holy Rosary, that, in conscience, she could not let me stay on here, for she was convinced that I would do more good in work of a definitely religious character. It was a terrific shock and so sudden and

* Veronica's sister, Josephine Burton, gave birth to a child who was painfully deformed and crippled; thanks to their intelligent and loving care, he grew up to be not just an ordinary man, but a man of great learning and culture, and a brilliant student at Oxford. Mrs Burton told the story of this triumph of maternal love in a book called *Crippled Victory* (Sheed and Ward, London); it was translated into French under the title *Le combat d'une mère* (published by Desclée De Brouwer, 1962), for which I wrote a preface.

unexpected, but it was also the most precious moment of my life, for never before had I a greater sacrifice to give our Blessed Lord, and I think I gave it to him without a second's hesitation.

In a flash I understood those lines of the "Hound of Heaven": "Naked I stand before thy love's uplifted stroke, my harness thou hast pierced from me bit by bit, and stricken me to my knee".

In a flash, too, I understood the silence of our Blessed Lady in all the great moments of her life, but especially in the flight into Egypt. Aroused at night, told to fly across the desert into Egypt; not knowing where to go, how to go, how long to stay, she had to leave her little home and go off into the night, carrying her precious burden.

She asked no questions, she asked for no star to guide her, she asked for no miracle to make the journey easier, she had to leave all she possessed; and yet a single wish from her would have been answered on the spot; but faith told her she held all the wealth of the world in her arms, as she also held all the joy and the happiness, so what could she fear? And what need had she to question? God Himself was with her, and he was bringing her there, where she would love and serve him best.

Kitten darling, understanding that, I could not ask any questions either, nor could I ask for explanations, nor could I even in prayer ask God why, or how, or where, or for how long. Will you, too, keep that loving silence with me, and refuse entry to even one single thought of opposition, or anxiety or complaint? I do not belong to myself, as you know, but to our Blessed Lord, and he has all the right to move me about here and there, to take from me this, to give me that, but all he does is dictated by his infinite love, and one can trust oneself to hands that have been nailed for me to the cross.

It is just a month ago today I was told, and since then I

47

have had the great privilege of being in retreat for these precious four weeks; they passed like a flash, and now I am down
on earth again and making plans "just for today", leaving
"tomorrow and its needs" safe in the keeping of our Blessed
Lady...

I wrote to Mother the other day, asking her, too, not to be
tempted to question the future. God loves you and me and us
all and that is more than enough. It would be a terrible sin
against trust to doubt this.

I long to hear from you, heaps of news about yourself especially, and you know the "yourself" which mainly interests me.

All my love, to each and all.

Lulu

That same day — as one door closed, blocking the future in one
direction — Mlle Charrat handed Veronica a letter from Frank Duff,
in which he told her that her vocation was definitely a religious
vocation and not a legionary one. He suggested that she should
move in that direction, contenting herself with simply praying that
the Legion of Mary would be introduced to France and that she
would become an auxiliary member.

Veronica received the letter as a sign from divine providence.
She replied to Frank Duff that she would give up all attempts to
found the Legion in France, but that she would remain in that
country, whatever happened (for war was about to break out); she
would live an obscure life of poverty, solitude and prayer, trusting
in the Lord to provide her with shelter and daily bread. She made
a vow to live in solitude for three years, offering this sacrifice for
the birth of the Legion on French soil.

During this time, she experienced extreme self-abandonment in
material terms. She earned a little money by doing housework and
by giving private lessons; she had a small card printed, listing
some of the subjects she was qualified to teach. At noon, bowl in
hand, she would queue with all the other refugees, for her daily
ration of soup.

She rented a small garret on the eighth floor of a building. The landlord, however, was afraid that she might be a German spy; only a few days after she had moved in, he decided to evict her. During that period, anyone and everyone was suspected of spying; Veronica was obliged to turn to the Irish Embassy in Paris for proof of her identity.

As a favour, she was allowed to move into a garage — but what a garage! Every night, rats would feast on the vegetables which were stored there.

A change of heart

Meanwhile, Frank Duff had received Veronica's letter, in which she agreed to give up all active apostolate, and chose a life of solitude. Frank Duff's reaction came as a further surprise — but this time orienting her in the opposite direction. He wrote to say that his previous letter should not be interpreted as an invitation to renounce the apostolate, and asked her actively to promote the Legion in France, adding that not he, "but the Blessed Virgin, had chosen [her] for this task".

Veronica interpreted this call as a sign of God's will, and immediately set out on her travels as a messenger of the Legion of Mary.

A first experiment in Angers

Once Veronica had obtained the authorisation of the Bishop of Angers to launch an experiment, her first thought was to place her initiative under the protection of St Louis-Marie Grignion de Montfort by going to pray on his tomb in Saint-Laurent-sur-Sèvre.

In February 1940 a praesidium was established in Angers. It was supported and assisted by several people, including the Robin family; the early days were full of promise.

When the bishop died, however, the vicar general who replaced him on an interim basis revoked the authorisation, "in order to avoid hindering the Catholic Action movement".

In Dublin, there were rumours that the vicar general's refusal

49

was due to some clumsiness on Veronica's part. In an attempt to clarify the situation, one of the founder members wrote a letter to Frank Duff. This letter is particularly revealing of the atmosphere of distrust which reigned – quite understandably – among those who surrounded Frank Duff. And indeed, it was not easy to believe in Veronica's absolute faithfulness to the rules set out in the *Handbook*, given the fact that she had received no proper formation before leaving, and had only attended one meeting in Dublin!

The letter correctly stresses the impossible situation which resulted from the fact that Veronica had never received proper credentials. I reproduce the letter in full, because it highlights the origins of the conflict which was to block the admission of the Legion as an instrument of the apostolate, on the grounds that the Legion was not an integral part of Action Catholique, the only authorised organisation.

Angers, April 10, 1940

Please forgive me for taking the liberty of writing to you. Last Sunday, I was with Miss O'Brien in the home of the sons of Blessed Grignion de Montfort, and Fr Lemmens, whom you know well, said he would mention me to you as a witness to Miss O'Brien's admirable efforts to spread the Legion of Mary. His introduction allows me to tell you that it would be most unfair to believe that Mgr Coste's refusal was the result of some fault committed by Miss O'Brien, and that I would be greatly distressed if this were to happen.

After high mass on the Feast of the Annunciation, Miss O'Brien and I went to ask Mgr Coste for his decision concerning the Legion of Mary. He told us that this new movement of Catholic action had been submitted for approval to the general assembly of the bishops, and rejected for the following reasons: "It is inappropriate at the present time, and there is already great confusion because Catholic Action in France already encompasses so many different groups."

It would take too long to give you a detailed explanation of all the objections that are being raised.

The organisation of Catholic Action in France is highly hierarchical, and no French parish priest will undertake any initiative without first seeking his bishop's authorisation. As Miss O'Brien has already told you, there is at least one parish priest in Angers who was only waiting for this authorisation to set up the first praesidium!

For these reasons, I take the liberty of emphasising Miss O'Brien's unlimited commitment, her talent, her tact, her zeal, her self-abnegation, her unfailing perseverance, her profound and edifying piety, and the many other qualities which she has brought to her activities and which have elicited the enthusiasm of some and won the respect of all those who have met her in recent months. Everyone, however, found it surprising that she has received no official credentials from the Legion of Mary, introducing her to the religious authorities and in particular to the bishop! This is surely the main reason — and perhaps the only one — for his negative response. In view of present circumstances, and in particular of the War, such documents were more necessary than ever, and I think you should know that the absence of such documents has led some to suspect her of being a spy!

You can see how painful this situation would be, if she did not know that her somewhat foolhardy audacity is nothing other than a great love for the Blessed Virgin. It is only thanks to her filial abandonment in total servitude to the Mother of God that she was able to bear with such courage the ordeal of this refusal, which has also been a great trial for me. Tremendous efforts had led to such great hopes, all of them dashed by one word from a higher authority! My admiration for this strong Christian soul mingled with compassion in this misfortune.

I would therefore like you to know that Miss O'Brien is a

woman who is entirely devoted to your work, entirely committed to it, ardently desiring the success of your Legion. She certainly deserves the gratitude of her superiors and their greatest respect. I realise that their concern is for the continued growth and development of their work, already so rich in results. I know, moreover, that supernatural as she is, it is enough for her to be pleasing to Mary. Whatever happens to her, be it joy or sorrow, her response is always the same: Deo gratias!

Do not think for a moment that I am exaggerating in praising her so. I simply believe that all that this beautiful apostolic soul has done for the Legion must not be left untold. I must add that the ease with which she expresses herself in French, her intellectual and cultural qualities, and her emotional stability have all been most useful during the many lengthy discussions, and especially during the meetings, which were held strictly in accordance with the *Handbook*, with which she is thoroughly familiar.

In April 1940, the situation in the diocese seemed to have reached a stalemate. Veronica went to Saint-Laurent-sur-Sèvres for the third time, for a three-day retreat. She began this retreat on April 16, the anniversary of the death of St Bernadette. This date is significant because of the "coincidence" which later took Veronica to Nevers.

At the sanctuary, pilgrims were provided with a notebook in which to write their intentions. Veronica wrote: "Blessed Grignion de Montfort, please let there be a Legion of Mary in France, and let it bring many souls closer to God."

During this same retreat, a priest of the order of Montfort, Fr Dayet, mentioned a young convert, Simone Bienaimé, whom he strongly recommended; as Veronica had just decided to return to Paris, despite the threat of war, he gave her Simone's address there.

A praesidium of Polish airmen

In Paris, events suddenly took an unexpected turn. The story of the founding of the first praesidium in Paris is quite amusing. When Poland was suddenly invaded by the German army, a group of Polish pilots fled their homeland and took refuge in France, where they remained, awaiting orders to resume combat. During a service in a Paris church, Veronica noticed a Polish officer. She decided that if he came back the following day, she would speak to him. He did; so she waited for him outside the church, walked up to him in the middle of the street, and began talking to him about the Legion of Mary!

At first, the officer was suspicious and reticent with this strange woman who had accosted him; but he began to relax when she showed him her miraculous medal and the *Handbook* of the Legion of Mary. He knew very little French, but he managed to convey that he would come back the following day with another officer who spoke better French.

The man who came with him was Colonel Urbansky. He welcomed Veronica's invitation, and soon became the president of the first Polish group of the Legion of Mary. They held three or four meetings; then the pilots received orders to leave Paris for London.

They gathered one last time to celebrate the Eucharist in the chapel of rue du Bac; two of the pilots served as acolytes. When it came time to say goodbye, Colonel Urbansky said to Veronica: "We have lost everything; but the discovery of the Legion of Mary is a grace greater than everything...".

When the War was over, Veronica and the colonel met by chance one day, in Frank Duff's office; one can well imagine their joy.

In later years, the colonel arranged for the publication of a Polish translation of the *Handbook*.

The Polish praesidium in Paris, which had taken the name of "Our Lady of Victory", was destined to have a very brief life; but it carried within it the seeds of the future.

5

NEVERS – THE FOUNDING OF THE LEGION OF MARY

Difficult things can be done immediately;
impossible ones take a little longer.

Exodus and arrival

We must not forget that all of these incidents were played out against the backdrop of the horrific events of May 1940. The Germans were invading the Nordic states, the Netherlands, Belgium, and France; bombs were falling by day and by night; roads were crowded with refugees fleeing under constant fire from hedgehopping aeroplanes.

Where to go? Veronica decided to leave France and travel to Spain. Simone Bienaimé, whom she had met earlier in Paris, offered to take her to the south of France with her own family, as far from Paris as possible – despite a certain reluctance on the part of her father, who did not really like the idea of taking this "foreigner" along. They had been travelling for many hours – for the crowded roads made their progress slow – when they came upon a road sign that pointed to Nevers.

"That's where St Bernadette is buried," Simone said.

Veronica thought that Nevers was not far from Lourdes; so she asked to be left there at the crossroads. She intended to go to Lourdes, and from there on to Spain.

She made her way to Nevers, changing vehicles from time to time, only to discover that somewhere along the way she had lost her suitcase. The first thing she did when she arrived was to ask directions to the convent where Bernadette had lived. When the door of the mother house of the Congregation of St Gildard was opened to her, a distressing sight met her eyes: in the inner courtyard, next to a small reproduction of the Lourdes grotto, a group of frantic nuns was rushing about, piling suitcases on to a lorry that was just about to depart.

She asked the sister who had let her in if she could speak to the superior general; she was so insistent that she was finally allowed to do so.

It was a brief interview. The superior asked, "What do you want, young lady?"

Veronica replied, "I am Irish, reverend mother, and I have come to France to found the Legion of Mary."

"Well, young lady, you have certainly timed it well!"

A first encounter — and a first failure.

When Veronica learned that Nevers was the centre of a diocese, she immediately went to see the bishop and requested his authorisation to found the Legion of Mary, in spite of the War. This second attempt was also a failure: Mgr Flynn raised his eyes to heaven, told her it was quite out of the question, and suggested that she leave Nevers immediately and go to Spain before the German troops surrounded the city. Veronica asked him for a letter of introduction to the Cardinal of Toledo, which the bishop wrote on the spot*. This, however, was to prove quite useless: due to the bombings and the rapid advance of German troops, Veronica was unable to leave Nevers. She found temporary shelter in one of the city's schools — the Saint-Cyr Institute — which provided space for refugees in the empty classrooms, which had been converted into dormitories.

Veronica, noticing a priest among the refugees, asked him to celebrate the Eucharist. The priest accepted; but they had no hosts to consecrate. Despite the bursts of gunfire, Veronica offered to go to the convent of St Gildard to look for hosts. She ran through the

---

* In the archives, I have discovered the note from Mgr Flynn, in which he warmly recommends Miss O'Brien to the Archbishop of Toledo.

deserted streets and knocked on the door. A nun, fearful and suspicious, opened it a crack. In the end, she agreed to go to the sacristy and bring back some hosts to be consecrated; terrified by the continuing sound of gunfire, she quickly thrust them into Veronica's hands.

Suddenly, as Veronica raced back through the deserted park between the convent and the school, aeroplanes roared overhead, tanks rolled into the city, and the sound of machine-guns echoed through the streets. She threw herself to the ground and remained there, the hosts clutched to her heart, while bullets whistled over her head. Finally the gunfire died down, and she was able to regain the school building and give the hosts to the priest, who celebrated the Eucharist.

The Germans occupied the city and imposed their own laws, and daily life gradually became more ordered. Veronica started eating one meal each day at the Carmelite convent.

Two years later, Mgr Flynn, Bishop of Nevers,* wrote an article in which he described his first meeting with Veronica, and its outcome.

In the midst of the chaos and desolation of the exodus, a young Irish woman stepped out of a car in Nevers, not far from the tomb of St Bernadette. She wanted to travel to Spain, so she asked me for a letter of introduction to Cardinal Goma, Archbishop of Toledo. However, no means of transport was available, and she was obliged to remain in my diocese. She had no resources but her fervent faith, her love for the Blessed Virgin, a rosary, and a copy of the *Handbook*; but she immediately set to work, and despite unbelievable difficulties, she succeeded beyond all hope. *Deus incrementum dedit.* (The Lord made the harvest grow.)

* Mgr Patrice Flynn was of Irish origin and was born in France in 1874; he was ordained to the priesthood in 1898, and taught at the Catholic Institute in Paris from 1897 to 1902. After working in various ministries, he was in charge of primary and secondary education in Paris from 1921 to 1924. He was parish priest at the Madeleine, in Paris, from 1924 to 1932, when he was appointed Bishop of Nevers. He was later to become spiritual director to the Legion of Mary in France. Mgr Flynn wrote an important article about the Legion of Mary which can be found in *Lumen Vitae*, vol.8 no.2, 1953

I must admit that my initial reaction was quite cautious. I would have liked to be the last French bishop to promote this movement: my name, and my Irish origin, lent themselves far too easily to the suspicion of a pious collusion; and this was made abundantly clear to me! Nevertheless, I felt that I could not forbid one or two experiments. As it turned out, they were a true revelation. After fifteen months of tolerant neutrality, I approved the Legion for my diocese.*

Mgr Flynn's story does not mention the happenings behind the scenes which contributed to his decision to grant his approval and support. Veronica went to the Carmelite convent in town to ask for the community's prayers. The prioress, Mother Jeanne de Jésus, was much impressed by her visitor; of her own accord, she asked the bishop to allow Veronica to give a talk to the community. The bishop agreed, with one restriction: Veronica would be allowed to speak about Mary, but not about the Legion of Mary.

Veronica's presentation to the Carmelites dealt exclusively with Marian themes. Afterwards, the prioress wrote a letter to the bishop, telling him that the members of the community had been deeply moved by Miss O'Brien's talk; she herself had experienced it as a great grace (as she was to tell me personally, some years later). One immediate result was that the entire convent was consecrated to Mary, in the spirit of St Louis-Marie Grignion de Montfort.

Some time later, the prioress advised Veronica to knock on the bishop's door once again, and suggested that August 15 might be a good day to do so. The date was chosen shrewdly: the feast of the Assumption was also the bishop's birthday. It was an excellent suggestion; this time Mgr Flynn greeted Veronica with the words "I can say 'no' to Miss O'Brien, but I must say 'yes' to Our Blessed Lady: the Legion is evidently her work."

Thus the Legion of Mary was born in France, not far from the

---

* From an article by Mgr Flynn, *Revue du Rosaire*, special issue on the Legion of Mary.

tomb of St Bernadette. This was Blessed Grignion de Montfort's answer to the written request which Veronica had made on his tomb a few months earlier: "Blessed Grignion de Montfort, please let the Legion of Mary begin in France, and let it bring many souls closer to God."

As for the incredible difficulties to which Mgr Flynn alluded in his article, the story deserves to be told in full detail – but that would be a book in itself.

To help us visualise some of the external difficulties which Veronica encountered, we should keep in mind the situation created by the occupying forces. Nevers was an occupied city, where people went about with flashlights, unauthorised meetings were forbidden, and a curfew was enforced at nightfall; it was no simple matter to start groups and hold weekly meetings in the evenings. In those early days, there were serious risks involved in being legionaries. They asked, in the words of one of the Legion prayers, for "a faith firm and immovable as a rock". They did not pray in vain: they were a living illustration of just such a faith.

Obstacles

The first personal obstacle which Veronica encountered was her total material destitution. She was on her own in a foreign land, with no home and no means of support.

The community of St Gildard, encouraged by the bishop, generously offered her shelter, giving her the use of a room next to the one in which St Bernadette had died. This put an end to some of the problems Veronica had shared with all the other refugees: improvised dormitories in schools, overcrowding, queues at public soup kitchens.

One danger still had to be faced daily: the occupying German authorities. On every wall in the city, official posters warned that anyone caught giving shelter to a citizen of an enemy state could be sentenced to death. Veronica had a British passport because, in 1905, when she was born, Ireland was still subject to the

British crown. As a foreigner, she was suspect in the eyes of the occupying powers; she was required to report once a day, at an appointed hour, to the Kommandantur, where her presence was duly recorded.

In order to be less conspicuous, she wore a novice's habit, provided by the nuns; but this was not enough to guarantee her safety. One day she was arrested at St Gildard itself, and taken, under military escort, to be questioned by the local commandant. More than once, she was subjected to intense interrogation. In the course of one of these sessions, a suspicious policeman sceptically pointed out to her that she was a little old to be a novice. She answered imperturbably, "At my age, sir, it is important to give these matters serious consideration before making any rash decisions."

This satisfied them temporarily; but the Gestapo did not give up. Some time later, a group of soldiers burst into St Gildard and demanded to be taken to her cell. Veronica, alerted by the commotion, quickly hid her British passport in a jug of water. When the soldiers asked for her identification, she produced a certificate which stated that her place of birth was Ireland. She held her thumb firmly over the date of issue – this was definitely not a birth certificate!

The officer insisted on seeing the date of issue of this so-called passport. At the last moment, Veronica noticed that a stamp on the certificate bore the date "1937": it was the seal of the university which had requested this certificate in order to register her for an exam. She pointed insistently at this date; the officer was satisfied, and Veronica was saved.

A man whom Veronica had met at some of the Legion meetings caused another crisis. This man's wife came to tell Veronica that her husband was convinced that she was an English spy; he felt it was his duty to denounce her to the authorities. Veronica was only saved by the fact that during the following night, the man had a mental breakdown. He was taken away to an institution, where he remained until the end of the War, when he regained his sanity.

Gales and storms

The first major obstacle to the Legion's implantation on French soil was the very fact that it was imported from abroad — "Can any good thing come out of Nazareth?"

Another difficulty was its use of Latin words (praesidium, curia, senatus, concilium), which had been adopted in Dublin in order to preserve a common terminology even after the Legion spread worldwide, as it was expected to do.

The main obstacle, however, was the *Handbook* itself. Frank Duff had written it himself, over the years, adding to it as he went; pages of spirituality are deliberately interspersed with the most trivial administrative details. The doctrine of the Mystical Body is discussed at length — which was rather unusual in the pastoral literature of the time — as is the fact that the president of a group must speak in a loud, clear voice, or be disqualified.

No doubt we can find much to criticise in the *Handbook* if we refuse to see the forest for the trees; if we are unaware of the genius behind it, of the depth of his soul, of his openness and active docility to the Holy Spirit through union with Mary. The mistake which must be avoided is that of reading the *Handbook* as an abstract theological essay, rather than as a handbook for apostolic action — unique in many ways — inspired by a breath of life which was not only to open five continents to it, but also to motivate astonishing apostolic accomplishments.

It was unfortunate that a well-known Jesuit theologian — Fr de Lubac, who was made cardinal in 1983 — decided to make a methodical and violent attack on the *Handbook*. It appears that he wrote it in response to a private request and did not intend his words to be made public; however, this merciless critique appeared in pamphlet form and was widely distributed among the clergy. No matter; since then, our dear Cardinal has written such magnificent lines about Mary that Frank Duff has no doubt forgiven him, from heaven, for the earthly skirmish which almost put an end to the Legion of Mary in France.

For the sake of historical accuracy, here is the vigorous response which the Bishop of Nevers wrote and sent to all the bishops of France.

Nevers, May 1, 1946

Most Reverend Excellency;

The Legion of Mary is sorry to inconvenience you. It would like nothing better than to continue to grow peaceably, in France and throughout the world, and to be spoken of only in the context of the consolations it desires to bring to those bishops who find it useful to their dioceses. However, the stubborn opposition with which it has met since its earliest days in France has now resorted to such intense propaganda and to such discourteous tactics that the Legion is obliged to respond. The Legion regrets this and wishes to apologise for this to Your Excellency.

The various means of hostile propaganda employed against the Legion include a typewritten pamphlet, universally attributed to Fr de Lubac SJ, which is being widely distributed; in some dioceses, almost every priest has personally received a copy. In this document, the spirit of the Legion is falsely portrayed in terms that can only be described as unjust and injurious.

I am convinced that the author wrote those lines without intending them to be circulated throughout France and abroad, and without measuring the full impact of his words.

Moreover, by his own admission, the author's condemnation of the movement is based entirely and exclusively on a reading of the Legion's *Handbook*. This *Handbook*, a compendium of rules and pious exhortations, does not claim to be a theological essay of unfailing and rigorous precision. The tree must be judged by its fruit; we recognise the excellence of the great movements of Catholic Action by the works and lives of their members, not by their handbooks. JOC [Jeunesse Ouvriers Catholiques] is not taught by correspondence!

Even in dealing only with the *Handbook*, the author should have been more subtle in his analysis, and should have respected basic rules of courtesy. The problems of Catholic Action, of the apostolate, of the different roles of the laity and of the clergy, are far from resolved. In March 1945, the ACA very wisely pointed out that "the development of movements of Catholic Action forces us to deepen the notion of Catholic action." In deepening, we enlarge. Today we see, far more clearly, how other active or auxiliary movements have a role to play alongside our praiseworthy specialised movements, and we are more aware of the immense areas that still need to be explored.

Whatever the label one wishes to give to the Legion of Mary, we can only judge whether or not it can provide a service by looking at its accomplishments within its concrete field of action.

Be that as it may, I cannot leave unchallenged a choice of words which indirectly but effectively discredits nearly four hundred cardinals, archbishops and bishops of the Holy Mother Church. I cannot disregard the insinuation that these numerous prelates, as well as those thousands of priests who support the Legion, are encouraging "a serious deviation from the Catholic notion of apostolate"; a "systematic deformation of the Catholic meaning"; a "total misconception of Catholic Action, or a desire to destroy it"; certain "affinities with leaflets promoting pharmaceutical products"; a form of "publicity that is crass and phoney," all of it "horribly lacking in Christian spirit or in any spirit whatsoever," "promoting a general stupor of the Catholic people," and "leading to a considerable decrease in the intelligence of Christianity."

One can only be saddened by such tactics.

Like yourself, Venerable Lord, I would like to see an end to these polemical outbursts — the sooner the better. Nearly half the bishops of France have already authorised the Legion. Its members are overworked; they are in no hurry to take on new dioceses. It is obvious, even to the faithful, that each bishop must be the sole judge of whether or not this Marian work is appropriate, and that his acceptance or refusal must in no way trouble the peace, the charity, the perfect union of the various pious groups and movements of Catholic Action.

I believe I can assure Your Excellency that the Legion of Mary fully intends to remain in its humble place as an auxiliary movement; that it will continue to be respectfully submissive to the hierarchy; and that it will endeavour to provide service to all, without harming anyone.

Respectfully yours, in Jesus and in Mary,

✠ Patrice Flynn, Bishop of Nevers

In October 1940 Yvette Dubois, who had been the first to join the Legion in Nevers, felt a deep calling to share both Veronica's life and her apostolate. Veronica did all she could to dissuade her, because she wanted to be completely free to go anywhere for the sake of the Legion of Mary. "Even to the Amazon," she would say, "and even if it means running the risk of being eaten by cannibals!"

In a spirit of faith, however, she suggested that they should pray about this matter until December 8. She asked Mgr Flynn for his advice, and he persuaded her to accept Yvette's offer; he was convinced that her desire was inspired by the Blessed Virgin herself.

And so, for well over half a century, Yvette has shared Veronica's life, freeing her as much as possible from the ordinary concerns of daily life; her common sense, her self-effacing ways, her good judgement and her unfailing devotion have been a source of constant wonder, as they still are today and always will be.

In 1942 Veronica asked Yvette to go to Paris to take a course in social work — an occupation that is rich in apostolic possibilities. This would also enable her to earn a living: the Legion of Mary supports none of its members except envoys sent to introduce the Legion in a new country, and even these are supported only on a temporary basis.

To this day, Veronica and Yvette continue to be united in the service of the Church. They have decided to be buried together, in Nevers, where this deeply moving lifelong bond was born.

Our Lady of Abandonment

Several other young women wished to join Veronica, to consecrate themselves fully, with her, to the legionary apostolate. On September 15, 1942 a small Association was created; it was known as Our Lady of Abandonment. Veronica designed an outfit for the members: a black dress, a colourful scarf and a sort of scapular. It could easily be adapted to different circumstances, thus freeing the members from slavery to the vagaries of fashion, and giving them more time for evangelisation. When Veronica arrived in Dublin, however, she realised that Frank Duff feared "a take-over by nuns", which would detract from the lay character of the Legion; she immediately gave up the idea of these outfits.

Each member of the Association chose a new name for herself: Veronica became *Marie de la Reconnaissance*, Mary of Gratitude; Yvette Dubois became *Marie de la Confiance*, Mary of Trust.

Today, "free associations of the faithful" are recognised in canon law; they are suited to every kind of apostolic action, and are now free of the traditional canonical limitations which existed before Vatican II. In those days, however, they were unknown.

This little team, which never numbered more than half a dozen members, founded the first legionary groups in France. Simone Bienaimé joined them and gave of herself with great generosity; she later became the national president of the Legion of Mary. She was particularly active in the group founded in Paris among the Russian community, "Unhoped-for Joy". In 1950 she chose to follow a different path.

War and bombings

The picture would not be complete without a few words about the suffering caused by the War: the rationing, the lack of food, the arrests, the bombings. One raid which struck Nevers was particularly bloody and devastating; the building which the Bishop had provided for the Legion was destroyed. On the day after this disaster, Veronica wrote to Yvette Dubois:

> Oh! how fully we must take advantage of all this pain, and be deeply thankful for this chance to share the chalice from which Our Lord has drunk.
> I have sent a telegram to Frank Duff, asking him to pray for us. I cannot help believing that this terrible trial must be drawing to its end; let us then taste all the bitterness of suffering, to the very dregs. If you have a copy with you, re-read the *Traité de la vraie dévotion*, or the *Lettre aux amis de la Croix*, as well as *Abandonment to Divine Providence*; I think they are more appropriate than ever.

In another letter, she wrote to Yvette, about air raid warnings and nights spent in the cellar:

> I lack courage, as always; but I am happy that I have this tiny drop of blood to pour into the chalice of the great sufferings of the world. (July 1944)

65

Although Veronica lived through the calvary of war, experiencing pain and suffering with those around her, there was always a deep serenity in her heart. One witness wrote:

> Yesterday Veronica told me that she deliberately does not hide her fear during the air raid warnings, because she wants to appear to be "just like the others"; in the depths of her soul, however, she is perfectly calm.

A strange requiem Mass

Veronica knew that her mother, who was gravely ill, might die at any moment. As she was leaving Nevers to give a talk in southern France, she asked one of her close companions to open her letters, just in case.

She gave her talk in a large theatre. As usual, a break had been scheduled halfway through the talk, to allow members of the audience to write down their questions. During the interval, one of the Nevers legionaries telephoned to inform the organiser of the meeting that Veronica's mother had died.

The organiser told Veronica immediately. He offered to make an announcement to the audience and cut the meeting short, but Veronica asked him not to. She answered questions with her usual liveliness and enthusiasm.

The following morning, she took the train back to Nevers. The first thing she did was read the letter from her sister which supposedly announced her mother's death. Much to her surprise, she read that her mother had spent a good night and had "fallen peacefully asleep". The English expression had been misunderstood: the sleep in question was a healing sleep, not the sleep of death!

But legionary groups in several dioceses had already been notified; the bishop had already agreed to celebrate the funeral mass, and a large number of priests had agreed to take part in it; messages of sympathy were arriving from near and far, expressing the legionaries' immense affection for Veronica and gratitude to her mother. What was she to do?

She could have informed everyone of the mistake, and put an end to this outpouring of prayers. In a spirit of charity and tact, however, Veronica decided to remain silent; she allowed the requiem service in the chapel at St Gildard to go ahead, and left it to the Lord to deal with the tricky situation which would result should anyone discover that her mother was still alive! Providence spared her this problem: no one in France found out. Her mother died a few weeks later, on December 27, the feast of St John.

Veronica had last seen her mother in August 1945. She described that last meeting in the following words:

> I went home just for three days, which included the Assumption and my birthday. It was a tremendous joy for my mother, and I was so happy to go on a pilgrimage with her to that sacred spot where I received the holy waters of baptism. Oh! to think that I might not have been baptised, like so many countless millions! Luckily, I shall have all of eternity to pray and sing my *Deo gratias*.
>
> All my family perfectly understood that, above everything else, "I must be about my Mother's business," and they let me go away very generously, not even trying to hold me back another day.

On the eve of All Saints' Day (October 30, 1945), two months before her death, Veronica's mother wrote her a letter — the last one she was to write. It is filled with the love of a mother who fully supported her daughter's apostolate. She was deeply grateful to all those who welcomed Veronica so warmly — in particular to the Deslondes family, whose daughter, Raymonde, is still a faithful member of the Legion of Mary in Nevers. Towards the end of her letter, Mrs O'Brien wrote:

> May the Holy Spirit help you to melt and to set afire those souls that are frozen, or cold, or which distance themselves from the Lord.

She thanked God that she was still able to meet frequently our "unchanging friend, the Lord" and participate in the Eucharist once a week. Her letter ends with these words:

> The saints and our departed ones are a permanent link between us. May the Lord bless your apostolate!

A first assessment

There is no doubt that God blessed Veronica's apostolate, despite the War and the many obstacles she encountered. The souvenir album which the Legion's national council in Nevers presented to Veronica, in token of thanks, provides an insight into the early results of her work. This album covers the period from August 15, 1940 to May 26, 1947. The opening words were written by Mgr Flynn:

"To her who placed her trust in Our Mother. Good wishes and prayerful gratitude from the Bishop of Nevers."

The text continues:

> The curia and praesidia which helped to create this album would have liked it to hold all their memories of seven years of hard work and of the unforgettable devotion of their president. With this in mind, they have filled it with words that are sometimes awkward, but always full of deep affection. It would be almost impossible to mention every event in the struggle which has led to the birth of the Legion; it would be even more difficult to enumerate the countless blessings and special graces which each of us has received. May the Blessed Virgin translate the deep gratitude of all the legionaries in France into a harvest of abundant grace for Sister O'Brien.

This introduction is followed by a large number of moving expressions of gratitude to Veronica, the determined promoter of the Legion — which at that point was already active in about thirty French dioceses.

With some surprise, I discovered that this book contains a page in my own writing! It reads as follows:

> The Belgian Legion of Mary wishes to join with all these French voices in expressing gratitude to the one who brought "this secret of Mary's" to Belgian soil, in Liège, in February 1946.
>
> Since then, the Legion has grown. The one who harvests is seldom the one who sowed. Five dioceses have opened their doors and the harvest is already ripening. May Our Lady bless a hundred times over, with her most precious blessings, the one who dared to believe and to hope!
>
> L.J. Suenens, Auxiliary Bishop

Apostolate — a mystery of redemption

Fruitful apostolate is a mystery of redemption. The seed must die in the earth if it is to sprout. As Veronica once said, souls are won at the highest price. The secret of her apostolic suffering belongs to God alone, and we will not attempt to unravel it; Veronica concealed her suffering so well that one lady, struck by her liveliness and joy, once said to her: "It is very obvious, young lady, that you have never suffered."

When, at St Clotilde, she chose the name "Veronica", she accepted in advance the sorrowful stations of every apostolic life; she offered herself to wipe the face of the Crucified Christ, and to defy human judgement.

Mgr Flynn gave her a portable set of the Stations of the Cross, in token of grateful affection; he knew the special significance that this gift would have for Veronica.

69

At Veronica's request, Henriette Talabot painted a small picture which deserves to be studied in detail. It is entitled "Our Lady of Abandonment". A cross stands out clearly against the background; on either side, we see an angel: one holds the chalice of the passion, the other the crown of thorns. In the foreground, Mary, her heart pierced by a sword, extends her protective hand over a person kneeling before her; this person represents Veronica, clothed in a simple uniform, with Mary's mantle covering her feet. In Mary's extended hand is an open book in which are written the words *"Deo gratias"*, which she wants Veronica to learn and to repeat "always and everywhere". The word "gratitude" is at the top of the painting, dominating it.

On the back of the painting is a prayer, which Veronica wrote herself, and which further explains the message of the painting:

> My Mother, my trust,
> Give me all that brings me closer to you;
> Take from me all that separates me from you;
> Teach me to thank you for all that comes from you.
> Lead me there where I may love and serve you best.

6

THE WAR AND ITS AFTERMATH
1940–1945

A thank-you from Frank Duff

In a personal letter to Veronica, Frank Duff wrote:

> In your letter of December 29, 1943, you wrote that you
> were celebrating the fourth anniversary of your first visit to
> Dublin, and you thanked us for accepting you as a member
> of the Legion despite our doubts!
>   Don't thank us. You must know that it was the quality of
> your spirit that opened the doors of the Legion to you, or
> rather I should say that it was the Blessed Virgin herself
> who brought you to the Legion. You have done good work.
> As they would say in America: "Local girl makes good."

When Veronica returned to Ireland at the end of the War, Frank
Duff wrote an article thanking her officially, on behalf of the
Legion, for her work as the Legion's envoy to France. This article
appeared in the September 1945 issue of the international magazine *Maria Legionis*; it speaks for itself, and needs no comment.

> On the 3rd August 1945, Veronica O'Brien, our Envoy to
> France, arrived in Dublin after her six and a half years of
> thrilling and unbelievably successful work for the Legion.
>   The amount of effort and suffering that she threw into
> her mission during that time was immense — and it has

left its mark large on her. As well, she contributed the sort of faith (including complete trust in Mary) that moves mountains. All of which was necessary, for mountainous was her task. She was unknown, without a friend, and at the most critical time – and for a long time – without a penny. In addition, it was hard to convince people that the Legion was required in France. It was not disputed that it might be good in itself, but the argument was that all the apostolic field was already covered by a close-knit, highly-developed system of works – so much so that the advent of the colourful Legionary system could only have a disruptive effect.

That is the type of reasoning which has to this day barred the Legion from innumerable places – even from whole countries. While we do not agree with that line of thought, let us at least try to sympathise with it.

As an argument on paper it is undeniably weighty – and indeed to those who do not know the Legion it is a conclusive one. So, the more effective and attractive that you prove the Legion to be, the more convinced become those persons that the Legion ought not to be let in; because if it is bad to have a rival, it is still worse that the rival should be attractive.

This was the position that confronted our envoy in 1939. With supreme courage she set herself to the task of persuading persons in authority that they should give a trial to this new society. Her ardour was intense, but so were those obstacles which stood in the way. That she succeeded is testimony alike to her own force and to the apostolic spirit of those to whom she addressed herself.

At the moment the Legion exists in probably 30* of the dioceses of France. This is the work of five years only. Having regard to all the circumstances of the case, the fact

---

* By 1948, the Legion was represented in forty-seven dioceses. I must point out, in passing, that during the first two years of the existence of the first praesidium, four of its members entered the seminary as late vocations

of such a result cannot be accounted for by causes of the human sort, and we are thrown back upon the one and only possible explanation: "It is the Lord; it is the operation of His Blessed Mother."

But this latter explanation does not take from the contribution made by Miss O'Brien: it rather enhances it, for the heavenly force utilised and leaned on the human agency which was striving so ardently.

The appraising and recording of the work of Veronica O'Brien is a matter for a higher court than any Legion one — in fact for the Court of Heaven. But at the same time, it would not be right — indeed it would be unnatural — for the Legion not to place on record its appreciation of what she has done for the Legion and to acknowledge the greatness of its debt to her.

Likewise, the Legion includes in this expression of its gratitude His Excellency the Bishop of Nevers and those other splendid persons who collaborated with our envoy in the bringing to pass of all those happy Legionary events which have been taking place on French soil.

Miss O'Brien spent five weeks in Dublin, which should by right have been a period of rest, but were far from being such. She had much to tell, much to see, much to ask — all of which meant continuous hard work for her.

On the 8th Sptember she set off on her return journey to France. She spent some days in London, and here let us acknowledge the great kindness which the Legionaries there bestowed on her.

* * *

In an article in *Maria Legionis* (no.3, 1985) Enda Dunleavy, who was president of the Legion at the time of Frank Duff's death, informed us that on the very day of his death in 1980, Frank

Duff was preparing to tell the story of the Legion in France; he felt that it was an exemplary and challenging tale. Enda Dunleavy also suggested that Veronica, "in whom the Legion found its Esther to plead its cause in high places", should tell this story herself: "Some day, Veronica's story must be told in full. Perhaps she will do us the honour of telling it herself, through the pages of this magazine. For now, I will simply say that the difficulties she encountered would have crushed a less noble soul."

Through an intermediary, and with some delay, his wish is now being fulfilled!

Return to Dublin

Veronica's letters to her companions back in Paris, after the War, are like snapshots capturing the changing climate: the War had ended, and people were slowly beginning to emerge from their deep and paralysing depression. These letters also reflect the Ireland of that time – a country still deeply imbued with ancestral faith. I reproduce them here in full.

A first letter from London

Wednesday August 1, 1945

Dear Everyone,

Yes, here I am, in the middle of great big London, as happy as can be, having found that the Legionary family is as kind and loving and delightful here as it is over there.

But first, a few words about my journey. Thank you, thank you, for helping me so much! Monday was a dreadful day to get my last papers; the whole trip almost had to be put off.

At 9:00 p.m., in London, three legionaries were there to meet me — three senatus officers, all of them charming, welcoming ladies. Yes, the Legion is truly a family — and what supernatural love inspires its members!

They took me to Santa Maria of London, a home for "street girls". I was deeply moved as I walked into the house; they were all terribly excited at the thought of meeting someone from Paris. I had to put on my beautiful hat and give them all a chance to admire it.

The girls who board here are perfectly at home and very happy, but what a life for the two legionaries who live with them! A lovely little chapel with the Blessed Sacrament is a source of strength and good cheer for the two women in charge of the house, and helps them to cope with the constant tension.

I could feel a little of Our Lord's love for the "smallest ones" of His children. I would have liked to speak to them on my knees, I was so aware of the grace in them; the divine hovers throughout the house.

Finally, dinner with the big "officers", the treasurer, Mr. Morris. They showered me with questions, and I did not get back to my room until a quarter to twelve, by which time I was more dead than alive.

I have only one regret, and that is that you are not all here with me. But I have an agreement with my Guardian Angel: he will send you twice as many graces as I receive here, so open your souls! Mass this morning brought us together beautifully. The communion of saints is truly so great!

I am filled with good resolutions to love my gentle Queen very tenderly, during these weeks, so that you may find me a little changed when I return.

In Ea,
Veronica

A second letter from London

Noon, August 4, 1945

Dear, dearest Everyone,

I have lots and lots and lots of things to tell you (does lots take an apostrophe?). Apparently my first letter was posted only yesterday, so you won't have heard from me in ages. And will you be able to read this one, with the train going at such a mad speed?

My report for Wednesday and Thursday of last week is very simple: we talked of nothing but the Legion from the moment I arrived.

All the legionaries are really extraordinary women; they all work, and are only free in the evenings. There isn't a single Sr Deslondes. The secretariat only opens after 6 p.m., but the home for young women (here they just say "girls") is the main legionary centre.

I slept in the house both nights, to breathe as much legionary air as I could; so I was there for the Santa Maria praesidium.

It was all very exciting and interesting. You can feel the extraordinary apostolic spirit, and the intense work. Everyone had something to say, and spoke with a great deal of ease and liveliness. Some of the details were really very entertaining, and I can assure you that life here is anything but monotonous. You never know what's about to happen or what's about to land on you. One poor sister was crowned with a cooking pan by a slightly overexcited girl – and the pan was full of water!

A legionary seminarian was acting as spiritual director. There are five praesidia in his seminary, and he would very much like to be in contact with his confrères in Nevers. After dinner – which we all had together, like a sort of picnic, in the most informal and relaxed manner — the young spiritual director gave a remarkable talk on the Mass.

I am gathering as much information as I can about the organisation of this house, in hopes of having one in Paris some day.

Life in London appears to be completely normal, and food distribution is very well organised. You must have tickets for practically everything, but there is no black market and you can find most of the things you need. But there's nothing to be done about clothing, especially shoes and stockings. I may be able to get some tickets.

The Lord is good, so very, very good: once again, early this morning, Mass and Holy Communion, quite unhoped-for. And now I am not far from the port, where the boat is waiting to take me to Dublin. I am told that there is no hope of getting on board, but a certain Brother Raybaud, here in England, has given me a letter for someone very important who will help me.

Don't forget to write to Mgr Van Hee.

Thank you, thank you, and thank you again...

In Ea,
Veronica O'Brien,
unworthy legionary.

A third letter

August 13, 1945
Returning to Dublin after the War

Dear Everyone,

I write you such long letters every day, but unfortunately they all stay in my head, and I never manage to get them down on paper.

My days are incredibly full, and they never end before midnight. Despite this, I feel that I am still learning my ABCs and will never reach XYZ by the time I have to leave.

Mr Duff is quite upset that I have to leave so soon, and he is tempting me greatly to stay on until the last possible moment, since my visa is valid until September 26. But I'm quite determined to be in Nevers for the retreat, as agreed — not to worry — but I may get there only just in time for the first meeting.

Make all the arrangements without me; think of me as a guest who is coming for the first time. You may leave the afternoon meeting to me, however, because I will have a thousand things to say.

Here, the spirit is marvellous, and the Legion is the great strength not only of the city, but of the whole country. You cannot imagine all that goes on at the secretariat, which is hardly more comfortable than ours. Simplicity and poverty are the hallmarks, and yet there is an incomparable spiritual wealth. This struck me before, in December 1938, but my impressions then were quite weak compared to what I feel now.

I would like to bring all of Nevers, all of France, to share in my joy when I see all this love for the Lord. The crowds in the churches, so quiet and prayerful, are wonderful to behold; and it takes time and courage to go to confession, the queues are so long! I can assure you that there is no place here for scruples or moral dilemmas!

I plan to leave Dublin on September 9, but I shall give you more details in my next letter. In any case, write to me in Dublin, because I shall not be in London for more than two or three days.

In Ea,
Veronica

An important decision

Veronica chose to stay with the Legion; she gave up the idea of creating a religious association in rue Boileau. She informed her little group of this decision.

Feast of the Assumption, 1945

My dear Sisters,

On this feast of our Most Gentle Queen, I would like to be very close to you, for you will need to lose yourselves in the depths of her heart as you read this letter.

I am not writing to tell you about the legionary life in Dublin, which goes well beyond anything I had hoped for; nor about Mr Duff, who is indeed the man of God of our century. I am writing about that which concerns you personally: our Association of Our Lady of Abandonment.

Frank Duff will not agree to it; nor will the concilium. I am not the first to have come up with this idea of a sort of congregation for legionaries. There are, here and there, a few congregations founded by legionaries; but they are quite separate, independent of the Legion. Their association — not actually a "congregation", according to canon law — is not acceptable either. So those who desire this kind of life must leave the Legion and form their association completely separately; then they can work as spiritual directors.

So I must make a difficult choice and an important decision, here, on the spot. Frank Duff's arguments in support of his views are so strong that I must recognise their validity.

This is the time to practise true abandonment, and to say "Blessed be your gentle, your holy will!" I am in darkness, in the night, but our Gentle Queen is there; a little

79

longer, and we shall see her will. Prepare yourselves to want her will, to be ready for anything with her — to want only God. Do not ask about the future; do not seek to know what will happen to you. I will keep you informed of my future conversations with Frank Duff; I will speak to him about you in detail, and I hope to have something definite to tell you very soon.

And there is more: our habit, our dearly beloved little habit, has met with total disapproval... "All I have is yours." Oh, let us give her all of this as well, if we find that she asks us to.

As for me, it seems very clear to me that Our Lady wants me in the Legion, at least for many years to come. And now you must tell me where your thoughts are leading you.

In Ea,
Veronica

Thus Veronica opted for the Legion of Mary, despite the great pain and the many difficulties which this decision entailed, not only for herself, but for her companions; and despite the problems which it raised, as we shall see, concerning the house at 41-43 rue Boileau, in Paris. This house had been given to Veronica by Mlle Ardant a few months earlier, to allow her to continue her small religious association.

PART II

MILESTONES OF AN ENCOUNTER
1946–1948

The Meeting of the Waters

7

MILESTONES OF AN ENCOUNTER

1946: The Legion of Mary comes to Belgium

Early in 1946, Veronica came to Belgium to introduce the Legion of Mary. Once more, her first task was to find a bishop who would be willing to support this idea. She decided to turn to Mgr Kerkhofs, Bishop of Liège, who had been mentioned to her as the one most likely to be open to a Marian initiative.

"Would you be willing," she asked him, "to bless such an experiment, even if the blessing is only lukewarm? Would you open the door just a crack?"

Mgr Kerkhofs replied: "I will give you a very warm blessing indeed, and I will open wide the doors of the diocese."

The Legion immediately began to take shape in Liège. Veronica founded the first praesidium among university students there. She remembers her first initiative with some amusement. Since the statutes of the Legion of Mary require that the parish priest grant his consent before a group can be formed in any given parish, Veronica, faithful to the rule, went to call on the parish priest. With her was a male student from the university, who was to be the president of the group. When the priest saw them coming into the sacristy together, he welcomed them kindly, invited them to sit down, and said: "So you want to get married, do you?"

They had to disillusion him and explain the actual purpose of their visit. Before long, they had obtained his permission.

Other groups soon followed. Support came from various local sources, including the Congregation of the Daughters of the

Cross. A thank-you letter, written soon after these first contacts were made, indicates the warmth and gratitude with which Veronica was received.

Liège, May 5, 1947

My very dear Miss O'Brien,

Our Reverend Mother has asked me to write to you to thank you for your visit, and I do so gladly and with all my heart. We are all deeply grateful to you, and our Reverend Mother has found a way of expressing our gratitude in a manner which I am sure you will appreciate. She has had six masses celebrated for you and six for your faithful companion, Miss Schmidt.

It is a joy and a privilege to work in union with the Legion of Mary.

With all our best wishes, and united in prayer, I remain affectionately yours in Jesus and in Mary,

Mother Carola Mary, DC

Veronica's specific mission was to set the Legion in motion and hand over all responsibility to others as soon as possible, since her own work required her presence in Paris. At her request, Dublin agreed to send Henriette Talabot, one of her close collaborators in France, to Belgium. For the next five years, Henriette worked to expand the Legion throughout Belgium, both in the French-speaking region and in the Flemish region, despite the fact that she did not speak Flemish. Those who are familiar with our political divisions in Belgium will appreciate the paradox that this represented.

I was at the time completely unaware of these early stages in the development of the Legion in Liège; I had never even heard of the Legion of Mary. I came to know it through a series of chance events.

A sculptor from Bruges, a Mr Dupont, gave a copy of the Legion's *Handbook* to a lay missionary in his diocese, who was about to leave for Africa. He asked her to read it carefully and send him her reactions. The missionary was reluctant to take the *Handbook* along in her suitcase, so she asked one of her friends to read it instead and write something about it which she could send to Mr Dupont. This friend was a parish assistant involved in apostolic work; I met her in Brussels during a retreat, and she asked me if I would be so kind as to read the *Handbook* and give her my opinion, which she would then send to Africa, so that it could be sent back to Mr Dupont in Bruges. I agreed to be part of this merry-go-round!

So it was that the *Handbook* happened to be sitting on my desk when a letter arrived for Cardinal Van Roey from a Belgian communist, a recent convert, requesting permission to found the Legion of Mary in the diocese of Malines. I met with him on the Cardinal's behalf. He told me in detail about his conversion and said that if I required more information concerning the Legion, I should contact the national centre in Paris, at rue Boileau. The authorisation was granted, and I promised to visit the centre as soon as I had the opportunity.

Paris, 1947: First Meeting with Veronica

The opportunity arose on July 7, 1947. I was then national chaplain of the Raphaelites – a Franco-Belgian association of railwaymen – and I had been invited to give a homily in Montmartre, in Paris, on the occasion of their annual congress. In the late afternoon, I found that I had some time to myself in Paris, so I went to No.41 rue Boileau. I had taken care to announce my visit, and when I rang the doorbell, I was warmly welcomed by one of the leaders, Yvette Dubois. She told me that Veronica O'Brien had been told of my visit and was on her way from Paray-le-Monial.

We met late that afternoon. When Veronica arrived, I was immediately impressed by her efficient and practical manner, her way of concentrating on what was most urgent and essential to the consolidation of the Legion's position in Belgium. She spoke of the soul of the Legion — the living alliance between the Holy Spirit and Mary.

I noticed that she wore a ring on which was represented a dove, the symbol of the Holy Spirit, whose wings overshadowed a diamond, symbol of Mary.* This echoed my own episcopal motto: "In the Holy Spirit, with Mary." During our conversation, she spoke of union with Mary as an opening to the Holy Spirit. I could tell straightaway that she spoke from personal experience, and with a rare depth.

At the end of our talk, Veronica asked me insistently to go to Dublin, to meet Frank Duff, whom she described as a saint and a great master in the field of the apostolate. I accepted her suggestion, but I postponed the date of the meeting, to give myself some time to become reasonably fluent in English.

1948: Decisive meetings in Lourdes

My second meeting with Veronica took place in Lourdes, at the beginning of April 1948. I was presiding over a military pilgrimage of about one thousand soldiers, who had promised to go to Lourdes if they came back alive from prisoner-of-war camps in Germany, where they were held during World War II.

Veronica was also in Lourdes at the time. This was not by chance. On August 28, 1942, in a letter to Fr Guynot, she had written: "I have begged Our Lady to take me to Lourdes when I have definitely found my vocation." She had written similar words in a personal note: "I have asked Mary for the grace of taking me to Lourdes when I have definitely 'found my path', when I am indeed where she wants me to be."

She had decided not to go to Lourdes on her own initiative, so as

---

* This double symbol is today represented on the medal of the FIAT rosary, of which there will be more later in the book.

not to interfere in any way with any answer to her prayer. Our Lady of Lourdes took care of that herself: Veronica unexpectedly received a free ticket for the Dijon diocesan pilgrimage to Lourdes. A last-minute cancellation had made it available, and the leader of the pilgrimage, Fr Mathey, who was already very involved in the Legion of Mary, sent the ticket to Veronica "on the off-chance" that she might be able to use it.

Veronica saw in all of this a smile from Our Lady. She went to Lourdes and stayed there for several weeks, in order to found a group of the Legion of Mary. At the time of our military pilgrimage, she had just embarked on a first attempt with the approval of the Bishop of Lourdes, Mgr Théas, and she had hoped to find in him the bishop she was looking for, the one who would spread throughout the world, in writing, the supernatural insights she felt she had received from the Lord. One of the first questions she asked him was "*Monseigneur*, can you write? Do you like to write?"

He answered promptly, "No. That is really not my charism."

The only support he would agree to give the Legion was his benevolent neutrality and permission for her to talk to the parish priest in Lourdes, at her own risk.

She managed to extract the parish priest's consent by the most original means, through an expedient that really belongs to the realm of the courage of the impossible.

One Saturday afternoon, Veronica, having gone to confession to the chaplain of the convent where she was staying, went to the presbytery once again, in search of the parish priest. She had already attempted, in vain, to see him: clearly, there were instructions that he should not be disturbed by unwelcome visitors. This second attempt failed as well: she was told that he was hearing confessions in the church.

So Veronica went off to the church. There was a long queue of penitents in front of the confessional, and she joined them and waited nervously.

At long last it was her turn.

THE PRIEST: "When was your last confession?"
VERONICA: "An hour ago, Father."
We shall never know what thoughts crossed the priest's mind at that moment. Veronica did not wait to find out; she immediately explained to him that she had received the bishop's permission to found the Legion in Lourdes, but that he had left it to her to convince the local priests. With intense emotion, she told him that Our Lady would be so happy if he would only agree to found one experimental group, and she begged his forgiveness for being so very bold!

The priest was won over by her apostolic courage, and the first parish group was founded with his very faithful support, as I was later able to see for myself.

I saw Veronica in the intervals between spiritual exercises with the military pilgrims. It was impossible to have a quiet conversation in a hotel lounge, and so, on various pretexts, we met in different convent parlours in Lourdes. We talked at great length; our conversations, in which her life and her soul were revealed to me, reached deeper and deeper levels.

One morning, on our way, we met Mgr Théas. I had been told that he did not look with favour upon the Legion, nor upon its delegate. He stopped to greet us, and said to me, with a big smile, "Miss O'Brien is not very pleased with me, but I am very pleased with her." He had evidently been struck by Veronica's spiritual depth, even though she had not succeeded in convincing him to support the Legion.

In spiritual communion with St Paul

During one of our conversations, Veronica told me that she loved St Paul with a very special love and that she lived in a kind of unique and continuous spiritual communion with him. One evening, while she was praying in the grotto, her fear that she might be deluding herself led her to beg him for some sign to confirm this inner presence. It was pouring rain. With some difficulty, Veronica opened her bible at random, protecting it beneath the folds of her cape, and, under the pelting raindrops, read a few verses from the Letter to the Colossians – Col 2:5. With deep emotion and intense gratitude, she received the words that St Paul had written to the Colossians: "I may be absent in body, but in spirit I am there among you, delighted to find you all in harmony and to see how firm your faith in Christ is."

One day this familiarity with St Paul, this mysterious spiritual telepathy, inspired her to ask him a precise and practical question. In prayer, she told him that she needed the visible, constant and concrete assistance of a bishop who could help her, here on earth, to transmit the graces that she felt she was receiving for the Church. She asked St Paul to help her to meet "a bishop who could write".

Only later did I understand why she had asked me so urgently, almost as soon as we met, "Can you write?"

I told her that I had never published anything but a brief essay entitled "Easter, the Centre of the Church's Devotion" and a few articles for newspapers and magazines; but I added that I enjoyed writing. Little did I know what consequences this was to have! I had no idea that I was to write more than thirty books, nor that one day the Académie Française would award me, for my writings, the Grand Prix de la Francophonie – which was both a great grace and a great surprise!

The outpouring of the Spirit

Our conversations in Lourdes opened new perspectives for me, and determined the direction of my pastoral ministry and of my future literary efforts. On a personal level, those days were extremely significant for me. On the last day – or, to be more precise, during the last night – which I spent in my hotel room in Lourdes, the Lord poured out his grace on me, in a way that marked my life for ever. What I experienced was an outpouring of the Spirit, a "baptism in the Spirit".

In those days, these were not familiar terms. Twenty years later, the Charismatic Renewal, beginning in the United States, spread and multiplied such experiences. Since that time, there have been countless testimonies, on every continent, to the fact that the Holy Spirit is even now at work with his gifts and charisms. The manner in which the Spirit takes hold of each person varies. But the one who experiences this comes closer to understanding St Paul's words: "It is no longer I who live, but Christ who lives in me." In extreme cases, the experience is not unlike that of being mysteriously emptied of self; of changing identity. Since the Renewal began, there have been innumerable witnesses to this.*

This mysterious experience of being seized by God varies in its duration and in its intensity. In my case, the full intensity lasted for about eight days, then began to fade. But this allowed me a glimpse, for a fleeting moment, of what it might be like to live in constant and conscious union with God – such a union as I have since discovered within Veronica's soul every day. Her original experience dates back to her first communion; it has continued throughout her life, to this day, with amazing constancy.

I also came to understand, once and for all, that there are not two Churches – one institutional, the other charismatic. There is only one Church with a double dimension, visible and invisible; and I came to understand that the fusion of the two is vital to the very mission of the Church.

In later years, during the Vatican Council, I had to plead the cause of the reality of charisms in God's Church today. The days I spent in Lourdes were, to me, an intensely experienced call never to separate those aspects which God has united, and an invitation to clarify the consequences of this unity.

---

* See, for example, *Pretres du Seigneur, témoins du Seigneur*, published by Pneumatique, Paris, 1981. An interesting book has also been published recently, in the United States, on the occasion of the twenty-fifth anniversary of the famous retreat at Duquesne University. At the time, one of the students in the group, Patty Mansfield Gallagher, edited a book of testimonies from the participants. On one of my visits to the US, she told me about the event, and added that she was reassured when she discovered the Vatican II document on the presence of charisms today. In memory of our conversation, she asked me to write a preface to the memorial volume, which has an introduction by Bishop Sam Jacobs, the American bishop in charge of the Renewal. The book is called *As by a New Pentecost;* it is published by the Franciscan Press at Steubenville University.

A key letter and its results

On my return from Lourdes, I received a letter from Veronica, written in Toulouse and dated April 15, 1948. Later I learned that she had written it in the chapel of the convent of Marie Réparatrice, in front of the Blessed Sacrament. She wrote:

> I am frightened and overwhelmed by all that has just happened. Nothing is more impressive than letting oneself be guided gently by Divine Providence, but there are moments when one feels crushed by the greatness of God's plan, which tends to make wonders out of nothing – on condition that those nothings let themselves be guided and so enter fully into the magnificent plan of the Master of the Universe. I feel that I am at such a moment.
>
> I discover in my soul an extraordinary union with you, a deep affinity and understanding, as though in some way I had been made for you. It is terribly daring to be thinking and writing such thoughts, but I am doing it very naturally. Is this an illusion? I don't think so, because at the same time, I am overflowing with insights about Our Blessed Lady and about what She will do, in you and through you, if you humbly and meekly receive from the hands of her poor little servant what She is putting into them. And She will put so, so, so much!
>
> I will be the insignificant and worthless child bringing five loaves and two fishes to the great Master, and with that He will feed the five thousand, and the many thousands of souls who are hungry.
>
> Would you, for your part, listen carefully to the whispering of grace in your soul, and see if it invites you to that sort of mystical alliance with me?

The field of my apostolate is the whole universe. With a handful of souls, I want to work for the conversion of the masses that Leo XIII dreamed of. Satan is trying to strangle me before I can communicate this "Secret of Mary". I dare to say that I have been chosen by Our Blessed Lady to communicate this atomic energy to the Church!

I was immediately aware of the sacred and solemn nature of this request. I understood at once that her offer represented a unique call from God, and I was reminded of something Claudel once wrote: "There are some things so sacred that they can only be asked once."

I did not keep a copy of my answer, but I have found her reaction to it.

Letter from Veronica, April 26, 1948

Yes, it is wonderful, isn't it?
My hands were shaking this morning, as I opened your letter; my own had been so bold, and any "sensible" person would have been horrified by it. But now — *Deo gratias*, a thousand thousand times. The other night, I was so afraid that I was fooling myself, so afraid of stealing something of you for myself, that I told the Lord of my fears, and I had a feeling that Jesus answered me, very tenderly, "I trust you." Oh, I do not want to betray that trust!

Letter from Veronica, May 12, 1948

In this letter, Veronica emphasised the importance of my exploratory trip to Dublin, and encouraged me to take an intensive course in English.

Your days there will be for you a Pentecost, a retreat, a time of Marian consecration, and I am preparing for them with you.

93

If you are faithful to the call of grace, the Lord will do unheard-of things in you and through you. Prepare for them with your heart, forgetting all your spirituality, all your methods, every kind of knowledge, other than Mary.

You must be Mary, so that Jesus may be at ease in you; be Mary to see Him, to serve Him and to love Him passionately, everywhere, everywhere; and above all, be Mary to receive the Holy Spirit, for this is your very reason for existing.

Your time in Dublin will be a time of incalculable importance for the Church, and you must also prepare for it with your mind, by studying English for hours and hours. It will be a grace that you must make known. It is very dangerous to keep a grace for oneself: you can only have it yourself by giving it to others. *Nunc cœpi.*"

Letter from Veronica, August 14, 1948

In a letter dated August 14, 1948, Veronica called upon me to live the present moment in faith, according to Fr de Caussade's doctrine of "abandonment to Divine Providence". The book of this title is particularly dear to Veronica, and she has promoted it throughout her life.

I have an even greater desire to know that you have entered even further into detachment and absolute abandonment of the future to God's will, never allowing yourself a single wilful thought that has no actual usefulness in the present moment. May your fondest aspirations always be infused with the feelings expressed in the words, "May your sweet and holy Will be done." We must take the utmost care to avoid meddling even the slightest bit, even in thought, with future divine action; for this takes us away from our duty of the present moment, which is nothing but to breathe Mary and to breathe the Holy Spirit — now, now.

Letter from Veronica, November 22, 1948

This letter further clarifies the meaning of our alliance, and indicates Veronica's desire to be an instrument of grace for the full development of my episcopal vocation.

I am answering by return post to try to tell you immediately how humbled and touched I am by this mission that our gentle Queen is entrusting to me. I take this very seriously, and I promise you, before Her, with the help of Her grace, to do my best to help you understand your vocation better, and follow it better, day by day.

Your supernatural success will be one of the main goals of my life, motivating me at every moment to be a docile instrument in the hands of my gentle Queen, so that, through me, She herself may guide you.

She has given you so many natural and supernatural gifts; it is primarily to keep you in a spirit of great humility and simplicity, of spirit and of heart, that She inspires you to continue this relationship with me, however unsettling it may be.

I do believe very truly that it is my tactfulness and faithfulness in the small things of daily life, and the constant renewal of my union with Mary, which will be the main instruments of my apostolate with you. I feel quite incapable of writing beautiful things or lengthy essays on interior life; but all that the Lord gives to me belongs to you.

The greatest joy I can have is to see the souls that are united to mine grow beyond me at every moment. I believe that I have a very special vocation: that of a policeman at a major crossroads. I wave everyone on, I send them onwards, while I stay where I am.

Every word in your letter is full of the supernatural and perfectly expresses an ideal which we must realise, if we are not to disappoint the Lord. With you I say, again and again, "Thanks to Our Blessed Lady".

Letter from Frank Duff, November 4, 1948

I had told Frank Duff of my meeting with Veronica in Lourdes. In reply, he wrote:

It is with great joy that the Concilium received your letter about Miss O'Brien, whom you met in Lourdes. Miss O'Brien is a dynamic force. There is no doubt that she has been chosen by the Blessed Virgin as an instrument to bring about great things in France. The greatest of these, however, has been the survival of the Legion in that country. Nowhere else, to our knowledge, has the Legion met with more obstacles and threats; happily, those times are now over.

PART III

THE PAST REDISCOVERED

EXPLORATORY JOURNEYS
1948–1951

8

NEVERS

Dublin

My first exploratory journey was to Dublin, to meet Frank Duff and his executive team. Here I discovered an astonishing and daring deployment of meagre resources in the service of evangelisation. I was to go back, later, on a number of occasions, once I had become more fluent in English – and better able to understand the Irish accent!

On this first visit, I attended the monthly meeting of the concilium*. At these meetings, guests from various parts of the world are given the opportunity to speak on behalf of their countries; I gave my very first improvised speech in English. I was immediately able to establish that I still had a great deal to learn. Seated just behind me on the stage was a Swiss priest; after each presentation by a foreign speaker, he would mutter in a loud whisper: "I didn't understand a thing." As soon as I had come to the end of my maiden speech, he leaned forward and whispered in my ear: "Thank you very much, Monsignor; for once I understood every word."

It was the worst "compliment" he could have paid me!

Nevers

My "legionary novitiate" took me from Dublin to Nevers, the cradle of the Legion in France. There I had long and intensive meetings with those who had witnessed the Legion's early days.

---

* The concilium is the central co-ordinating body of the Legion; it is based in Dublin.

Three witnesses

In Nevers, Providence placed in Veronica's path two priests who were to play an important role in her life: Canon Guynot, superior of the major seminary and professor of theology, and Canon Cordier, superior of the minor seminary. Their understanding, their unfailing support, and their testimonies were most valuable to me when I set out to write these chapters. It seems appropriate, at this point, to digress briefly in order to explain their backgrounds.

Canon E. Guynot

Canon Guynot is the author of *The Life of Saint Bernadette*, a fresh and lively biography based on memories and anecdotes which he gathered from elderly nuns who had known the saint personally.

A theologian by profession, he was imbued with the spirituality of the French school: Bérulle, Condren, Olier and Eudes were his masters. He was also known and appreciated for his skill as a speaker, and his friends referred to him as "our little Bossuet".

He ran the seminary in the traditional style of his time: the emphasis was on theology and spirituality; initiation to direct apostolic pastoral work was not part of the programme. Veronica spoke to him with deep concern about this deficiency. One day she had the audacity to put him to the test: she asked him, point blank, if he had ever spoken of God to the gardener who took care of the seminary grounds. He admitted that he never had, and agreed to break this "sound barrier".

Much to his surprise, he discovered that the kindly gardener was not a practising Catholic, and that no one had ever talked to him about God. Some time later, after a few more chats, the gardener was back at church.

Veronica took full advantage of the healthy shock which had resulted from the discovery of such neglect; she asked Canon

Guynot to form a voluntary legionary group among the seminarians during the following academic year. With intrepid faith, she added:

"If you agree to found such a group in the seminary, I can promise you that this seminary will not have to be evacuated to make room for the Germans."

The very next day, however, the occupying authorities ordered the evacuation of the premises within twenty-four hours. A lorry was hired to move the students to a seminary in the neighbouring diocese, where they had been offered hospitality. The students boarded the lorry, but the convoy had barely set off when the lorry broke down. Despite a number of telephone calls, no mechanic could be found to repair it. Finally, the students were permitted to spend one last night in the seminary.

The following morning, a German officer arrived to announce a counter-order from headquarters, instructing the Germans to leave the premises immediately, and returning the seminary to its legitimate owners!

Canon Guynot saw in all of this a sign and a smile from the Lord, and the legionary group was established.

His later contacts with Veronica made a deep impression on him. In a letter written in November 1940, he tells her as much with touching humility:

> My very dear child, why did you not come to Nevers thirty years earlier! I would have specialised in the study of our admirable Mother, and I would not have become the little apprentice I am today, who can only babble when he tries to speak of the Holy Trinity's masterpiece. This is my one reproach to you – one which I am sure you did not expect. I have nothing else with which to reproach you.

The Canon's humility was legendary. When people saw him in the street, stooped and bent almost double, they would laugh and say: "He walks along hugging the walls, as if to apologise for his very existence."

For many years he was Veronica's spiritual director. He died in Nevers at the age of 104, in serene abandonment to the Lord, clear-minded to the very last.

After my meeting with Veronica in Lourdes, I wrote a first letter to Canon Guynot:

Archbishop's House, Malines   May 8, 1948

Dear Canon Guynot,

I find it very difficult to believe that I do not know you yet, for I feel in such deep communion with your writings on the Legion, and with some legionaries who have spoken to me about you. So, without further ado, I will tell you that Sister O'Brien, with whom I have spent unforgettable moments of grace in Lourdes, has asked me to write to you. A mystery of unity occurred at that time; it has left a profound mark on my spiritual life, and I believe that the responsibility for it lies entirely with Our Lady. Sister O'Brien will no doubt speak or write to you about this in greater detail. I simply wish to submit the entire matter to you, who are her spiritual director, leaving you complete freedom to ask her for all the facts. I truly believe that all of this is pure gift.

The Lord, who wishes to give Himself to us through Mary's mediation, no doubt continues to grant His graces through instruments of His choice. We would be grateful for a word from you to each of us. Perhaps I shall have the opportunity to meet you within the next few months.

I wrote to him again in December 1951, to ask for his judgement on his former directee, in the hope that he would give me an overall picture of her. I was not disappointed: his letter was a rich and vivid portrait.

Paris, December 29, 1951

To His Excellency,
Mgr Suenens
Auxiliary Bishop of Malines

Your Grace,

Your Excellency does me the honour of asking what I think of Miss O'Brien — of her personal qualities, and of her legionary activities in France. I hasten to respond on both points, but I must apologise for doing so in a hurried and perhaps a rather rambling manner.

I remember that Canon Mathey, director of works in Dijon, was once asked a similar question, to which he responded: "Miss O'Brien is a genius and a saint." I am not qualified to make judgements concerning either sanctity or genius. I can only say that, in my long life, I have never met a man or a woman who has given me such a powerful impression of both natural and supernatural superiority. I found her to be equally remarkable in the area of abstract thought as in that of practical matters; dominating situations as she dominates audiences; as comfortable dealing with the most elevated matters as with the complexities of personality and the workings of human psychology, which she grasps with a perspicacity verging on the miraculous.

What I have most admired about her, however, over the ten years of our close acquaintance, during which she confided in me and informed me of her trials, was her total detachment from herself and from all creatures; her spirit of faith, which seemed to come naturally to her; her constant union with the Blessed Virgin; her perfect docility to the Church and to the hierarchy; her extraordinary respect for the priesthood; the manly – more than manly – courage with which she faced the incredible difficulties she encountered. She had the patience to tell me all about her past – her childhood and her youth – and I am convinced that some historian will find in her life uncommonly rich material for a biography.

The work she has done in France, from 1939 until these recent months, has been truly unbelievable. The suffering she endured, the walls – I should say the mountains – she has had to climb, bring to mind St Paul's words in his letter to the Corinthians: "In difficulties on all sides...consigned to death every day." She has been for us the accomplished model of the legionary, or rather of the Legion itself – the living, walking Legion, which is disconcerted by nothing because it does not rely on itself but on its head, who is Mary.

There is one particularly interesting aspect to this apostolic work which she carried out in almost sixty French dioceses: the influence it has had on so many priests. Several have told me that since their consecration to the priesthood, they have received two special graces: the first was being introduced to the Legion of Mary and, through the Legion, to the *Treatise on True Devotion*; the second was meeting this Irishwoman. Miss O'Brien did not seek this kind of seemingly paradoxical influence; Providence used her for work that presents certain analogies with the activities of St Teresa of Avila among the Carmelites of her own time.

Your Excellency is not unaware of the good she has done to many of the faithful; among these are several young men who, having been counselled by her, have become fervent Christians and admirable apostles. I would not like to exaggerate, nor to overuse historical comparisons, but I cannot help being reminded of St Catherine of Siena among her disciples. In mentioning the names of Teresa and of Catherine, I am in no way drawing parallels. I would simply like to say that what I have seen as I observed Miss O'Brien has helped me to understand a number of events and situations from the past which, at first glance, may appear to defy common sense.

Moreover, I can testify that both in this apostolate — which is by nature particularly delicate — and in her relationships with priests, Miss O'Brien has always remained within the limits of the most careful prudence and the most scrupulous docility to the advice of her spiritual director.

These many qualities and accomplishments account for the high esteem in which she is held by many religious and clergy noted for their learning and their virtue. The venerable Cardinal Suhard valued her at her true worth; our Bishop of Nevers, Mgr Flynn, has always spoken of her with reverence; religious superiors have asked her to speak to their communities; bishops have asked her to address their priests and seminarians. All of these guarantees and testimonies allay in me the fear which one always experiences in such matters — that of having allowed oneself to be led away from reality by naïve admiration.

I beg Your Excellency to forgive the deficiencies of this letter; the words that have come to my pen are quite incapable of realistically conveying the countenance which is indelible and vivid in my memory, but I have no time to do better. I know, at least, that I have come sufficiently close to truth, as it was given to me to know it.

Please accept, Your Excellency, my best wishes for the New Year, and the respectful regards of your humble servant.

This letter was very valuable to me; it confirmed my own impressions, on every point. Canon Guynot had mentioned St Catherine, to whom such a variety of followers gravitated; I was struck by the analogy. I had just finished reading a book by Joseph Wilbois on Saint Catherine of Siena,* the introduction to which ends with the following words: "A heart burning with such fire could not but radiate light. Around her was gathered, not a court – no word could be less appropriate – but a tribe of disciples, whose piety was kindled by her fervour. Happy are we if, one day, in some corner of Paris, we chance to meet her, and, recognising her, follow in her wake, to be caught as in a fisherman's net."

Canon Cordier

Canon Cordier, superior of the minor seminary, was a friend of Canon Guynot, and occasionally replaced him as Veronica's confessor. He kept careful notes, day by day, of his conversations with her; unbeknownst to her, he copied some of her letters into his notebooks. In this way, he prepared a very useful file for the future biographer. There are twelve notebooks altogether, written in a beautiful hand. Canon Cordier gave me these valuable documents during one of my visits to Nevers, late in 1987, thus leaving his memories and his own personal journal to my discretion. He died recently, on August 24, 1992. Only a few days before his death, he ended his last letter with an apology for writing his goodbyes with a hand that was no longer steady. May he rest in the peace and joy of the Lord.

I have gleaned a few revealing items from his notes:

An elderly sister at St Gildard once said to him, "In 1866, the Blessed Virgin showed us how much she loved us, by sending us Bernadette; today, she shows us how much she still loves us, by sending us Miss O'Brien."

"More and more," Canon Cordier wrote, "Veronica gives me the impression that she has at her disposal a superhuman courage, a

---

* *Sainte Catherine de Sienne, l'actualité de son message,* Editions Casterman, 1948

strength of soul for which temperament and character alone cannot account."

Describing a meeting at St Gildard, he notes: "The previous
evening, the rehearsal had left Veronica worried: too many
details were still unresolved. In the morning, she said to the
Blessed Virgin, 'Now it's up to you. In heaven you have thousands of angels who have nothing to do; send one to each person
who comes here tonight, to tell them what they must do.'"

Once, when he was ill, Canon Cordier received a note from
Veronica:

I am delighted to know that as a result of your illness you
have been somewhat neglected; you will have time to
think about eternity and about the salvation of your soul.

But if you are very good and very obedient about getting some rest, I can promise you that in a short while you
will be as active as ever, for you do not at all deserve to go
to heaven so soon and at so little cost.

So get well soon, so that you may soon be back in the
midst of the fray.

Very much united in Ea,
V. O'B.

Here, lastly, is a poem by Canon Cordier. It was in no way intended for publication, but it fits very naturally among these testimonies of those early days.

Blessed be the day I met her!
The day your hand, O Lord,
Guided her steps to my door,
I was as if asleep – I never imagined
The road which would be shown to me
Through her.
Blessed be the day
On which I met her!

For at the sound of her voice
My sluggish soul
Begins to shake off the numbness
And I feel that her call
Pulls me to You
Drawing me in her wake
As I hasten to follow.
Blessed be the day
On which I met her!
Glory be to you for this,
O Immaculate Virgin!

The Eve of the Epiphany, 1942

In a letter dated August 24, 1952, Canon Cordier wrote to me:

I have just finished reading the life of Edel Quinn*.

I have made this book my daily spiritual reading, to be savoured in small sips. I never knew Edel Quinn, except through your book, and I must admit that what I see on every page is the portrait of another daughter of Ireland, whom I know very well indeed, and whom you also know. It is in essence the same holiness, expressed in two masterpieces which differ only in minor details — the Divine Master never repeats himself; neither Mary nor the Holy Spirit engages in mass production.

While I humbly congratulate you on your beautiful book, I find myself hoping that the same pen will one day reveal to the world the wonders that the Blessed Virgin has worked in and through Sister O'Brien.

Now, forty years later, his wish is being fulfilled. I had planned to give him a very special acknowledgement; but he will have to read it in heaven.

---

* Edel Quinn was a delegate of the Legion of Mary in Africa. I wrote a biography of her which has been translated into about twenty languages. The cause for her beatification has been introduced.

109

A letter from Canon Cordier to Veronica and Yvette (February 12, 1971) reveals both his sense of humour and his faithful memory; I quote:

> I was beginning to believe that you had both become increasingly elusive and untraceable, flitting about from one continent to another, waiting for a 'cosmobus' to whisk you off to some other planet.... Thank you for your kind wishes. What can I wish you in return? That the Holy Spirit may continue to be your chauffeur, in Our Lady's car, to the very end.... Along the way, please ask her that I may complete my journey without too much damage done.

He goes on to speak of his own death, which he felt was near, and of "the last few miles along this road".

Sister Jeanne de Jésus

Another witness of these early days was Sister Jeanne de Jésus, prioress of the Carmelite convent in Nevers. On December 20, 1940 she wrote to Canon Cordier describing her own reaction, and that of her community, to their first contact with Veronica.

> Miss O'Brien may not be aware of this, but she does me so much good. With a soul like hers, how could it be otherwise? She lives and radiates her faith. I cherish her little sayings, which seem to me to come from the Blessed Virgin: "Now that you love the Blessed Virgin more, do you not feel a special attraction to the Holy Spirit? If you do, please tell me about it. Many here have had this experience; it is a wonderful grace!"

On January 29, 1941, she wrote:

> I was delighted — and, I must admit, a little surprised — by the rare wisdom, the supernatural prudence of our young

apostle of Mary. It is obvious that she has a good teacher: the Holy Spirit Himself — He alone can thus enlighten souls and grant them His gifts. I have blessed her for this with all my heart, for many are the souls who will benefit from this. I will therefore end my letter with a hearty *Deo gratias.*

Her correspondence with Veronica ended, by mutual agreement, in November 1950. It ended with these words, full of humour and faith:

I have taken note of your wish not to see me again in this life. Oh! how I agree with you! I am ready — and with what joy! I remain in union with you for all time and all eternity.

Letter to Mgr Flynn

In a letter to Mgr Flynn, I attempted to summarise my own reactions to my contacts with the witnesses of the early days.

For me, the Legion has the freshness of a chapter of the Acts of the Apostles, where everything is true, simple, spontaneous and direct. I had already sensed its atmosphere of primitive church, through the rumours that reached me; but the joy of discovery is yet another special grace.

I have no doubt that Our Lady and St Bernadette are watching, with pleasure, this little corner of France, and the bishop who has dared to believe in and bless the miracle.

9

PARIS

The transfer

Veronica was anxious to establish the central office of the Legion of Mary in Paris as soon as the War ended. She asked Yvette Dubois to move to Paris in order to study to become a social worker and to lay the foundations of the future organisation. On a brief visit to Paris, Veronica met Canon Brot, archpriest of Notre-Dame; he helped the Legion to find a meeting-place, and a first praesidium was established and given the name of "Notre-Dame". Canon Brot's vicar, Fr Couly, was the first spiritual director of this group.

The number of groups increased; some were attached to parishes, others to communities. Veronica came to Paris at regular intervals, to check on their progress. Yvette was assigned the task of finding a home for Veronica's first little team, and to set aside a room for the secretariat of the Legion of Mary.

Yvette was still searching, in vain, when Veronica, back in Nevers, had an extraordinary spiritual experience, one that belongs – in the most compelling way – to the realm of the "hidden hand of God".

Rue Boileau

Veronica was praying the Stations of the Cross, as she did every day, when she heard an inner voice say to her, "Go to the 'Oeuvre des Mourants' – the 'Institute for the Dying'." This continued to happen for a full month.

She asked Canon Guynot whether this striking experience was

merely an illusion, and whether she should act upon it. He suggested that she find out from the Archbishop's House in Paris whether the "Oeuvre des Mourants" actually existed. Veronica went there, but no one could answer her question. She watched as the Diocesan Directory was consulted in vain: no institute by that name was listed.

She decided to return to Nevers. Before leaving Paris, however, she went to an afternoon meeting of a praesidium of Russian emigrants, named "Unhoped-for Joy". At the end of the meeting, as she was saying goodbye, she enquired about the "Oeuvre des Mourants", on the off-chance that someone there might have heard of it. The chaplain of the group, a Russian Uniate priest, said, "Indeed I have; it's just around the corner, on rue Boileau." He explained that the official name for it was "Oeuvre des Grands Malades" – "Institute for the Terminally Ill", but it was more commonly known as "Oeuvre des Mourants".

Veronica immediately went to the house. She met the director of the Oeuvre, Mlle Ardant – the successor of the foundress, Mlle Noualhier – who welcomed her and told her about the origin and the history of the institute.* Veronica, in turn, told of her search for a building to house her little team.

At the time, only four members of the Oeuvre were still living, and the youngest was seventy-two years old. On that very day, the group had finished a novena to the Sacred Heart, asking the Lord to ensure the continuity of their institution. Mlle Ardant saw her meeting with Veronica as the Lord's marvellous answer to the prayers of the group. This meeting was a great joy to her; she immediately realised that she should entrust the future of the Institute and of the house to Miss O'Brien.

Veronica was suddenly faced with a completely unforeseen situation. At first, she simply attempted to continue the work along the established lines, with the help of her own team. In July 1945, she and her first companions moved into the house.

---

* Gaétan Bernoville tells the story of this house in a book about Mlle Noualhier, who founded the Oeuvre in Limoges in 1883, then brought it to Paris in 1900.

During her first stay in Dublin after the War, however, Veronica learned that the Legion's concilium would not allow the creation of any religious association within the framework of the Legion, for fear that the Legion might lose its lay character. This was a painful surprise for Veronica and the members of her team. However, she resolutely opted for the Legion, sacrificing her dream of community. As soon as she returned from Dublin, she informed Mlle Ardant – Mother Fanny, as they called her – that the little community which had formed around her would not be recognised by the Legion, and that consequently Veronica felt she should step back and allow some other community to take over.

The decision made in Dublin gave Mlle Ardant great pain; however, she unexpectedly remained convinced that Veronica had been sent by providence to inherit the house at 41 rue Boileau. She therefore insisted on confirming that she had given the house to Veronica, for the present and for the future. This was later supported by her successor, the Countess Boudet, in a handwritten letter dated August 25, 1961, which was intended to prevent any confusion in the future. This is the Countess's will:

Paris, August 25, 1961

I hereby certify by the present letter that the property legally known as "Société immobilière Boileau Molitor", located at No.41-43 (formerly No.41) was given to Miss V. O'Brien by myself and by Mlle Fanny Ardant in 1945, and this to her personally and not as a representative of any organisation or institute of apostolic work.

Mlle Ardant, who, before she died, had known Miss O'Brien for ten years, always believed that Miss O'Brien was the person sent by God to use these premises in accordance with God's own will.

I request that this house be left in the hands of Miss

O'Brien and of the team which, under her direction, ensures the continued good management of the house.

It will be left to Miss O'Brien's discretion to ensure the continuity of leadership in the house. I have the greatest confidence in her; I am certain that in this, as in all her undertakings, she will act for the greater glory of God and of souls, in accordance with the guidance of divine Providence and of her spiritual director.

Louise Boudet

For Veronica, the fact that the house in rue Boileau contained a small chapel was a special sign of the loving attentiveness of Divine Providence, an answer to the prayer she had once addressed to the Lord:

"I refuse to work for money, because I want to be completely available for evangelisation. Lord, you are my Spouse, and according to human laws, you would be expected to provide food and lodging for me. Please take care of all of that, so that I can be fully available for evangelisation. And since you are all-powerful, I also ask you, as a special grace, to give me a house with the Blessed Sacrament."

This brings to mind the Master's promise to his disciples:

"I tell you solemnly, there is no one who has left house, brothers, sisters, father, mother, children or land for my sake and for the sake of the gospel who will not be repaid a hundred times over, houses, brothers, sisters, mothers, children and land – not without persecutions – now in this present time and, in the world to come, eternal life" (Mark 10:29-30).

This is a truly astonishing promise, both in its sorrowful and mysterious aspect and in its radiant aspect. All of this was to come about, word for word, in Veronica's life of apostolate.

Veronica's little team, who lived with her at 41 rue Boileau, were divided into two groups. One group remained at the house and took care of the sick; among these was Marcelle Gandit, who had studied nursing in order to meet legal requirements. The others worked outside to earn the money they needed in order to pay their own expenses, provide for the elderly people they took in, and finance the medical care of the sick, which they gave free of charge.

As had originally been agreed, a small part of the house was set aside for the secretariat of the Legion of Mary. In addition to her regular work, each member of the group gave some of her free time to the secretariat.

In the house, there was a surprising mixture of social classes and backgrounds: Sister Gernez, who was in charge of the kitchen, was the president of a praesidium which included two generals and a marquise! At legionary meetings, everyone referred to each other as "sister" or "brother". This in itself represented a Christian revolution.

At first, Veronica continued to follow the methods and inspiration which had originally guided the Oeuvre des Mourants . Very sick people were taken in from various hospitals in Paris; they received medical care in the house, thanks to the help of three doctors who provided their services free of charge. On my way through Paris, I have on occasion administered the last sacraments to those who were dying in the house.

However, a small private charitable institute such as this could not possibly keep up with the demands which were made on it. Soon it became necessary for patients to remain in hospitals, and a new approach had to be developed. Until then, members of the community had visited patients in hospitals, and brought those whose condition was most serious to the house in rue Boileau. Veronica now decided to assign a few legionary groups – in particular the one that met in rue Boileau – to visit patients in hospitals without offering to transfer them.

Mgr Leclerc, Auxiliary Bishop of Paris, was consulted on this matter. He responded with this letter:

Archbishop's House, Paris   July 2, 1953

Dear Miss O'Brien,

I have received the report on the *Oeuvre des grands malades*, and I have read it with the greatest care.

I was once in charge of the little Society of the Daughters of Jesus and of the work to which they devoted themselves.

In this capacity, I can confirm that the orientation described in the report does indeed correspond to the constitutions of the Institute — constitutions with which I am familiar, and of which I have a copy.

Since the religious society in question no longer exists, the *Oeuvre des grands malades* is at an impasse. It would appear most appropriate to adopt a new approach, while remaining faithful to the spirit of the foundress. Mlle Noualhier's main concern was the apostolate to those who are spiritually neglected, and in particular to non-Christians among the sick.

The approach proposed in your report is imbued with the spirit of the foundation; it is dictated by circumstances which can be seen to reflect the guiding hand of Providence.

I therefore encourage you to embark generously on this path, and to do much good.

I send you my blessings.

Mgr Leclerc,
Auxiliary Bishop of Paris

The beginnings of legionary activity

The Legion's apostolic initiatives were many and varied. As I have mentioned, Veronica had asked Yvette Dubois to train to be a social worker. This gave her access to two areas of activity

117

among prostitutes in Paris: in her professional capacity, she participated in a survey organised by the youth tribunal in co-operation with the observation centre of Chevilly-la-Rue, whose director, Dr Le Moal, was a psychiatrist; at the same time, through her apostolic work as a legionary, she established contact with the prostitutes in the Saint-Denis area.

The legionaries were also involved in other kinds of social work; they established and ran a welcome shelter for tramps and former prison inmates. This institute was called "Morning Star", as a tribute to Mary. The Cardinal Archbishop of Paris officially inaugurated it and encouraged the initiative. Due to the magnitude of the task, this project was later handed over to the State authorities.

One of the directors of the shelter, "Brother" Thiénard, was by profession a police officer. He managed to conceal his identity so as not to frighten off the clients and so as to be able to assist them more freely. I have just found a description of Brother Thiénard in a book by Fr Jean Debruynne;* it captures vividly the image of this man which is still alive in my mind and in the minds of many of the Paris legionaries. The author, who was chaplain of the Christian Community of Policemen in France, writes:

> After a day's work, Gaston Thiénard frequently spent the night serving soup to tramps, on a voluntary basis, in one of the shelters which opened in Paris to serve the poor. He often said to me: "When I arrest a burglar, I'm doing my job, serving justice. But the burglar is also a man, a human presence. I can stop the act while treating the man with respect. Every time I question a thug or a burglar, I see Jesus hidden in the eyes of the suspect." To live this kind of faith, Gaston needed long hours of prayer. He liked to go up to Montmartre and spend a night in adoration, before engaging once again in terrible face-to-face encoun-

---

* *L'Evangile du poète,* published by Le Centurion, Paris, 1990

ters with criminals. He told me that he had found himself serving soup to wretches whom he had personally sent to jail...

Later, after he retired from the police force, Thiénard expressed the desire to become a deacon. He had started his formation when he was suddenly taken ill; he died a few months later. Veronica and Yvette were informed in time; they visited him a few days before his death. Veronica asked him, "What is in your heart at this very moment?"

He replied: "My Mother! My trust!"

These were the words of a prayer which Veronica had made popular in the early days of the Legion. Many members have adopted it as their favourite ejaculatory prayer. It is also the prayer which Pope John XXIII murmured at the moment of his death.

As she was leaving the dear dying man, Veronica asked him for a parting word for me. He whispered one word, asking her to tell me to "continue."

The Senatus moves to Paris (January 1950)

At this point, the Senatus — the national authority of the Legion of Mary — had to be moved from Nevers to Paris. In a way, this was the official consecration of Veronica's work.

When an article announcing the move appeared in the Paris-based magazine *La Croix*, Veronica received a touching letter from her former spiritual director at St Clotilde, in Eltham. He knew better than anyone the suffering that had led to this magnificent apostolic accomplishment.

My dear child,

It is with all my heart that I joined in your Magnificat as I read, in this morning's *La Croix*, the great news of the transfer of the Senatus from Nevers to Paris. Canon Guynot is one of your most fervent supporters, and it is a great joy to read his account of the progress you have made during the past ten years. The Blessed Mother has guided your every step, since the decision you made in Dublin. When I think of all your tentative efforts, Mary's plans for you become utterly clear.

I think of you very often when I celebrate mass at Eltham. It has now been turned into a special school for difficult children, and is in the hands of the Sisters of Mary. We have been their chaplains for the past two years. The house was fairly well converted after the War.

Happy New Year, dear Veronica, and may the Blessed Virgin shower upon you her tenderness and her blessings.

Affectionately yours,

Benedict Cara, AA

The Legion takes root in Paris

From the beginning, the Legion was well received by Cardinal Feltin and by his auxiliary, Mgr Leclerc, who became his personal permanent delegate to the Legion. Mgr Leclerc was already familiar with the *Oeuvre des grands malades* in rue Boileau, as it was under his jurisdiction.

On October 8, 1956 Cardinal Feltin attended one of the meetings of the Senatus in Paris; after listening carefully to the various reports, he gave his own reactions in these words:

"I have heard your reports; in simple and direct terms, they speak of life in schools, in novitiates, in convents; they span every age and social class. As I listened, I tried to think of some form of apostolic work which you might have overlooked. I could not find a single one. Your movement could be described as 'an encyclopaedia of apostolic activities'. Each and every soul can find in the Legion the means to satisfy its apostolic needs."

Plans for a trip to Poland

Earlier in this book, I told the story of the legionary group which
Veronica founded among Polish pilots in Paris, at the beginning of
the War. In view of that precedent, after the War Frank Duff asked
Veronica to prepare the ground for the Legion in Poland. He was
very conscious of the importance of sowing the seed at the earliest possible time, in view of growing hostility from the communist
regime.

Veronica accepted this mission and prepared for it as best she
could. In a letter to Canon Cordier, she informed him of her proposed trip.

April 2, 1947

I am very much in need of rest, and the Easter holidays
would have been a welcome break; but I must stay in Paris
for six days, to gather information for a trip to Poland.

Yes! I am going to Poland, but only for a short visit of a
few months. Things are going very badly there, it seems,
and Mr Duff feels that we must do all we can to make some
inroads while it is still possible – assuming that it still is.

So I must concentrate all my efforts in that direction –
arrange for the *Handbook* to be printed, and so forth; it has
already been translated and duplicated. Say nothing of this
to anyone; I want to have more information before I let anyone know. Apparently the Irish Government has yet to
recognise the Polish Government, so this will make things
more difficult.

In addition to Poland, I am still in charge of France, as
delegate. I received the good news in Saint Sebastian, and
you can imagine my joy and my gratitude to Our Lady, who
has kept me on in her Legion, despite everything; for I feel,
more and more, that this is my life.

You cannot imagine the intense joy it gives me to speak
of the Blessed Virgin to priests and religious...

121

I believe that in Saint Sebastian I received special graces, the greatest of which was to see how little courage I have had, and how un-spiritual I have been, through the trials of this past year.

Poor Mary – I'm afraid I did not pass that particular test with flying colours. But I hope that next time I shall at least be better prepared as a result of this experience, and that I shall have the courage to keep the sword in my heart without a word to anyone, anyone at all.

Oh, how important it is to remain silent when we suffer! Otherwise we spoil everything. And that's just what I did, even though, at the time, my weak nature found all sorts of good reasons to talk, to you and to others. More and more, grace calls me to be alone, very alone. And I know you will help me there, won't you?

I rely on your daily Mass. It is such a grace for me, and the only way I can ever thank you enough for your faithful affection is by trying at every moment to be more truly holy – in other words, more truly lost in communion with Mary in the adoration of the Most Holy Trinity.

This letter is also for Canon Guynot: it is a great joy for me to share all that I have received during the past weeks with my two fathers. I hope you will be able to give me a little of your time to talk about all of this.

Very humbly and affectionately yours,

In Ea,
V. O'B.

Veronica was due to leave for Poland on August 15: she has always liked to link all of her important projects with some Marian date. Everything was ready, including her plane ticket – which she had placed, as she always did before travelling, at the foot of the little statue of Our Lady. At the time, Mgr Roncalli, the future Pope John XXIII, was nuncio in Paris; he had entrusted Veronica with five pectoral crosses to take to the newly consecrated Polish bishops, and she had even obtained a suitcase with a false bottom, in which to hide these crosses.

At the last minute, however, Veronica's departure was cancelled; an employee at the Polish Embassy in Paris warned her, through others, that her name was on a list of suspicious persons and that she would be arrested as soon as the plane landed in Warsaw. Veronica, ready to run the risk despite everything, telephoned Frank Duff to ask him what he wanted her to do; he told her not to go. Together, they entrusted the future to the care of Our Lady of Tzestochowa.

After the war, the Polish religious authorities in Paris awarded Veronica a medal in grateful recognition of all she had done, through the Legion of Mary, for Polish refugees in France – in particular in the diocese of Autun. She wore it only once: at a private audience with Pope John Paul II, at which I was present. The Holy Father was well aware of the story behind the medal.

A friend in Paris – Mgr Benelli

Our friendship with Mgr Benelli began in Paris. For almost thirty years, it remained steadfast and constant. At several points in our lives, it was to be an instrument of Divine Providence.

When Veronica first met him, he was a young auditor at the nunciature in Paris. He had just arrived from his previous post in Ireland. In Dublin, he had often met Frank Duff, and had quickly become aware of the man's apostolic genius. He was immediately welcoming to the Legion of Mary and to its delegate.

He was also quick to grasp Veronica's spiritual depth, and she became a guide in whom he placed filial trust. She asked him not to remain enclosed within the boundaries set by the diplomatic life, but to become involved in some pastoral activities as well. She asked him to be the confessor of the legionaries in rue Boileau, under the assumed name of Fr Eli. Meanwhile, I had agreed to preach a day of retreat there every three months. It was inevitable that we should meet.

Because of his affection for the Legion of Mary, Mgr Benelli requested and obtained from Pope John XXIII a large subsidy for the construction of a building in the grounds of the house in rue Boileau; he also helped to break the ice between the Legion and some groups within the Catholic Action movement in France. We owe him the first friendly article about the Legion, signed G. Hourdin and published in *Informations catholiques internationales*.

I owe him my first driving lesson. It was in the Bois de Boulogne; there was to be no second lesson, for, as I told him, there were far too many trees for a beginner!

When Mgr Benelli left Paris for his next diplomatic post in Rio de Janeiro, *La Croix* published a farewell article expressing the friendship of everyone who had known him during his stay at the Paris nunciature. These are by no means empty words of politeness.

> All those in Paris who have met Mgr Benelli — and they are many, as his stay was a long one — look upon his departure with great sadness. They will cherish memories of his lively intelligence and constant kindness, of the charming welcome and the unfailing availability that were always hallmarks of his hospitality. They will also remember his intimate knowledge of France, and the understanding and friendship he has always shown to the French people. He will be missed by everybody. His friends at *La Croix* and at *La Bonne Presse*, to whom he has so often shown his kindness, wish to express their sadness at his departure and to assure him that, as he has asked, they will remember him in their prayers.

10

DIJON, CITEAUX AND OTHER PLACES

For some years, Veronica continued to promote the Legion of Mary, as the envoy of the Concilium in Dublin. Throughout this period, she and her little team lived at 41 rue Boileau, in the house which she had discovered and received like a mysterious gift from heaven.

OBSTACLES

To follow her travels from day to day, we would have to spread out a map of France and trace her path through the dioceses, towns and villages she visited. In each diocese, her mission was to convince the bishop, then the directors of institutes – who were often allergic to the Legion, which did not fit in easily with their established plans and structures. Finally, she had to win the support of each and every parish priest. Often she herself had to seek potential members and oversee the establishment of the group. In short, she had plenty of obstacles to overcome.

A formal ban

The very first hurdle was a daunting one. In March 1944 the cardinals and archbishops of France, gathered in assembly, had banned the Legion of Mary from the country, "to avoid possible negative effects on Action Catholique, and to avoid overlap".

From a strictly canonical point of view, this assembly had no legal authority over individual bishops, who remained free to follow or ignore this directive. Nevertheless, such an official stance represented a major handicap, especially as it is an absolute rule within the Legion never to move into a diocese without obtaining prior consent from the local bishop. I can even recall a case where the Legion's faithful obedience to this rule impressed a bishop, who had rejected the idea, to such an extent that he changed his mind and granted his authorisation. The bishop in question was Mgr Renard, then Bishop of Versailles, later Cardinal of Lyons. He told one of the Legion leaders:

"I forbade you to introduce the Legion in my diocese and you obeyed. It is rare to see such loyal obedience – so you have my consent."

Convincing the bishop was not necessarily synonymous with success: the bishop still had to convince his collaborators. Once, after Veronica had given her talk, the local bishop said to his priests, "Someone has just set your churches on fire; do not become firefighters."

Some typical objections

Certain objections recurred frequently, at all levels. For example, people often said to Veronica:

– "We have a perfectly well-organised apostolate, run along well-structured lines; any new work would simply be disruptive."

– "You have an Irish faith, Miss O'Brien; it is obvious that you know nothing about France."

– "At best, the Legion of Mary might work in rural areas, but it certainly would not work in cities" (or vice versa).

– "The Legion makes very heavy demands – weekly meetings, clearly defined and supervised apostolic work, and so on; it is all far too burdensome; you will never find volunteers."

– "The Legion's spirituality is imbued with that of Grignion de Montfort; it is old-fashioned and unacceptable."

– "Direct religious apostolate is no longer appropriate; we must 'humanise first, envagelise later'." This "theology" had become pervasive, and was often a motive for refusals.

From a Marian standpoint, one episode has left a particularly vivid memory in our minds. Veronica was to give a talk to a group of priests; before she had even started to speak, a professional theologian launched into a vigorous attack against "Marian exaggerations", taking a rather aggressive tone and backing his arguments with scholarly quotations. Veronica took in this theological attack very calmly; then she responded, with kindness and respect for the man, but with a doctrinal confidence which greatly impressed the audience and won her a lengthy ovation — which, incidentally, annoyed her considerably.

Her weapons were her living union with Mary; a faith strong enough to move mountains; and her Irish humour, which no audience could resist. She responded to these typical objections as best she could, humbly pleading the Legion's right to exist and to experiment.

Thanks to Veronica's letters, we can follow the development of the Legion in a few dioceses in France.

Clermont-Ferrand — 1945

On Wednesday I spent the day with the Holy Ghost scholastics and with the directors and priests of the area. In the morning we had a big meeting, and I spoke as best I could. Then, though I tried to beg off, I had to eat lunch with Fathers X, Y and Z, who were like three little children happily gathered around their Mother. Their humility and their simplicity were very touching.

After lunch, I had fifteen minutes to rest, then another long meeting. I'm told it went off very well. There were a few very delicate questions concerning Marian theology; they were asked in writing, and I had to respond on the spot. But our gentle Queen helped me out, and everyone seemed quite satisfied.

I came back here on my bicycle, and then — at 10.20 in the evening! — another meeting, this time with the

127

Auxiliaries. I could hardly keep my eyes open, but everyone was very considerate. There were well over a hundred people in the audience! It's fantastic, for a little place like this.

On Friday afternoon, another talk for the priests – twice as many this time, and many had already been there in the morning: there were two vicars-general, both very sympathetic to the Legion and very faithful auxiliaries. One told me that he had never once missed his legionary prayers, and even said them when he was not feeling well.

In the evening, there was a praesidium meeting at the major seminary, a few miles outside the town. My impression was excellent; the group could well be recognised before long. There are only seven members, but they have the right tone and the right spirit.

Next, a one-hour conference for the whole seminary. Apparently it is an unprecedented triumph for the Legion to be given the opportunity to speak, as I did, at the seminary and to the seminarians.

Very late the same evening, I had a meal alone with Fr X in the refectory of the Sulpicians; the superior served us personally! Then he lent me a legionary seminarian to escort me back to the convent, because it was quite dark by then, and the convent is quite far away.

And so to bed, empty-headed, or rather with my head over-heated from so many talks in one day.

They woke me up at 5.30 the following morning, so I could be at the university at 6.30 for mass with Fr X. Then on to the praesidium – this time, boys and girls together – seven altogether, and at least seven guests. The meeting was still poor, but the spirit has certainly improved greatly. I gave a brief talk, and managed to discourage the new girls completely – there will only be three girls left, as a result.

Fr X is absolutely thrilled, and he wants so badly to make his legionary promise; it's really touching.

I met the two presidents separately. The young man seems listless; he lacks vitality and enthusiasm. The girl is a little better. Both promised weekly confession and a good routine of prayer, so there is reason to be hopeful.

Back to the convent: breakfast, prayer, packing and off to Saint-Bonnet. I had a long wait for the bus to Riom; from Riom I got here on a bicycle.

Here, they are busy preparing for tomorrow's Acies;* they are hoping to have a procession through the village, but today the weather is dark and cloudy.

Mgr Van Hee SJ has just arrived. He is increasingly involved in the Legion, and considers the *Handbook* to be truly inspired. He is beginning to give talks all over the place about "The Legion and the missions".

Valence — 1946

Then off to a parish about twenty miles from Annonay, but belonging to the diocese of Valence. The parish priest had been warned the previous day, and received us with icy coldness. Five people had come to hear me, along with two legionary brothers from Annonay. Monsieur le Curé became more and more terrible, and I became sweeter and sweeter. I talked for an hour. Result — the poor distraught curé succumbed to my attack, surrendered unconditionally, and a praesidium was established, which included the five men who were present; four officers were appointed on the spot.

We travelled back at top speed. I had half an hour to eat at the home of a lady who had prepared a delicious supper for me. Then — a big meeting with the auxiliaries. I am told that it was perfect. In any case, the audience vibrated with enthusiasm and smiled and was moved at all the right places.

---

* The Acies is the solemn annual assembly during which all active and auxiliary members renew their consecration to Mary.

129

Yet again, I didn't get to bed until midnight.

Today, I found that in Valence nothing had been prepared, nothing at all, not even the praesidium — and now I
shall not be able to see them at all. However, there will be
a meeting of the auxiliaries this evening at the Young
Women's Hostel where I am staying.

I shall tell you more when I see you. Now I haven't a
minute left.

I thank you, each one of you, for being so astonishingly
good to me.

Ever so seriously yours,
in Ea,
V. O'B.

Angers — 1953

At the beginning of 1940, Veronica had obtained permission to
found the Legion in Angers. However, the bishop died soon after
the first group was established, and the vicar general who was in
charge during the interim period rescinded the authorisation.

In 1953, the new bishop authorised the Legion once again.
After a private meeting with the local leaders, Veronica gave a
lecture in the main hall of the university; as a result, she was
given the go-ahead for the diocese.

An amusing letter describes the details of this new beginning:

Yesterday was the big day — the triumphant entrance of
the Legion into Angers, after my important lecture in the
presence of *Monseigneur*, the vicars-general, and a large
crowd of priests and religious, all gathered in the main
hall of the university.

All the various communities were represented, some by
fifteen or twenty members. There was a large contingent of
OPs, OPMs, etc., professors, rectors of the university semi-

Kathleen Leahy O'Brien,
Veronica's mother

Dr O'Brien with Lulu, the twelfth of his
thirteen children

The O'Brien Family

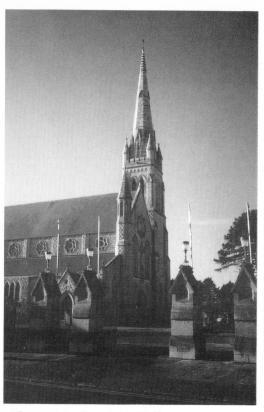

The parish church in Midleton

Veronica on the eve of her entrance into the convent of St Clotilde

Midleton House, the O'Brien family house

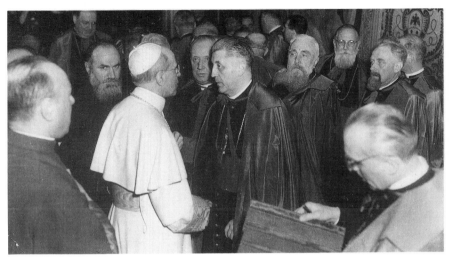

Cardinal Suenens at an audience with Pope Pius XII

Cardinal Tisserant on a visit to the Legion of Mary's house in Lourdes

On the Isle of Tinos, in Greece. The Mother Superior of the Ursulines and Mother Camille (on the right), holding the Handbook, were the Legion's apostles on the island. Sister O'Brien, on the donkey, is already heading for new horizons

Veronica O'Brien in Greece

The annual Legion of Mary Pilgrimage to Lourdes, 1957

Veronica's car after her accident

The Congress on Apostolate and Religious Life, in the United States

To Veronica O'Brien, on the occasion
of her Seventieth Birthday, praying that the
Lord may give her light and strength and
love, in order that she may continue in
her service of Christ's Church with undi-
minished generosity and fidelity, we cor-
dially impart our Apostolic Blessing.
From the Vatican, 16 August 1975.

Paulus PP. VI

Pope Paul VI's birthday greetings to
Veronica

Cardinal Benelli, Substitute at the
Secretariat of State under Pope Paul
VI, and a close friend of both Cardinal
Suenens and Veronica O'Brien

Margie and Peter Grace with Veronica

Veronica at an audience with Pope Paul VI

Veronica and the Assistant General of the Christian Brothers

Cardinal Suenens with Chiara Lubich

Cardinal Suenens prays at Frank Duff's grave

Cardinal Suenens with members of the Concilium of the Legion of Mary, at Frank Duff's house

Cardinal Suenens at the ceremony marking the 65th anniversary of his ordination

Cardinal Suenens with his successor, Cardinal Danneels, Archbishop of Malines-Brussels and Primate of Belgium

Veronica O'Brien keeping the neighbourhood tidy – 1993

Our Lady of Gratitude

The FIAT rosary

nary, so on and so forth – all in all, close to five hundred people. *Monseigneur* was astounded to see such a crowd.

In spite of this, things were looking very bad. I had been told unofficially that he is a difficult and moody man, and that he was having a very bad day because he has been very overworked recently. When Mr Robin asked him to introduce me to the audience, he refused point blank, and he refused to meet me when I arrived. You can imagine how I felt. I waited for him in the hallway, and asked him very humbly if he would be willing to open the meeting with the Veni Creator and a Hail Mary – which he agreed to do. He looks older than his age – about fifty – large and heavy.

The legionary altar was in front of my conference table – I always insist on this; it gives the proper atmosphere. Standing on a high platform, I launched into my speech. I was reasonably calm, but in close union with the guardian angel of each person in the room. I talked and talked, and people laughed at the right places, were serious when they were supposed to be serious, and now and then broke into prolonged applause.

And there were also moments of deep silence, when I spoke of the union with our gentle Queen, of the moments when we can experience the shadow of the Holy Spirit. I think I can say that I deserved ten out of ten, and that the audience – including the bishops – gave me twenty out of ten.

After a full hour, I stopped and gave the audience a chance to breathe after this whirlwind trip around the world – after such a climb to the very heights of Mary's influence.

At the end, *Monseigneur* arose: he spoke magnificently, saying that when he came in, he had been determined not to speak, but that etc. etc. – he went on to praise poor little me to high heaven, in all sorts of emotional terms.... He ended by saying that he was overwhelmed, and that he hoped to see the Legion spreading throughout his diocese. After this, I spent a few minutes with him in an atmosphere of almost tropical heat, and received his permission to speak in the major seminary. He will personally make all the arrangements with the superior.

That's all.

In Ea,
V. O'Brien

Aix-en-Provence – 1955

In this letter, Veronica begins by describing her arrival at the home of the Aix-en-Provence legionary group's president, whose name was truly providential: Esperendieu – Hope-in-God.

The president's name really is Esperendieu. We ate at his house yesterday; the second spiritual director joined us, and it was very cosy. However – minor source of concern – he did not ask me a single question about his new responsibilities.

What a meal! I suppose this is what people mean when they speak of the best of French cuisine. Madame would have been heartbroken if I had not eaten everything – and there were wines, and then champagne, and then liqueurs. My head was on fire and my face bright red by the time I left for the archbishop's house to give my talk.

Veronica goes on to describe her 3.00 p.m. meeting with fifteen priests and about fifty nuns; this was followed by another meeting with a group of men.

I was off again, to give a talk to thirty-five men at 6.10 p.m. – note the time; I would never have thought they would come so early. This allowed me to schedule another talk for 8.30 p.m.

At the first meeting, the men were mostly middle-aged or old, but very open; I'm sure we will get a few more active members from among them. Again, about ten books were sold. Make sure more books are sent on before each visit.

I passed around the photographs I had brought along. One gentleman will give me the address of his nephew in Istanbul – he works in a bank, and is a faithful churchgoer.

Then came supper with Monsieur le Curé. It was a real disaster: I was exhausted and I could feel that I was just about to be sick. I dragged myself to the chapel, and my insides settled somewhat, but I needed a real miracle to be able to give another talk at 8:30.

This time, there were about fifty men, younger, many of them workers. Monsieur le Curé spoke first, for about fifteen minutes. When I finished, I felt almost well again. I made many contacts this time, and there will certainly be quite a few active members from this group.

It was very late by the time I got to bed. I read the life of Gounod – very interesting. I will be able to appreciate his *Ave Verum* much better now that I know under what circumstances he wrote it.

That's all for now.

In Ea,
Veronica

OASES

Dijon

Nevers was the cradle of the Legion of Mary, but the Diocese of Dijon soon became a valuable support. The Bishop of Dijon, Mgr Sembel, welcomed and encouraged the Legion, as did the director of institutes, Fr A. Mathey (who later became vicar general and national spiritual director for the Legion, as assistant to Mgr Flynn).

I have before me a report prepared for his bishop by Fr Mathey when he was still a young vicar in St Joseph's parish in Dijon. In it he describes, with deep emotion, his discovery of the Legion; his work with young people was transformed by the new spirit that breathed through it. "I used to have a 'functioning' youth group; today I have a youth group that is alive." We still think of him as a close friend. He left us in 1972; I look forward with joy to seeing him again in heaven.

The Abbey of Citeaux

Veronica was in the habit of going to religious communities, in particular to Carmelite communities, to beg for their spiritual support, as she had done in Nevers in 1940. She felt comfortable and happy in the company of consecrated souls who breathed the same air she breathed. As a result, many lasting bonds were established over the years; and many of the religious houses which she contacted in this way agreed to become auxiliary members of the Legion.

A letter from a Carmelite nun in Angers, dated June 1, 1954, includes the following words, which provide a good summary of the general reaction to Veronica's visits: "The chaplain described the talk as 'pure theology, supported by a living experience. Those are indeed unforgettable moments.'"

Among those places of deep prayer which have been particularly dear and familiar to Veronica, one played a special role, and her relationship with the monastery of Citeaux deserves a special mention.

A few letters which have somehow escaped destruction reveal her spiritual intimacy with the monks of Citeaux. In some of these letters, monastic austerity goes delightfully hand-in-hand with humour. I will let two of the monks speak for themselves.

On October 22, 1951, Fr Marie-Bernard wrote to Veronica:

Dearest Miss O'Brien,
Dearest Sister,
or dearest Mother,

I am hard put to choose which of these forms of address is most appropriate, for in truth you deserve them all! You are Miss O'Brien, as well as my sister in Christ, and our mother in the Legion of Mary, since you are the foundress of the Legion in France. Personally I prefer the second form.

We often speak of you in our little praesidium of Our Lady of Citeaux, and I may add that everything we say is good. We do our best to keep alive the flame which you came to rekindle, or rather to revive, during your brief stay among us.

Another monk wrote these quick-witted lines to Canon Guynot:

It's just too bad for Sister O'Brien if she is a saint — there's nothing I can do about it! I'm simply stating a fact. If this statement infuriates her, no doubt it is a holy rage — like Moses'; he was "very meek, more than all men that were on the face of the earth", and yet the Bible tells us that seven times he became very angry indeed.

Veronica herself, writing from Citeaux on January 23, 1943, commented:

The Abbot and the Prior are as fervent as Mother Jeanne de Jésus (of Nevers). I went to this great centre of prayer and contemplation because I was in urgent need of two days of silence. Instead, I talked from sunrise to sunset! I

even gave a long talk to some priests whom the abbot himself had brought in from all over the place. There were
about thirty curates, and they were all very, very eager to
get started; they all agreed to be auxiliaries of the Legion.
Then they brought a microphone into the hall, and all the
monks listened in from behind the wall!

Everywhere, everywhere, I can see great graces, wherever souls accept in simplicity and humility what the Legion
offers.

And now, here is a report from Veronica:

The Abbot, completely won over to the Legion by the
legionary priests in Dijon, invited me to give him some
additional information. In this sanctuary of silence, I never
stopped talking for two whole days. I even had to be merciless and send away the brother who brought my meal, so I
could at least eat!

This brother and the prior have become auxiliaries, so
they will now recite the rosary every day.

I gave a lengthy talk to a large group of priests whom
the abbot convened to Citeaux by telephone. The monks
who deal with the outside world were present; the other
trappists (even the novices) were behind the wall, but they
heard every word, thanks to a microphone which the
abbot had the courage (!) to install that morning.

The Blessed Virgin has done marvellous work. The
atmosphere was extremely friendly; every one of them,
with very few exceptions, has registered as an auxiliary,
and about ten curates would like to begin as soon as possible. The prior and the doorkeeper have their pockets full
of pamphlets. Even before I arrived, the abbot had
arranged for more than six hundred francs' worth of
copies of the *Handbook* and of *True Devotion** to be

---

* Louis-Marie Grignion de Montfort

bought; after my talk, he sent a brother off to Fr Mathey to bring back some more! The booklet and a few other articles were read out loud in the refectory; most of the *Handbook* was read at the chapter, and now they will read *True Devotion.*

I wonder what St Bernard thought when he heard a woman's voice within the cloisters of Citeaux! But don't you think this is yet another proof that Our Lady herself is guiding the Legion? And She has a master-key which takes her wherever She wants to go.

Humour and humility

Veronica tells of an amusing conversation she once had with Dom Bélorgey, the Abbot of Citeaux,* on the subject of humility.

I was surprised at the ease and the emotion with which I spoke to the abbot about our gentle Queen. At the end of the conversation, I told him the secret of my boldness – that this secret is my profound humility! Naturally, I elaborated eloquently on the theme, which can be found in No. 213 of *True Devotion,* in which Louis-Marie Grignion de Montfort describes himself as a snake, a toad, a slug – in short, a whole menagerie; and the abbot listened to all of this with the greatest attention.

He used it well, too, the following morning: instead of giving the homily he had prepared for his monks, he gave them Sister O'Brien, down to the smallest detail, adding that this was the very first time in his life as an abbot that he had met someone who insisted on highlighting her own humility!

He ended his speech to the monks with the words, "She says she is humble... and what's more, I believe her."

---

* Dom Godefroid Bélorgey is a well-known author of spiritual works, including *Sous le regard de Dieu – Initiation à la vie intérieure* and *La Pratique de l'oraison mentale,* a work in two volumes, the first concerning ordinary prayer, the second dealing with mystical prayer.

Even the most solemn monks were laughing till they cried, so I am told — I have been hearing stories and comments about the whole event from all the monks; each one of them managed to invent some excuse to come and see me!

Veronica was asked to write a few lines in the visitors' book at Citeaux. On April 23, 1951 she wrote to me asking for my approval of this text:

Places of retreat are arsenals of grace; but we must find soldiers who are willing to use these weapons in hand-to-hand combat with the enemy. My thanks to Citeaux, to the Most Reverend Father Abbot, to dear Father Robert, and to each and every one of the monks — who, by their heroic silence and their voluntary stability, capture the supernatural high-voltage current so that the Legion of Mary can use it! Their silence gives us the strength to speak out loud and clear; their stability allows us to travel to the four corners of the earth.

To conclude this section on humility, I include another one of Veronica's letters, which dates back to the same period and which is to be read in the same spirit of natural and supernatural realism. In this letter, she speaks of the praise that was showered on her as she travelled, and in particular of one priest who was deeply moved and overwhelmed by her aposotolic words.

I am told that when they left me, they were "overwhelmed", all of them exclaiming "It's wonderful!" and so on and so forth, and there were all sorts of admiring words about me.

It is a hard and bitter pill to swallow, and it happens very often on occasions like this. But it is such a relief, and such a consolation, to know that God at least knows the real me, the one you stubbornly refuse to recognise.

How I cling to my gentle Mother at such times! I offer her Immaculate Heart to Our Lord, and then I repeat, with her pure lips: *"Vulnera tua, merita mea* — Your wounds are my only pride."* This gives me the strength to continue, even at the risk of fooling people so completely and so terribly.

I am bombarded with compliments, but practical results are not as good...

What frightens me is seeing how they appreciate me. But I imagine that the Lord himself blinds people so that they do not see the real me, which would fill them with disgust.

You, at least, know who I am, and this is very restful to me.

Still on the Road

Knock and it shall be opened unto you

"Il faut marcher, toujours marcher, une valise à la main — We must keep walking, walking on, suitcase in hand." Gilbert Bécaud's song is a perfect description of Veronica, travelling along the roads of France. With her knapsack on her back, she crisscrossed France for many years, carrying a small typewriter and clothed in a severe black cloak — a left-over from the War, which, in its classical timelessness, made her independent of changing fashions. Veronica took literally the Master's order to his servants to "travel the big roads and the small".

She went from bishop to bishop, to obtain the necessary authorisations; then from priest to priest, encountering obstacles and adventures of every kind, but never failing in her steadfast perseverance. Although the price she paid was heavy, the Lord visibly blessed her work. Whenever people gave her defeatist advice, she reminded them that the Master assured his disciples, "Knock and it shall be opened unto you" — but never specified how many times we would have to knock. She also quoted the Legion's *Handbook*, which states that "a failure is only a postponed success".

Because she was constantly on the move, Veronica never had a fixed address, and reaching her by mail was no easy matter. Her elusiveness led to an amusing exchange with the editor of the magazine *Le Rosaire*. He wanted to reach her so badly that he resorted to a rather unusual expedient: he published a desperate call in his magazine. Veronica heard of this SOS from a reader of the magazine, and immediately wrote to the reverend father. Her letter opened with the words, "Well, dear Father, that was certainly an original way of writing to me!" In the following issue of his magazine he responded, very pointedly, "And how else would you suggest that I do it?... I will have my readers know that Miss O'Brien is still out there on the road. If she is in Nice on the 15th, you can be sure that she will be in Lille on the 20th, in Bordeaux on the 25th, in Quimper on the 30th, and so on.... Where are we to write to her? The day Miss O'Brien is canonised — as she surely will be — she will, just as surely, become the patron saint of globe-trotters, vagabonds and wanderers. Will she then make them all, in her own image, into God's travelling salesmen?"

An apostolic visit to a chateau

From the very beginning of her apostolic activity, Veronica took very seriously the Lord's command to his disciples: "Go to the very corners of the earth and preach the gospel to all creatures." (Mark 16:15) She made her own the words of the *Handbook* (p. 240) which insist on the duty to go to all men everywhere, to the humblest and to the greatest, to those near, to those remote, the nearest and the farthest, even to the keeper of "the loneliest lighthouse".

In her mind, the great – those who belong to the uppermost classes – are, in a special way, the most remote; even when they support good works and movements, they remain isolated in their palaces. Veronica called them "the untouchables".

She told us about the very first time she decided to ring the doorbell of a mansion, with no introduction, simply trusting in God. It was in France. The gate was wide open, so she ventured up the main drive, without ringing the bell at the gate. No sooner had she entered the grounds than an impressive German shepherd rushed out to meet her, barking ferociously. Veronica called on her faith in Divine Providence, and bravely continued up the drive. As she reached the front porch, she felt something heavy pulling her back: the dog had seized the back of her coat in his teeth, and was furiously trying to stop her. At last, the lady of the manor appeared to investigate the uproar.

So began this apostolic initiative. When she told me this story, Veronica concluded: "The Legion rules state that, as a precaution, we must always go visiting in pairs, never alone. So you see, I was perfectly in line with regulations: there were indeed two of us – the dog and me!"

This story is here not only to entertain the reader, nor merely as an example of apostolic courage. It has a certain symbolic and prophetic value; it prefigures the *apostolat des salons* – the drawing-room apostolate – which was to become such an integral part of Veronica's life.

PART IV

IN APOSTOLIC COMMUNION

A. THE LEGIONARY PERSPECTIVE

11

A PRIVATE AUDIENCE
AND ITS UNEXPECTED
CONSEQUENCES

Having discovered the extraordinary apostolic worth of Frank Duff and Veronica O'Brien, I felt it was my duty to inform the Holy Father, so that he might personally discover their tremendous apostolic potential for the Church as a whole. No one spoke, in those days, of the charisms of the laity — Vatican II was not yet in sight. However, having met these two outstandingly charismatic people, I felt compelled to take this step. I was aware of the fact that, as an obscure young auxiliary bishop, I did not have much credibility, and that the initiative I proposed to take was quite unusual. However, I had read and re-read in the *Handbook* of the Legion that when faced with an apostolic task which appears quite impossible, the most important thing is to take the first step — the "symbolic action". This is stated clearly and explicitly:

"When faced with the apparently impossible ... take one step at a time. Take one step... there is no need yet to worry about the next step; so concentrate on that first one. When taken, a second step will immediately or soon suggest itself. And after a series of them...one finds that one has passed through the portals of the impossible." (*Handbook*, p. 250)

These words challenged me. Without a word to those concerned, I decided to take the first step by approaching Pope Pius XII. This was to lead to a completely unexpected second step!

My request was granted readily: the audience took place on

145

January 9, 1952. I began with a plea for Rome to express, in more explicit terms, its approval of the Legion of Mary, whose entry into a number of European countries was blocked due to the monopoly held by "Catholic Action". Five years later, I was to address the subject again, this time in a memorandum, which the Pope appreciated; later, he personally made the substance of it public.

I then came to the actual purpose of my visit. The Pope heard me out very kindly, but made no promises concerning my suggestion of a meeting. Clearly, I had failed in my goal: we were not on the same wavelength.

At the end of the audience I went, as was customary, to pay my respects to Mgr Montini, substitute in the Secretariat of State. Our conversation was easy and relaxed; I told him of the real purpose of my visit. As I was about to leave, I said to him, "You don't have to believe me, but you should see for yourself. Miss O'Brien is here in Rome at the moment, on a retreat. This is the telephone number of the convent where she can be reached."

I must confess that I was rather sceptical as to whether my suggestion would have any result; it is sometimes difficult to tell where polite attention ends and serious commitment begins. I was therefore pleasantly surprised to hear that Mgr Montini telephoned Veronica soon after I left, and, of his own accord, summoned her to his office. This first contact was to have far-reaching consequences.

Mgr Montini was an excellent diplomat; his pretext for this first meeting with Veronica was a desire to enquire about the situation of the Legion of Mary in France. After this meeting, Mgr Montini invited Veronica to come and see him again the following Sunday morning, at the Vatican; then they would be able to continue their conversation in a more leisurely fashion, as there are no audiences on Sundays.

Here is a description of these first two meetings, in Veronica's own words.

146

A letter to Frank Duff

I interrupted this letter to go and see none other than Mgr Montini, who gave me a tremendous surprise by ringing me up, the other day, and asking me to come and tell him about the Legion of Mary in France. It was last Thursday, just as I was leaving the house where I had spent some days on retreat. Mgr Suenens had spoken to him about me and my various experiences in France; he took my address, and this was the sequel.

I went along at once, feeling very frightened indeed, for every word would have its full meaning, and every second would be terribly valuable to the Legion. I had exactly twenty minutes with him; I was able to give a brief survey of the different activities of the Legion, and touch on the special difficulties we meet with.

He seemed to have only a vague notion of the Legion, and asked me the most elementary questions about its organisation – but all this in a very friendly and open way. He just mentioned Mgr Suenens' name, and also the fact that he had met you. I think he realised all of a sudden that something very important for the Church had come his way, and that he had a role to play; for when the audience was over, he thanked me very warmly, asked me to pray for him, and then invited me to return on the following Sunday, for a longer talk.

So here I am now, still a bit dazed after this morning's interview. When I arrived at the Vatican, the different officials on duty found it hard to believe that he had given me an appointment for a Sunday morning. This very fact, small in itself, speaks loudly. I was received at 12.25, and I had one hour and twenty minutes with him. I touched on many aspects of the Church in France, and showed him how the Legion seems to be the providential answer to many serious pastoral problems; I particularly emphasised the excellent formation it gives to seminarians. Then I was able to go deeply into the Legion spirituality, and show clearly where all this wisdom, and these initiatives, spring from.

It was obvious that he was deeply moved and impressed. He questioned me about you, and about the Legion in general, and I think he saw all of a sudden that the moment had come for Rome to recognise its influence, for he repeated several times, "We must see what we can do to help the Legion." And he asked me if there was any special function approaching which would give the Holy Father the occasion of making some public announcement.

I could only suggest the Dijon Congress, which is being held in March, and he took note of it. I did not dare to suggest a letter from the Pope directly to the Dublin Concilium, since I thought such a suggestion on my part would be outside my role...

I tried to keep to France as much as I could, and gave him Miss Ingoldsby's name [the delegate for Italy]. But I yearned to suggest a letter to the Concilium for the Acies [the annual assembly of the Legion, held on March 25, the feast of the Annunciation], the main feast of the year, and I submit this idea to you.

Mgr Montini repeated at least four times that there must be more personal contact with the Vatican, and that they are not sufficiently informed; he asked me to send him the *Handbook* and some Legion literature; and when I knelt down for his blessing, he knelt with me and suggested that we say together a Hail Mary, which we did, he adding the invocation "Seat of Wisdom, pray for us."

Then, as I was leaving, he abruptly said he thought it would be very useful if I were to see the Holy Father, even though His Holiness could not give me much time, and added, "I think we could manage that."

I told him I had not dared hope for such a favour – for

indeed I had abandoned that desire, since Mgr Suenens thought there would be no possible chance of its being realised. Mgr Montini finished by saying he would ring me up again soon, as he wished to continue the conversation.

And there I was back praying at St Peter's tomb at 2.00 p.m., leaving all that had been said safe in his hands. I pointed out to Mgr Montini that I have no official role now in the Legion, and I prepared the way for Miss Ingoldsby as well as I could.

In the antechamber, before the audience, I was looking through a Swiss magazine, and came across a very good article on Ireland, "only yesterday the poorest and most backward of English provinces, today a nation, strong and free". There were a few very telling lines about the Legion which ended thus: "The Legion of Mary, which has now spread to every continent, is a source of great hopes for the Church." That was a real pearl, and I read it out to Mgr Montini, who allowed me to keep the magazine.

From then on, there were more meetings with Mgr Montini, who was to become Archbishop of Milan and later Pope, supreme pastor of the Church.

I have found a letter from Mgr Montini which reveals an openness which, over time, became increasingly more spiritual and trusting.

> From the Vatican, March 30, 1954
> To Miss Veronica O'Brien
> The Green,
> Hampton Court, Surrey

Dear Miss O'Brien,

I have just received your letter of March 22 and I would

like to thank you without delay for your thoughtful gesture, which touched me deeply.

The Holy Father, to whom I have communicated your filial wishes and your prayers, has asked me to thank you. He entrusts your tireless Marian activity to the maternal protection of the Immaculate Virgin.

Please accept the assurance of my religious devotion.

Mgr Montini

12

PORTS OF CALL

Free of her mandate as delegate for France, and exhausted by twelve years of unremitting apostolic activity, Veronica felt the need for a long rest to prepare for future missions. This was made possible by a decision of the main council in Dublin: to thank Veronica for her work — which was described as "a work of lasting historical import" — the concilium offered to finance six months of well-deserved rest, to allow her to regain her strength.

Veronica accepted this offer, and decided to use the time profitably, to prepare herself for an apostolate "to the four corners of the earth," which had never ceased to be her dream. She chose to divide the available time into two parts: first she spent four months in Italy, to learn Italian and breathe the Roman air; later she spent two months in Spain, studying Spanish.

ITALY

In a letter to Yvette Dubois, dated February 26, 1952, Veronica described, in some detail, the price she had to pay to learn Italian. She stayed, as an au pair, with an Italian family, of which her letter gives a lively and colourful portrait:

> ...And now, a few words about the place where I am staying. There are two old ladies, who chatter away during meals; generally they say very sensible things, for they are both intelligent and well-educated.
>
> Their little niece, a nine-year-old orphan, is delightful and reminds me of Felicity at that age. I meet them all at

meals and also, briefly, in the evenings. I join them in
their drawing room and bravely read out loud for about
half an hour; I sew a little, and this gives me the opportunity to listen in on their conversations, and occasionally
make a few remarks of my own. The two ladies are very
active in the house. They have a very dirty housemaid, a
widow with three children. She has taken a liking to me,
and she pours out her trials and tribulations to me. This
of course goes on in Italian, so I am happy to listen, and I
even encourage her – not in her suffering, but in the sharing of it.

The food is excellent, well presented, but normally I
would eat twice as much as they give me. Each mouthful
is carefully measured out in a most unpleasant way; but
it's excellent mortification. From that standpoint, I welcome it, because I don't need as much food now that I am
not working under great pressure... and I have a great
many sins to atone for in that area.

The best food goes to the little girl, who eats twice as
much as I do; but she enjoys it so much that it's a pleasure
to watch her. She is all round and chubby – what will she
be at eighteen!

My room is very nice, with an electric heater. The housemaid sleeps in the bathroom, which is only a cubby-hole,
and I suspect she uses my towels and my powder – and,
who knows, perhaps my toothbrush as well – for the
wretch does not seem to have even the barest necessities; I
am glad to share it all.

Rome in a faith perspective

Here are a few of Veronica's reactions to the city of Rome:

I don't think you need be embarrassed by my reactions to
Rome. I can feel in every fibre of my being that I am in a

holy city, the holy city, a city which links the past to the future.

Every stone has a story to tell; each story seems to be a different one, but in the end, it is always the same, proclaiming the victory of grace over sin and suffering and death.

However, I must admit that I have little interest in the human side of it all, and I cannot stare at the ceilings for more than half a second.

But my heart beats with those of all the saints and martyrs who have loved and suffered here. 'Do not look on our sins, but on the faith of your Church' – this prayer is constantly on my lips as I wander through the city. And I could weep for joy at being able to breathe the air of Rome for four full months. Thank you, thank you, St Peter and St Paul!

In spite of it all, I do try to remember – because it is the thing to do – those things that every visitor is supposed to keep in mind when in Rome; and I can now tell St Mary Major from St Peter's Basilica!

Lecture timetable

Veronica's daily schedule, and the list of courses she attended, were rich in variety:

February 26, 1952

My study programme is positively Herculean; I want to take full advantage of all the very interesting opportunities in Rome, since this is my only chance to do so. In the morning, right after breakfast, I go to the University of Rome, where I attend three philosophy courses which are taught respectively by an atheist, a free thinker and a Jew.

In the afternoon, I take courses on a variety of subjects

ranging from propaganda methods in the media to courses on aesthetics and government — all of this at the Pro Deo University. Three afternoons a week, I take theology courses at an important institute near the Vatican; on Saturdays and Sundays, I have a course in humanism, which includes a few lectures on Dante, at the Angelicum.

SPAIN

In another letter, Veronica gave an account of her stay in Spain:

I spent two months in Madrid, to learn Spanish as best I could. This marvellous opportunity was offered to me at early Vespers in Notre-Dame de la Merci. You can imagine how grateful I was!

I had been tormented by the thought that I was not really preparing myself to be of service to Our Lady in Latin America. Then suddenly, yesterday morning, a letter arrived from Brazil, telling me that my plan to spend some time there next October was all settled. I was given the names of a dozen mothers general of congregations who would be happy to receive me. Now I must write to them to tell them that I am going to postpone my trip until after Christmas.*

I am told that educated people there speak Spanish; so I need not worry about Portuguese. I know just enough to follow an ordinary conversation.

Veronica's stay in Spain was marked by a fortuitous meeting which would one day greatly assist our joint activities in the United States.

One day, as Veronica was passing through Malaga, she noticed a priest coming out of a church; she greeted him in Spanish, but he answered, "I don't understand Spanish, I'm Irish."

They burst out laughing, and introduced themselves. The priest

---

* The trip to Latin America was finally postponed until after the Vatican Council.

turned out to be the famous Fr Peyton, world-wide promoter of the Rosary, from the United States. He told her that he was preparing a film on the fifteen mysteries of the Rosary; it would be shown at the 1958 World Fair in Brussels. He also mentioned that he did not know anyone in Belgium who could help him to publicise the film. Veronica gave him my name, in case it might come in useful.

When the World Fair opened at first, few people visited Fr Peyton's stand; I went there myself and met Fr Peyton, who complained about the low attendance. I promised that there would be an announcement from Cardinal Van Roey in the local papers, urging the faithful to visit Fr Peyton's stand; I wrote the note myself, and the Cardinal was happy to sign it. As a result, the number of visitors increased considerably, and Fr Peyton was very grateful.

This sequence of events had long-term consequences. Fr Peyton was a close friend of the Grace family; Peter Grace was an important American businessman who supported Fr Peyton's apostolate, and his wife, Margie, belonged to the Legion of Mary. She had always wanted to meet the author of the *Life of Edel Quinn* – in other words, me! A first meeting with the Grace family, in Paris, led to more than thirty years of friendship and extremely productive collaboration – especially for our apostolic contacts in the United States, both before and after the Vatican Council.

The film, which was inspired by Fr Peyton, contains a scene I have never forgotten. On her deathbed, Mary is shown talking to Peter; by way of goodbye, he says to her, "Tell the Master that I love him." Mary answers, "Peter, the Master knows it well." Peter replies, "Yes, of course; but he will be so much happier to hear it from your lips."

I have often quoted these words; they encapsulate a whole Marian theology.

13

MISSIONS TO GREECE, TURKEY AND YUGOSLAVIA 1955–1956

Difficult things can be done right away;
impossible ones take a little longer.

G. Santayana

The risk of hoping

More than once, when some apostolic endeavour seemed doomed to failure – whether because of particular circumstances or of the people involved – I advised Veronica to give up the idea. But unless the Church, through her spiritual director, ordered her to abandon a project – in which case she scrupulously complied – she invariably chose to run the risk of hoping; to reach for "that unreachable star...even to breaking point". She never hesitated "to go where no one dares to go".

She played Jacques Brel's recording of "The Man of La Mancha" countless times, for everyone she knew. She once said to us, during a spiritual sharing session,

I am happy to share with you all that is in my heart as I listen to this song. It is as if I were hearing it for the first time, with the heart of an eighteen-year-old. Every verse speaks to me, awakens in me a great yearning – a passionate feeling which makes me want to speak to the world about Jesus and about his love, to pour out my life for him, "to go where no one goes", to fight his battles "without strength or armour", "to love till love tears me apart". Oh Jesus, bless those who wrote this music, bless this song, and bless this wonderful singer.

I was deeply moved; it was as if I was hearing, for the very first time the part where he sings, just as he is about to die. The time is approaching when, on my deathbed, I shall jump up in my bed and sing, at the top of my voice, that I too am on the point of reaching what will no longer be an unreachable star. (April 12, 1977)

Many years ago, I once wrote to her, on the subject of her intrepid faith:

Your faith is like magic; it transforms everything it touches, it knows only victories, and turns everything into bounty. "Happy is she who believed!" – I know these are the first words you want to hear when you reach paradise. I will do my best to be there before you, to prompt the angels on the welcoming committee; however, if I should still be lagging behind in purgatory at the time, I am sure St Paul will give them the message.

Veronica never underestimated the risks involved in any apostolic initiative; but she belongs to the race of those Irish monks who braved violent storms to spread Christianity throughout Europe.

Her faith inspired me to write the following lines, which have become famous throughout the world:

> Happy are those who dare to dream dreams
> and are willing to pay the price
> to make them come true.*

It is a faith which abandons itself to God; and it shines through clearly in these three adventures.

GREECE — 1955

During one of her visits to Malines, Veronica received a telegram from Frank Duff, asking her to go to Greece to lay the foundation for the Legion of Mary. She was very touched; she jumped up and told me, "I'm going!" Greece was to be the first stage in a journey which would take her on to Turkey and Yugoslavia.

She left for Paris that same evening, to prepare for her journey. The date of her departure for Greece had been set for March 29, 1955. Her plan, which she had worked out in agreement with Dublin, was to stay in Greece for three months, spend three weeks in Turkey, then move on to Yugoslavia; after that, she intended to go back to Greece for another six months.

In March 1955, the Legion of Mary newsletter carried this item: "The concilium has just given Veronica O'Brien a new and important mission: she is to go to Greece and then to Turkey, to found the Legion of Mary." This was followed by enthusiastic letters of recommendation from Cardinal Feltin, Archbishop of Paris, and Mgr Rupp, Auxiliary Bishop of Paris in charge of foreign nationals.

The article ended with these words: "On her way to Athens, Sister O'Brien will visit the dioceses of Aix, Fréjus, and Nice; she will also make a brief stop in Rome to entrust her mission to St Paul, apostle of Greece."

The article discreetly avoided any reference to the fact that the concilium had also entrusted to Veronica the "impossible" task of implanting the Legion of Mary in Yugoslavia, at the heart of a communist nation which was bitterly hostile to the Church.

* *A New Pentecost?*, p. 13.

Veronica wrote to Canon Finet, in Chateauneauf-de-Galaure, asking him and Marthe Robin to pray for the success of her mission. Back in the pioneering days, Marthe Robin had welcomed Veronica with open arms to her Foyer de Charité; and a praesidium of the Legion has been active there ever since the earliest days. I have been there several times on retreat, and have been comforted by the warm and friendly atmosphere. Marthe Robin once said of Veronica, "She is so limpid, so transparent and so intelligent; and what courage she has!"

Now let us watch that courage in action.

Ventimiglia — a first adventure

Veronica decided to travel to Greece via Milan and Rome. Her journey began with an adventure which I find delightfully picturesque and amusing. I will let her tell the story in her own breathless style!

En route to Milan

When I arrived in Ventimiglia, I had to go through customs and change trains. Instead of calling a porter, I stupidly tried to drag the suitcases myself; I thought that the station was very small — but alas, it got bigger with every step! Finally I came upon a group of middle-aged gentlemen, and two of these, moved by compassion, took my suitcases. They were Swiss and they were travelling to Genoa and Milan for a chess tournament! I had to chat and laugh with them to thank them for being so kind, but all the formalities — changing money, and so forth — were taking up a great deal of time, and the train was waiting impatiently...

At last, we made it through. In the crowd I tried to keep an eye on my gallant knights, but — but... need I say more? I'm sure you have guessed...

I rushed on to the train with one suitcase; the hatbox had disappeared, and the train was starting. The porters all witnessed my distress, but there was little they could do. There was still some hope that my gentleman had managed to climb on board at the other end of the train. I left all of my possessions in the care of two Italian soldiers, and began to make my way, with great difficulty, all the way down to the other end of the train; the corridors were jam-packed with what looked like a whole fruit and vegetable market, with a few chickens thrown in for good measure.

At last I made it to the other end, more dead than alive. I found a compartment reserved for the chess players — but, much to my consternation, my "hatbox gentleman" had missed the train.

I did not know whether to laugh or to cry; so I did neither. No doubt he would take the evening train, but since they were to spend the night in Genoa, they would only reach Milan the following day — only a few minutes before I was due to leave!

I decided to give them my address in Milan, on the off chance — but my address book was nowhere to be found. Could it possibly be in the suitcase I had left with the soldiers? Off I went again, all the way back; by that time, I was beginning to have cramps. Finally I got there, and under the pitying eyes of my good soldiers I took everything, everything and everything out of the suitcase. Nothing and more nothing! In despair, I decided to have my hats sent to Mgr Montini, since at least I know that he lives in the Archbishop's House. By then, I was practically in tears!

But yes, you've guessed — I found the horrid little book; it was right under my nose. So off I went again, all the way down the train.

But where had I put my glasses? I could not read Mrs Otto's address! Please, please do feel at least a little sorry for me! Everyone helped, and between us, we managed to make out the address and I laboriously wrote it out.

Sad and resigned, I stood up to go. We had only been on our way for an hour, but just then, the train came to a stop – and there was my gentleman! He climbed into the train with my suitcase, and they both fell into my arms! Hurray for Switzerland, for ever and ever!

When he saw the train leave without him, this gentleman had grabbed a taxi and chased the train. He missed it at the first stop, but caught up with it at the next one. I almost kissed him! And everyone shared in my happiness. Then there was another big search through the other suitcase, to find a holy card to give him as a souvenir; I found one of Our Lady of the Road, and on the back was the "Driver's Prayer" which I had had made for Madeleine two years ago. I wrote my name on it, and "Legion of Mary", and when we reached Genoa, I went and gave it to him.

And now – a deep breath. But first I must tell you in a whisper that in Ventimiglia, I handed in my ticket for Milan, by mistake! But the angels are watching over me, and the ticket collector brought it back to me.

You see what's become of me! and I've only gone as far as Ventimiglia – and I have to go all the way to Asia!

At last, weak with hunger and with all the excitement, I let myself be tempted by a "hot lunch box" for which I paid 666 Lire; I was handed a horrible plateful of macaroni, sausages swimming in grease, two big dry bread rolls and a piece of chicken dating back to Noah's ark, along with a bottle of wine: on a scale of one to ten, a great big zero!

Let this be a lesson to us all!

I arrived in Milan, and Mrs Otto was there to meet me,

with her son and a magnificent car. Another half hour — and some more lire — later, I had my big blue suitcase; and then we were off to make an appointment with Mgr Montini. Mgr Macchi telephoned around ten o'clock the following morning, and I immediately went to see him.

And now — off to Rome!

A stopover in Rome

On her way to Athens, Veronica spent two days in Rome. She hoped to increase the Roman hierarchy's awareness of concrete methods of evangelisation. Her first letter from Athens describes this lightning visit to Rome with exuberant humour; it is full of lively sketches of the people she met: Cardinals — Ottaviani, Pizzardo, Tisserant, Valerio Valeri; Vatican prelates — Dell'Acqua, Samore, Van Lierde, Veuillot, Glorieux, Civardi; and Miss Goldie of International Catholic Action.

With such a busy schedule, it is hardly surprising that she never found the time to pray on St Paul's tomb, outside the walls, as she had originally planned to. However, she entrusted this task to St Peter; she asked him, among other things, to help her walk on the water and kindly to apologise on her behalf to St Paul outside the walls. She also thanked St Peter for responding so magnificently to the prayer she had addressed to him in October 1937, when she had asked him to enlighten her about her vocation.

At work in Greece

In Greece, Veronica found that nothing had been done to prepare for her arrival; due to a misunderstanding, the delegate from Dublin was not expected for another three months.

In Athens, Veronica stayed at a convent of Greek nuns of the Eastern rite. Here she set up her headquarters. Her first step was to call on Mgr Calavassy, the Catholic Uniate Bishop of the Eastern rite. He explained to her, in great detail, the complex situation with respect to the Orthodox Patriarch of Athens. Mgr Calavassy was involved in a court case with the Patriarch because of a church which he wanted to build, and for which he had already purchased land. This was, as it turned out, the fifteenth court case he had been involved in – a clear indication of the tensions existing between the Greek Orthodox Church and the Catholic Church. Uniate priests of the Greek rite were obliged to wear lay clothing in the streets, in order to establish the point that Uniates had no claim to the Eastern tradition. As we all know, anti-Roman feelings are still very strong within the Greek Orthodox Church, which does not participate in any way in current efforts toward an ecumenical *rapprochement.*

After visiting the Uniate Catholic Bishop, Veronica went to see the Latin Catholic Archbishop of Athens, Mgr Micrionitis SJ. He received her warmly, but later retreated into benevolent passivity.

Against this background, Veronica was to attempt the impossible task of setting up legionary apostolic groups. She had to take into account not only local tensions, but also the general climate, which was hostile to any form of evangelisation, and thus – *a priori* – to the Legion. In spite of all this – and despite her health, which was poor at the time – Veronica multiplied her contacts and her meetings, first in Athens, then in a number of little islands in the Aegean – Syros, Naxos, Tinos-Sirias – and in the city of Salonica.

One photograph shows her riding a donkey up the side of a steep mountain, with a group of nuns who had been won over to the Legion.

In addition to these external difficulties, a number of adjustments had to be made to the Legion's usual approach: the statue of Mary had to be replaced by an icon; the Rosary had to give way to the hymn of Akathistos; and there were problems with the Greek translation of the *Handbook.* All of this had to be done in a rush, as Veronica's passport was only valid from April 1, 1955 – the day of her arrival – until June 10.

163

In her last report to Frank Duff from Athens, she describes the concrete results of her work: ten praesidia had been established, of which four were of the Greek rite, one was among the Armenian population, and one was among Americans. She left behind a temporary liaison office, which would need to be strengthened by the future delegate, whose path Veronica had prepared.

At the end of her letter, she announced her departure for Turkey – yet another "impossible" mission. She was to return to Greece, but only to hand over responsibility to the envoy from Dublin, Mrs Zacherl, an Austrian legionary; she also met her briefly in Turkey, for the same purpose of transferring responsibility.

Veronica left a lasting impression in Greece. Ten years later, she received this telegram: "Athens Legion of Mary celebrating tenth anniversary of foundation May fifteenth expresses deep gratitude to the one who by her ardent zeal first sowed fertile seeds in Greece – Athens Curia."

TURKEY – 1955

Groundwork

Before leaving for Greece and Turkey, heading into the unknown in a true spirit of adventure, Veronica wrote to one of our Belgian friends, Fr Pirnay SJ, superior of the retreat house of Xhovémont in Belgium. She informed him of her plans and asked him for an introduction to his cousin, who was the Belgian Consul in Istanbul.

Here are Fr Pirnay's two letters, one to Veronica and one to his cousin.

Retreat House of Our Lady of Xhovémont,
Liège,
March 12, 1955

Dear Miss O'Brien,

When I heard of your new mission, I was surprised, but above all filled with great hope. I pray with all my heart that this mission will be crowned with a spiritual success comparable to that of your previous missions to France and to Belgium.

For some years now, I have been able to witness personally the excellent effects of the Legion of Mary, and I consider this a great gift from the Lord. My brother, who is parish priest in Oudenval, has founded a praesidium in each of his parishes. He has invited me to several meetings, and each one — and I say this to you in all simplicity — has left me profoundly moved, comforted, and, if I may say so, a better priest as a result. At these meetings, I experienced God's promise: "Where two or three are gathered in my name, there I shall be among them."

My cousin, Fr Devos, is parish priest of Saint-Gilles, the most popular parish in Liège; he too has invited me to meetings of his praesidium. As in all the other praesidia of the Legion of Mary with which I have had the grace of being in contact, I found men and women from very modest backgrounds who, even in their outward attitudes, radiated something of the purity, the prayerfulness and the gentleness of Our Blessed Lady. I also discovered in these meetings a real understanding of the concrete apostolic needs of a parish. As I was leaving, a friend said to me, "At last, a real meeting — a meeting that involves more than just chatter. This is real prayer, and good work." This was exactly my own impression.

In the course of the many retreats I preach to the clergy, I have had the opportunity to meet priests who, having attempted various forms of works, were becoming, in middle age, somewhat tired, disappointed, and discouraged. I have often advised them to introduce the Legion of Mary in their parishes. All, without exception, have been deeply comforted by the legionary life. They have had the comforting experience of finding a realistic and efficient method — one that, when it is lived faithfully in every detail, leads unfailingly to supernatural life. Often, they have also had an experience that has enhanced their own lives: that of finding a true spiritual family within which they are respected, obeyed and loved, no longer merely as organisers of works, propagandists or religious bureaucrats, but as men of God who have a specific priestly mission to accomplish. Because they are seen as such, they have become better priests.

And this is why, dear Miss O'Brien, I hope with all my heart that your mission to Greece and to Turkey will be blessed by Our Lady. My prayers and my respectful friendship go with you.

I have written to my cousin, who has been posted to the consulate in Turkey, in hopes that this may be of some assistance to you.

Pierre Pirnay, SJ
Superior
Retreat House of Xhovémont

Mr Robert Nokin
Belgian Consul
Belgian Consulate
Taksim Beyoglu
Istanbul, Turkey

Liège, March 12, 1955

My dear Lily, dear Robert,

Miss Veronica O'Brien, a young woman for whom all of us here have the greatest esteem, has been sent on an apostolic mission to Greece and to Turkey. I have taken the liberty of giving her your address, and of insisting that she must visit you in Istanbul. I would be very grateful if you would welcome her as you would welcome my own sister, and do all that is in your power to make her stay in Turkey as pleasant as possible.

Miss O'Brien, who is Irish, has been living in France for more than fifteen years; she has also lived in Spain and in Italy. She graduated brilliantly from university, and is gifted with the most beautiful qualities of spirit and of heart. Thanks to her extraordinary energy and generosity of heart, which all who meet her cannot help admiring, she has accomplished magnificent spiritual work in the countries she has visited. I am sure she will tell you all about it herself, and I can promise that you will not be bored. She has a lively, original and captivating manner of expressing herself. And when she talks — and this is perhaps her only shortcoming — she is irrepressible!

I am not yet sure whether she will begin her odyssey in Greece or in Turkey. If she goes to Athens first, she will be in Istanbul in early June.

First steps

The position of Christians in Ataturk's country was worrisome, and tension was still growing. The Orthodox Church was also experiencing difficulties.

Veronica and Frank Duff had agreed that from Greece she should make a side-trip to Turkey and do her best to introduce the Legion there; so she attempted to "move mountains", to awaken apostolic vocations and provide a supportive framework for them. She made contacts in Ankara, Istanbul and Smyrna (now known as Izmir). She had an important conversation with Mgr Descuffy, Archbishop of Smyrna, who invited her to accompany him to Ephesus; the city is traditionally associated with Mary's dormition, and the Archbishop was hoping to reawaken interest and stimulate pilgrimages to it.

A painful volleyball game

In a Moslem country bitterly hostile to the Catholic Church, it is no easy matter to establish the Legion of Mary. Where does one begin?

One Sunday, Veronica noticed a few young people at Mass; she started talking to them, and learned that they were going to play volleyball on a little island in the Bosphorus. Anxious to be "all things to all people", as St Paul recommends, she joined them on the beach, found the necessary equipment in a beach cabin, jumped into the water with them and played with great enthusiasm. All went well until the ball, which had been blown up to capacity, was thrown forcefully in her direction. She expected a very light ball which she could catch on her fingertips; but the ball hit her so violently that she sprained both her thumbs. As there was no doctor nearby, she received no medical attention; to this day, she suffers from the painful consequences of that volleyball game. It was the price she paid for her first contact with those young people whom she wanted to win to the apostolate.

Veronica had noticed that at Sunday Mass, none of the young couples received communion. She pointed out to the Archbishop this sad anomaly, which was due to the impasse surrounding the issue of birth control. This, she told him, was the main obstacle to all apostolic initiatives, and she urged him to propose a careful study of natural birth control methods, which could be a step towards resolving the deadlock. The Archbishop was impressed; he suggested that Veronica should go to Rome on her way back, to pursue this conversation with Cardinal Ottaviani himself.

When the time came for Veronica to leave Smyrna, the Archbishop thanked her publicly for the work she had done, saying that her visit and her message had done more good to the Church than all the other attempts at religious reawakening which he had witnessed in his diocese. Veronica's goodbye present to him consisted of eight praesidia of the Legion of Mary in his diocese.

I do not know what became of the groups set up in Turkey. In 1977, however, when we were on a pilgrimage to Nazareth, a group of pilgrims from Turkey recognised Veronica; they belonged to a praesidium she had founded in their country. I was able to see the exuberant joy with which they greeted her. It was a touching moment of fraternal love.

YUGOSLAVIA

The following year, 1956, Frank Duff asked Veronica to go to Yugoslavia. On the way, she was to stop in Turkey to consolidate the work she had done on her previous visit.

On May 13, 1956 she left Ankara by aeroplane and arrived in Yugoslavia. The purpose of this visit was to found a few apostolic groups which might in time become praesidia. Veronica had to do this from scratch; she knew no one, did not understand the language, and was unfamiliar with the place. In addition, she found herself at the heart of a fiercely communist country.

Veronica wrote a long report on this experience; it covers the

169

period of May and June 1956, and was intended for the authorities in Rome. One of the striking things about this report is the frequency with which it mentions the oppressive regime and the propagandistic skills used to promote communism.

Here is the introduction of the report on the early days of the Legion of Mary in Yugoslavia.

May-June 1956

At the request of the concilium of the Legion of Mary, I travelled to Yugoslavia earlier this spring, on an exploratory trip. In appearance, I was there as a tourist; in reality, I was there to explore the possibility of establishing the Legion of Mary. In any case, this trip provided an opportunity to express the concern and solidarity of Catholics and religious authorities of my country for the people of Yugoslavia.

As a precaution, I have kept no names or addresses; I am writing this report from memory, and I must apologise for any minor inaccuracies it may contain. I shall describe my journey chronologically and provide some background information on the situation and on possible openings in the various locations.

From Turkey — where, during a previous stay, I had established twenty-two praesidia of the Legion of Mary — I left directly for Yugoslavia. On the eve of my departure, I was able to obtain only a three-day visa, instead of a regular tourist visa, which is valid for five weeks. This seemed to indicate that the Turkish authorities had been alerted to my religious activities. I had to decide whether to go anyway. Under the circumstances, the whole venture seemed quite impossible; but the *Handbook* invites us, in desperate situations, to attempt "the symbolic action" and to divide the impossible into small portions. The situation was made even more delicate by the fact that everyone had advised me not to go; also, I had been able to obtain very few useful addresses, since everyone was afraid of compromising people. I was left with nothing but faith and trust in Her whom I had promised to serve.

I arrived in Belgrade by aeroplane, and went to the Jesuit residence. At first, they greeted me with total distrust (I will come back to this later). Despite their extreme reserve, they finally agreed to give me the name of a lady of Irish origin, married to an English diplomat, who they said might be able help me with the problem of my three-day visa.

At 7.30 in the morning, I went to see this lady. She was still in bed; I woke her up and asked her to get dressed and accompany me immediately to the passport office. I hoped that this would give the impression that I had friends in Belgrade who were expecting me. You can well imagine the lady's outrage and panic, her doubts and hesitations. Finally, with a complete lack of enthusiasm, she agreed.

At the passport office, I was told that what I asked was quite impossible. I insisted so much, showing them the dollars I had brought with me "to spend in the country", that the employee agreed to refer the matter to her superiors, and told me to come back that evening. Finally, physically and emotionally exhausted, I was granted a five-week visa. Then I had to find a place to stay. I will not go into the endless complications that this involved, everywhere I went. I will simply say that each time, a regular battle had to be fought; for corruption is rife, and everyone is at the mercy of the highest bidder.

And at last, my adventure could begin.

At first, I introduced myself as an Irish tourist involved in Catholic action; I gave no further explanations, and did not reveal the true purpose of my visit until I was sure of

171

the Catholics I was meeting. I expressed an interest in the social problems of the country, and said that I wanted to take back some information to the nuncio and to the Archbishop of Dublin, and also to express their goodwill.

My task was complicated by the fact that even the priests and religious could not be trusted. It is known that the government has set up an association of priests who support the regime. As the result of an intervention from Rome, this association was banned by the bishops at the episcopal assembly of September 1952. But the harm was done: many priests, both secular and regular, belong to it. In Slovenia, this association is known as the Association of Saints Cyril and Methodius; in Bosnia-Herzegovina, it is called the Association of the People's Priests. Members must commit themselves to do nothing against the regime and to be exemplary "patriots", which involves participation in communist meetings and in work teams. Only those priests who register in these Associations have legal existence and enjoy privileges such as a salary, free medical care, and an old age pension. These priests are recognised as priests of the people; the others are known as "persons of independent means" and are therefore subject to exorbitant taxes. It is easy to understand why the temptation to register is great. This made my task particularly complicated, since it was difficult to know in advance which priests belonged and which ones did not.

Freed from the fear of being deported within forty-eight hours, Veronica travelled through the country. During the few weeks she was authorised to stay, she went to Belgrade, Zagreb, Ljubljana (in Slovenia), Rijka (Fiume, Croatia), Dubrovnik, Cetinje, Split, Zadar, Opatija and Pazin.

Her report is a historical document on the religious situation under Tito's regime. I will reproduce a few excerpts, in order to

172

give the reader a taste of the prevailing atmosphere and an idea of the risks involved in any kind of religious apostolate during that time.

Belgrade (Serbia)

My journey began in Belgrade.

The city looks very strange. New buildings have sprung up all around the entrance to the city. There are no cars or bicycles. It is a bit like Paris at five o'clock in the morning; the feeling is of an immense, indefinable and expectant lull, as after a night of bombing. Its shop windows are half empty; to disguise the emptiness, the few available items are spread out across entire displays. The only clothes to be had are 'all-purpose' items made of coarse cloth, and these are exorbitantly expensive. The most essential items are treated as first-class luxuries. Life begins at seven o'clock in the morning and goes on till about three or four in the afternoon. Work is interrupted for a quick snack — on the spot, to avoid travel expenses. To supplement salaries, which are much too low, people work in the evenings; so they are always exhausted, especially the women and mothers. No one is polite to foreigners; the feeling that the people own the country is very strong. To get a room in a hotel, one must bribe the staff — and the bribes are high. As I said earlier, finding a place to stay is one of the most difficult problems for all foreign travellers.

My first call was to the Jesuit church. The priest who let me in refused to speak to me because I had not brought my passport (I had been instructed to leave it at the hotel). The following day, I returned with my passport, but he still would not trust me; he asked me if I wore a holy medal, and said that before he would speak to me, he must hear my confession. He was obviously a very frightened man. As it turned out, he had spent a number of years in prison.

173

At last, his suspicions were appeased. He showed me a card with the Legionary prayers, which he kept in his breviary, and asked me "Are you the envoy?" The card had been given to him last year by an Irish journalist who had promised that "one day, someone will come." This priest spoke English. He went to fetch his superior, with whom I spoke Spanish. The superior authorised me to talk about the Legion to the four young Jesuits in the house. During this first talk, the superior kept watch in the corridor, keeping an eye on everyone who passed by.

Zagreb (Croatia)

I will also include the section of the report in which Veronica describes her meeting with Archbishop Seper, who later became Cardinal and Prefect of the Holy Office; his friendship with Veronica continued after he moved to Rome.

From Belgrade, I flew to Zagreb.

The Jesuits have a magnificent church here; Mass is celebrated daily, and there are always large crowds, both in the morning and in the evening. There seemed to be a large number of priests.

After some difficulty, I was allowed to see the superior. At first, he was extremely reserved and fearful; but very gradually, his reserve melted. He told me that the State confiscated the large building they used to have; now, about twenty novices and young religious are confined to one small room. He seemed exhausted, and saw little hope of improvement.

I managed to see the archbishop, who received me "against all the rules", as he told me later; he added that he considered this meeting to be a very special grace from the Blessed Virgin. He did not want me to get in touch with the auxiliary bishops, or with the priests working

174

within the Archbishop's house; he said that he could trust no one, with the exception of one professor of dogmatics in the seminary, to whom he later introduced me.

The Archbishop gave me his authorisation to try to establish a legionary group; he also gave me the names of two people (a professor at the seminary, and the superior of the Ursulines, with whom he arranged a meeting) who might be able to ensure the success of such an experiment.

I found a wonderful and immediate rapport with the professor at the seminary. He is a priest, and he has read and enjoyed *Theology of the Apostolate*, from which he quotes in a book he is writing about the formation of priests in seminaries. He speaks French and Italian poorly, but understands them very well.

He has agreed, with the Archbishop's approval, to speak to the seminarians about the Legion, and to give them the appropriate apostolic formation. Once a month, he meets with three or four country priests who give each other spiritual support, and he will share with them all that he knows about the Legion.

Until now, he had only known Catholic action in the form of study groups, lectures, sermons. For him, the Legion is a tremendous discovery — he sees it as a powerful instrument of salvation for his country. With the Archbishop's approval, he will find someone to translate the *Handbook* into Croatian.

My meeting with the Superior of the Ursulines — Mother Marguerite — also went very well. These Ursulines live in a small annexe of their big house, which has been confiscated. They live in one room, with no garden, all year round; as a result, some of the younger nuns are ill and very tense. They are forced into a contemplative lifestyle, simply because they will on no account abandon their habit; this makes it impossible for them to find work or to be present in the outside world. They live from day to day, making paintings for the church. They have no conception of the leadership role they could play among laywomen, who are left completely at a loose end.

I had very long talks with Mother Marguerite, who is a very special and saintly soul – ready for anything, capable of anything, and joyfully receptive. She understands the incompleteness of the lives of the thousands of nuns who concentrate on their immediate tasks – the children and the sick – and neglect their leadership role among the laity. She is aware of all this apostolic energy which needs to be channelled towards mission. She immediately brought together six young women, all around the age of twenty, who agreed to found the first praesidium, despite the risks involved. Their goal is to visit former students who are now dispersed and who, like themselves, have received no preparation for the apostolate. The first visits had wonderful results. The praesidium calls itself "Our Lady of First Aid". Mother Marguerite was very impressed by a letter she had received from their house in Athens, in which they described my visit to found the Legion in Greece and spoke of the Legion with great enthusiasm. In other words, I found an open door. The first meeting of this praesidium was held in accordance with all the rules. We could feel the Holy Spirit hovering over this little cenacle with its closed doors – closed, not for fear of the Jews, as in Jerusalem, but for fear of communists.

The report ends with a few general reflections and some practical suggestions encouraging "apostolic tourism" by Christian holiday-makers to this country. She tells her readers that they should go there during the summer months, not in winter; that they should avoid asking for directions; and that the foreign languages used are, in decreasing order of usefulness, Italian, German, French and English.

In conclusion, Veronica wrote:

It is not for me to draw conclusions; but I would like to stress how desperate the situation is, and how important it is to act without delay. In my opinion, the Legion of Mary could be an effective instrument to set things in motion. Given the circumstances, I would not recommend that the Legion be established in all of its usual forms, which can only be deployed in a free society. But it would be possible to establish praesidia, basic cells which would provide the foundations for future apostolic action. This would be a dangerous undertaking; but is this not the kind of risk which is inherent in our faith?

14

ON THE MARGINS OF
THE WORLD CONGRESS FOR THE
LAITY

ROME, 1957

An impasse

One of the major difficulties which the Legion encountered in
many European countries – particularly in Belgium, France and
Italy – arose from the fact that it was not recognised as an
authentic form of Catholic action. As a result, it was banned in a
number of dioceses, in order to avoid competition and disrup-
tion. At best, it was accepted as one of many devotional movements; this was tantamount to a denial of the very nature of the
Legion, whose goal was to translate prayer into action, inviting
us to "act out our prayers". It took a great deal of time and
patience to break down the monopoly held by Catholic Action.

Veronica made many efforts to alter this situation. Among
other things, she devoted several pages to the subject in a booklet entitled *The Legion of Mary*,* which provides a succinct but
thorough description of the Legion, illustrated by various concrete examples of apostolate.

On the same subject, I wrote:

There is no doubt that the Legion of Mary embodies those
qualities by which we can recognise a genuine form of

---

* Published by Légion de Marie, Paris.

Catholic action. This is true whether we consider its essence — its purpose, method and structure; whether we look at its work — in which we see an active, organised, systematic and controlled form of evangelisation, in close and constant partnership with the clergy and the hierarchy; or whether we examine its worldwide accomplishments in the many dioceses where it is active.

In addition to these elements — which could be called intrinsic, as they stem from the Legion itself, from its nature and activities — there is an external criterion which entitles it to the label of Catholic action: hundreds of bishops and apostolic vicars, in every part of the world, already recognise it as belonging to this category.

Mgr Garrone's recent statement is clear and unambiguous, and it is with joy that the Legion calls attention to his words. Writing about movements such as the Legion of Mary, the Archbishop of Toulouse stated:

"Today, as a result of a more clearly defined apostolic orientation and of various official statements, we can no longer reject their claim to a place within Catholic Action. Some may legitimately reject the methods of the Legion of Mary, but it is impossible to refuse to grant it the title and the status which it has in every way deserved."

If these words are accepted, we may hope that they will put an end, once and for all, to the painful malaise which has already lasted far too long; that they will open the doors to a time of fruitful and fraternal collaboration.

For a harmonious co-ordination of the various forms of Catholic action, pluralism must be at the very heart of the expression "Catholic action". There is a need for openness — not in the definition of Catholic action, which is not being questioned, but in the attribution of the label. Such openness would help to avoid a hardening of established situations; would allow life to evolve; and would allow new

authentic and valid movements to emerge in future, insti-
gated by the Holy Spirit, at the very heart of Catholic
action. There is no question of attributing the label of
Catholic action randomly to any movement, or of including
devotional associations. Once criteria and conditions for
admission are established, however, the present exclu-
sivism must give way to co-ordination, thereby forestalling
dispersion of energy while enhancing different activities
and allowing them to converge.

The openness for which I was pleading gradually gained support
and acceptance at the World Congress for the Laity, which was
held in Rome in 1957.

In 1955 I had published a book called *L'Eglise en état de mission.** My goal throughout this book was to call for broader apostolic horizons and for a wider range of initiatives enjoying
greater freedom of action. Mgr Montini, Archbishop of Milan,
wrote a preface to the Italian edition.

The enthusiastic welcome which the book received – in particular from Mgr Cardijn, founder of JOC – allowed me to hope that
it would be widely understood. In an issue of *Notes de pastorale
jociste* (no.5, 1955), Mgr Cardijn addressed the following words
to JOC chaplains and to all members of JOCF:

Every priest, every religious and every believer should
read this book and reflect on it! The author, who is a bishop, follows in the footsteps of Pius XI and Pius XII in calling, with episcopal authority, for a general mobilisation of
all Christians, so that, through our joint efforts, the
Church of the twentieth century may be a missionary
Church.

This book is by no means a dry analysis, restricting itself
to defining and explaining the essential mission of the
Church, or the missionary vocation of every Christian –

---

* Desclée De Brouwer.

whether priest, religious or lay — or the call to community and solidarity of Christians as a whole, united in the most indissoluble apostolic co-operation. It is rather an enthusiastic and insistent invitation to a more intense awareness of the missionary duty of each and every one of us. Above all, it is a solemn plea for religious education and pastoral programmes which include formation and initiation to the apostolate — in other words, a plea for apostolic apprenticeship.

There is a need among Christians for religious education which provides — in addition to a deep formation to the spiritual, sacramental and liturgical dimensions — a doctrine of Catholic life, practical training in apostolic action, a commitment to the apostolic organisation which is necessary to the mission of the Church in the twentieth century.

The book's originality — especially when we realise that it was written by a bishop — lies in its insistence on the need for direct formation and initiation to the apostolate, and in the methods which it promotes. *L'Eglise en état de mission* would make an excellent introduction to the Second World Congress on the Apostolate of the Laity, which is to be held in Rome in 1957. It could provide a starting point for further research.

Mgr Suenens dwells at some length on the apostolic role of auxiliaries of the clergy and that of nuns in traditional congregations; he deals boldly with the crucial problem of their collaboration in the various sectors of education and of charitable and religious assistance...

...I can only repeat, to all chaplains and leaders of JOC and JOCF: read Mgr Suenens's book, encourage others to read it, and use it in your study groups and in your team meetings.

A surprise

I had sent Pope Pius XII a detailed memorandum on the subject of the "monopolised mandate". It was a joy and a surprise to me when the Pope, in his opening speech, called on the Congress to reflect on a suggestion which he said (without mentioning the source) he had just received, and which he quoted at some length. Everyone understood that he was in favour of greater openness; the effect was explosive in some influential circles at the Congress, especially in one group of bishops and cardinals, who complained to the Pope.

He told them that the suggestion which he had passed on had come from the Auxiliary Bishop of Malines, and that he wanted to leave the matter open to discussion. Since he had explicitly requested the opinion of the forty bishops − all of whom were chaplains of the movements participating in the Congress − we held a meeting. Mgr Larrain, of Brazil, was chosen to defend the position of the status quo on behalf of all the bishops (except one), and they agreed to hear my arguments as an opening.

I had reason to fear that the report intended for the Pope would only reflect the majority opinion; I had therefore drafted my own report, just in case.

Towards the end of the Congress, Pope Pius XII granted me a private audience in Castel Gandolfo, to hear my report on the meeting.

A letter from Mgr Benelli

Mgr Benelli, who shared our point of view, wrote a letter to Veronica, describing the Pope's perspective on the situation. He asked her to share this letter with me.

> The Holy Father intended to give an orientation, not an order. Nevertheless, the orientation is clear. All are invited to reflect, debate, and so on; however, it is expected that

this reflection will take into account the Holy Father's orientation. It is not an order. In his commentary on the Pope's speech, Fr Lombardi said that the Holy Father wants, requests, proposes this and that; he has regretted this commentary. For the time being, the debate must remain open at every level. Once the membership has given its reactions, we shall see what needs to be done.

He went on to describe in detail the reactions of various cardinals, bishops, and so on; he concluded with those of Mgr Veuillot, of Paris.

Veuillot absolutely agrees that the monopoly must end. He is anxious to point out that, in the last few days, he has tried to make this clear to the leaders of the French Catholic Action. According to him, the Holy Father will come back to this issue in a while (as he did with the question of the Eucharistic fast). He will then make whatever decision seems appropriate in the light of reactions to his speech.

At the end of his letter, Mgr Benelli wrote:

I will keep you informed of any further reactions. My impression is that there is neither optimism nor pessimism here; everyone is simply waiting to see what the reactions will be. An idea has been launched; now it is up to the interested movements to send letters from bishops who are in favour of the Legion — or at least are opposed to the existing monopoly — directly to the Holy Father.

15

EXPERIMENTS IN FORMATION FOR EVANGELISATION

BELGIUM, FRANCE AND ITALY

Experiments in formation for evangelisation

Veronica has always believed that the problem of formation for evangelisation, both of priests and of male and female religious, is crucial to the future of Christianity. As we have seen, it was precisely conflict on this issue that determined the direction of her life.

At her behest, I wrote *The Nun in the World*. Although I wrote every line, she wrote what lies between the lines.

Veronica's entire life has been a sorrowful and heart-rending call to reform seminaries, novitiates and active religious communities, in order to introduce and train their members to direct religious apostolate through personal contact. This unheeded cry in the wilderness has been – and still is – the greatest sorrow in her life and in mine. Mr Gallup, the great expert in statistical surveys, has compared the Catholic Church to "a sleeping giant" where evangelisation is concerned. This sluggishness begins in our houses of formation, and it is due to a lack of appropriate instruction.

Veronica, in the hope of shaking us out of our apathy and our blindness, has used analogy after analogy. She asks, "Have you ever seen a swimming school where swimming is taught in a classroom, and students never go into the water? Or a medical school where students are taught about every disease that ever existed, in the past and in the present, and never spend time with patients? Or a military academy where students learn the history of every war that was ever fought through the centuries, and never perform any manoeuvres?"

Out of this concern sprang a number of concrete pastoral experiments. Partly to avoid having to develop a methodology from scratch – but also because the Legion of Mary already existed on every continent and provided a flexible and simple method which could be adapted to every situation – Veronica suggested that some experiments be undertaken along the lines of legionary practice. This was to be a temporary solution; we expected that more elaborate methods would be developed to meet the needs of specific religious communities, novitiates and seminaries. We asked Frank Duff if we could use the legionary method for one year; I met with him in London to discuss this, and obtained his authorisation.

BELGIUM

Malonne

Thanks to Brother Philippe, Assistant General of the Christian Brothers, several experiments got under way in this Congregation. They involved both the large St Berthuin Institute in Malonne and the Ecole normale of St Thomas in Brussels, where I personally gave a number of lectures which included supervised practical work. This experiment was specifically aimed at future lay Christian teachers, but a few of the brothers participated in the learning experience. One of the young students was Remy Van Cottem, who is now Auxiliary Bishop in charge of the Walloon Brabant.

Veronica's activities were centred in Malonne. The Congregation there appreciated her immensely: on October 22,

1960, in a solemn ceremony at the St Berthuin Institute, the Superior General, Brother Nicet, awarded Veronica a certificate of affiliation to the Congregation itself. The document was signed in Rome on September 15, 1960; as I mentioned in chapter 2, in connection with Veronica's departure from Aigle, this date has special significance for her, and she saw in this "coincidence" a smile from heaven.

The official text begins with these words: "Aware of your deep devotion, and wishing wholeheartedly to recognise the Marian and apostolic stimulation for which our humble congregation is deeply indebted to you, we believe that spiritual offerings are the most appropriate expressions of our profound gratitude, and also the ones that would mean most to you."

In this spirit, the Congregation gave Veronica its highest proof of esteem, promising that prayers would be prescribed throughout the Congregation "as soon as we learn that you have reached the end of your pilgrimage in this land of exile".

Veronica has the gift of awakening apostolic conscience and bringing about simple initiatives of the kind that are within everyone's reach. Concretely and with a great sense of humour, she taught those around her how to love God with all of their imagination. "Get your brain cells working," she would say, as she pointed out the thousands of ways in which we can "witness to the Lord always and everywhere".

Br Mutien Clément, spiritual director of the third-year students at Bordighera, wrote a lively description of Veronica's apostolic challenges and suggestions, and mentioned some of the objections that were most frequently raised. I have this paper in front of me; its title is "Is Sister Veronica O'Brien's message – as we have understood it – viable for our communities?" It begins with a question: "Why do we need a lady to come and tell us what we should be doing? Do we not have superiors and a founder?"

Br Mutien then goes on to answer this question.

"God chooses his own messengers. In Lourdes, he chose an

ignorant little girl; in Fatima, a few small children. We would find it much more logical if Our Lady's messengers came to us from the pope; and yet the Lord chose to use these particular messengers. This has often been the case in the history of our Holy Mother Church. When it became necessary to reawaken the evangelical meaning of poverty, the Lord used Francis of Assisi, who was neither pope, nor cardinal, nor even priest. The messenger is unimportant; what matters is the message."

The Missionaries of the Congregation of Scheut also accepted Veronica's initiative and welcomed it with great openness. Thanks to the wholehearted support of their Superior General, Fr Degryse, similar experiments took place in their seminary in Jambes (Namur). Fr Lefèvre, a member of the Congregation, wrote to Veronica:

> This inspiration comes from God, who wants you to be His instrument. I am convinced that Providence has reserved for you a unique role in the Church.
>
> Fr Degryse said to me one day (I only mention this because his words had a decisive influence on me) that he was happy to place the Congregation at the service of a saint who is visibly inspired by God.
>
> (All Saints' Day 1961)

Nivelles

Inspired and encouraged by Veronica, almost fifty communities, representing about twenty congregations in Belgium and France, agreed to be involved in similar apostolic experiments. I would remind the reader that these were all active congregations; contemplative orders were not involved. In *The Nun in the World*, I explained at some length the reason for these initiatives. The key passages are on pages 36 through 38:

One can only marvel at the admirable sum of devotion

which makes up the lives of women religious. However, devotion and apostolate are not always realities which coincide. The question that must be foremost in the mind of every pastor of souls is this: in today's world and in today's Church, what is the apostolic yield of women religious, who are so admirably devoted in every other way? Is there in these women an apostolic wealth which could be used to greater advantage? Are there any new fields of apostolic endeavour which are lying fallow, awaiting their contribution?

It seems that these questions must be answered in the affirmative. But first, we must clearly define what is meant by apostolate, and in what ways it differs from devotion. Only then will it be possible to see where the deficiencies lie and how they can best be remedied.

Let me point out once and for all that when we speak of deficiencies, we are in no way criticising or reproaching today's religious women. They are not to blame if they have not been invited or prepared to undertake certain missions which have become necessary in our time. Later we shall attempt to unravel the original causes of this situation.

The Community of the Sisters of Nivelles was one of the first women's congregations to enter upon this path of "legionary" experience. Sr Marie-Emilie, who was Superior General at the time, has written a booklet which tells their story.

This was also the congregation which Veronica convinced to adopt a new religious habit – distinctive yet modernised, and designed by a famous Paris couturier! Veronica wrote to the designer, asking for her assistance; the letter, I think, is quite amusing:

Sunday, October 13, 1963

Dear Madame Marguerite,

I have a very special favour to ask of you.

As I know your kindness, your thoughtfulness, and your desire to do as much good as you can whenever the opportunity arises, I thought that you might be able to assist me in my apostolic work, in a way that fits in perfectly with your own activities.

You are no doubt aware that a number of religious communities are making great efforts to adopt a new habit – one which, while preserving its religious character, is more appropriate to our times.

This, of course, is the great difficulty: the desire to have both of these aspects. Several congregations have asked me to help them; they realise that they have not yet found what they are looking for, but they do not know what other changes they might make.

I am touched by their good will, especially since all of this involves a great deal of expense for them, and I have promised to help them discreetly.

But I badly need your assistance! This is why I am writing: to ask if you would be willing to contribute to the Council's work by helping me to find that little touch that will make them more in tune with today's world – that will help them to look neither countrified nor like little old maids!

If you are willing to participate in this effort, I can bring you some photographs or samples of what has already been attempted and needs to be improved.

Naturally, I must ask you to be most discreet about this matter, as indeed I am myself.

I feel sure that you will not refuse to help me in some-

189

thing which will certainly have far-reaching consequences, and which, through these few congregations, will help many others who do not yet dare to begin because they do not know what would be suitable.

I thank you in advance for all your help, and I remain affectionately yours...

At the level of the Universal Church

The same apostolic concern spread to Italy, as is evident in a letter Veronica wrote to Mgr Montini – by then Pope Paul VI.

Rome, Saturday June 20, 1964

Most Holy Father,

When I had the honour and the joy of seeing you last, at a special audience with Mrs Peter Grace, I spoke to you of the experiments under way in a few religious congregations; these congregations are attempting to acquire an apostolic formation within their communities, in order to train both their own students, and all the people who will be indirectly entrusted to their care, in the field of apostolic work.

At that time, Holy Father, you were kind enough to tell me that you were personally interested in this matter and that you wished to be kept abreast of developments in this area.

Since then, the Congregation of the Ursulines of St Charles, in Milan, who have a special fondness for you, have expressed a great interest in some of the experiments in Brussels. The Superior General sent two of her assistants – Sr Maria Ignazia de Prosperis and Sr Marie-Madeleine Knerich of Florence – to see for themselves what has been accomplished. Upon their return, the Mother General strongly encouraged them to prepare the way within the entire Congregation for this kind of apostolic training. They have since made a few attempts at apostolic meetings in some of their communities.

I even had the joy and the surprise of discovering that they have translated and printed the little handbook which contains some practical ideas based on the experiments in the diocese of Malines-Bruxelles; they plan to distribute it throughout the Congregation. I am therefore taking the liberty of enclosing a copy of the Italian translation for you.

I am staying in Rome for a few days, till next Wednesday, June 24 (my plane leaves Rome at 1.05 p.m.). With me is Yvette Dubois, who has been assisting me in my work for almost twenty-five years and who comes from Nevers, the land of St Bernadette. May I ask Your Holiness to grant me an audience before I leave for the United States, where I am to undertake an important tour?

I have received personal invitations from a number of religious congregations, and I am happy to be able to tell them that lay women, whom I represent, need them to inspire them and to train them in the apostolate. In a sense, I am, in every convent, a beggar on behalf of lay women.

I dare to hope that you will grant my request; may I inform you, Most Holy Father, that I am staying at Salvator Mundi, the big American hospital in Viale delle Mura Gianicolensi, where the sisters are also deeply involved in this approach of "apostolic training".

Most Holy Father, I beg most humbly and respectfully for your blessing.

Meetings with the Roman Congregation

Because of pre-conciliar ways and traditions, and the rigid interpretations of canon law which prevailed at the time, these experiments caused some problems.

Veronica, however, has always been anxious to maintain ecclesial communion. For this reason, she went to Rome several times, in order to inform the authorities of the meaning of these experiments; she explained how essential they were, and emphasised the urgent need for the Church hierarchy not only to tolerate, but actively to promote them.

In Rome, Fr Van Biervliet, a Redemptorist who was much appreciated by religious congregations, was wonderfully receptive to Veronica's ideas, and supported her efforts. He was a renowned canon lawyer, very open to the concept of apostolic action, and he had a marvellous sense of humour. At their first meeting, he said to her, "You shall be the rushing river, and we canon lawyers will prepare a bed for you!"

Veronica once complained to him that certain obstacles to apostolic work were due to the fact that women religious were bound by excessively restrictive regulations, which contrasted greatly with the freedom granted to men within the same congregation, established by the same founder. He smiled mischievously and said, "Miss O'Brien, we men practise holiness by proxy."

He fully shared her pastoral concern, however; he asked her to provide him with written documentation, with a view to promoting her initiatives, if possible, through an official Roman document, possibly one signed by the Pope.

She was also very warmly received by Cardinal Valerio Valeri, Cardinal Prefect of the Congregation for Religious, who had previously been nuncio in Paris.

The formidable Cardinal Larraona received her less coolly than we had expected; Cardinal Ottaviani had told Veronica that he was the key person to contact, and had telephoned him to announce her visit. Veronica wrote me a letter describing this meeting:

> I found a hefty Spaniard, overburdened with duties, allergic to any kind of nonsense. Van Biervliet had warned me

that he might not be very friendly, as he is incredibly over-worked; but he added that I had to win him over at all costs, because he is the key man. I believe I can say, in all humility, that I got 100 out of 10. The meeting only lasted twenty minutes, but all the essentials were said. He promised me that the matter would not end there – *but* on condition that I send him all of my suggestions in writing.

Fr Dezza SJ also welcomed Veronica very warmly. He was confessor to Pius XII for a time; he has also been the Rector of the Gregorian University. Pope John Paul II appointed him to head the Society of Jesus during the interim period. Today he is a cardinal.

He was extremely understanding; Veronica described him as "a delightful, friendly, easygoing, gentle person – simply a saint." As for the subject of their conversation, she said he was "as receptive as a sponge"!

I personally invited Fr Dezza to come to a meeting of women religious who were already interested in apostolic experiences, and he accepted my invitation. He came to Brussels and reassured them about the interpretation of the year of novitiate: it is incompatible with external activities, but not, he said, with activities of evangelical initiation; these are inherent in the baptism of every Christian, and should not be left on a back burner in active congregations.

Veronica did not waste a single moment in Rome; she made many useful contacts. She wrote to me:

> I make endless telephone calls, trying to set up appointments, which is a complicated matter here. On the streets, I pray incessantly, and my prayer is often "Lord, I am not worthy", or, in the same spirit as St Peter, "Go from me...". But at the same time, I offer the Immaculate Heart of Mary. I am like a fish in water, happy all day long to be

using every bit of my strength in the service of the Divine Master. My constant purpose is as clear as the sun. I think people here are gradually beginning to see it more clearly as well; but it is all so time-consuming, and it is so essential to explain things in person! Everything I say seems so new to them; and yet every word is there in your book.

In another letter, she described a fifty-minute meeting with Cardinal Tisserant, underlining the following words: "I forced him to listen to me." That, I must say, was quite an accomplishment! The meeting went very well.

She also described a visit to another prelate, who agreed to support her apostolic views. In spite of this, however, she preferred Dezza to this man; this particular high official of the curia seemed "too charming, too much of an artist, too sublime, too ethereal for me". When all was said and done, however, she felt he was "a real ray of supernatural light in that dark dungeon".

Apostolic teams

These practical experiments along the lines of the legionary method caused some difficulties, especially with some religious circles in France, who feared that the Legion would intrude into the life of religious communities. There were also difficulties with Dublin, where it was feared that the Legion would lose some of its specifically lay characteristics, and that these new praesidia, however temporary, would slip away from the control of the local legionary authorities.

In order to avoid these dilemmas, Veronica abandoned the legionary approach and developed "apostolic teams" in total freedom; these retained the same basic principles, but had no link whatsoever with the Legion itself.

In 1957 she wrote a booklet of initial instructions adapted to religious communities, entitled *Women religious in Mission — a Belgian Experiment*. A religious community in Milan, which had a close relationship with Archbishop Montini, translated and published the booklet for its own use. Later, it was also translated into German and English.

Fr Philippe OP, whom Veronica had already met when he was in the Holy Office, had just been appointed Prefect of the Congregation for Institutes of Religious Life, much to Veronica's joy. This meant that we could hope that Rome would give some support to our experiments. We continued to have an excellent relationship with Fr Philippe, even after he was made cardinal. On December 27, 1959 Veronica wrote to him from Paris:

Paris, December 27, 1959

Most Reverend Father,

You will have received my telegram by now, so you already know of the great joy with which I welcome your appointment to head the Congregation for Institutes of Religious Life; this letter is simply to express my joy more fully, and to give you more detailed news of the experiments under way here in Belgium.

In Rome, and again in Paris, I spoke to you about a number of experiments in initiation to apostolic action, involving nuns and brothers; on a temporary basis, these experiments consisted essentially of one year of training in the methods of the Legion of Mary. I clearly stated to all concerned that the Legion had only one ambition in this matter: to disappear as soon as possible, once the experiments had proved their point in a conclusive way.

Since no one had ever seen an institute in this field which was anxious to hasten its own disappearance, I had to overcome a certain amount of scepticism. However, even the most sceptical have had to bow down to evidence: we have put a complete end to all legionary training courses for the professed (the Legion continues to exist in novitiates, where it has been active for a long time). We have now entered a phase of "apostolic teams", which, structurally, no longer have anything in common with the Legion.

Mgr Suenens has set up a small private committee to draft a handbook for these apostolic teams; it includes a few superiors of congregations of nuns and brothers, who have been through the legionary training course, and I am working with them on the handbook. We will submit the draft to you as soon as it is ready, to make sure that there is nothing in it which does not meet with your full agreement. A few religious canon lawyers have promised to assist us, and we are hopeful that this instrument can be used for a few years on an experimental basis, before it is redrafted in final form. However, this would require the personal contact that is so dear to the Legion, and an opportunity to give you all the details and nuances.

I will be travelling to the United States for a series of lectures in spring. I hope to stop briefly in Rome, both on my way there and on my way back, and I hope to have the joy of meeting with you and submitting the draft to you, with Mgr Suenens' full agreement.

More and more, I realise that apostolic effectiveness could be multiplied a thousandfold if only our women religious were ready to play their role of animators of adult lay people. This, however, presupposes a reform of the novitiates – so much needs to be done at that level.... I am overwhelmed with joy at the thought that you are now heading the congregation, for you have in your hands the key to open a kingdom.

With all my respect, I remain, Most Reverend Father, yours, etc.

Finally, in order to make clear that our initiatives had nothing in them that was imprudent or unorthodox, Rome, through the official channel of Cardinal Valeri, Prefect of the Congregation for Institutes of Religious Life, invited me to give a lecture on the subject to the International Congress of Religious in Rome, in 1957.

16

A SERIOUS CAR ACCIDENT AND
A TURNING-POINT
1958

THE ACCIDENT AND ITS CONSEQUENCES

In 1958, Veronica's life came to a sudden and unexpected turning-point. A very serious car accident determined and precipitated her decision to move from Paris to Brussels.

The accident

One glance at a photograph of what was left of Veronica's car is enough to show us how serious the accident was: the car was reduced to a scrap heap. The consequences might easily have been tragic, not only for Veronica and Yvette, who were on their way to Malines, but also for the occupants of the other car, who were going in the opposite direction, and whose car skidded into the wrong lane as a result of slippery driving conditions at Zemst, near Malines.

I will let Yvette Dubois describe the nerve-racking event in her own words.

Here are a few details of the terrible accident in which Sister O'Brien and I were involved on Tuesday, December 16, on the road between Brussels and Antwerp.

Veronica and I were travelling together, with Veronica at

198

the wheel, and we had just invoked the angels of the road and prayed that the Lord might inspire us and guide us in a major decision that we had to make. We had invoked Edel Quinn, whose prayer we prayed each day and whose picture we carried, and we were just finishing the invocation to the Holy Virgin: "My Mother, my Trust, guide us where we can love you and serve you best..." Then the accident took place.

A few moments later, we saw a car coming towards us from the opposite direction; the car skidded across the road, then managed to get back into its own lane, which brought a sigh of relief to our lips. Just as it was passing us, however, it skidded once again, in such a manner and with such force as to throw us off the road and down into the field on our right. There was nothing we could have done to avoid it. We saw it coming, we screamed, and a moment later, with a tremendous crashing sound of breaking glass and crumpling metal, we were flung into the ditch. The car landed upside down, and I was jammed in the right-hand corner; Veronica fell on top of me, unconscious. In the impact, her head was forced out between the broken windscreen and the windshield wiper. I thought she was dead. There was nothing we could do to get out, as she had lost consciousness and I was caught in such a way that I could not move.

The first ambulance took the five wounded people from the other car to the hospital in Vilvoorde. We would have been taken there as well; however, by an extraordinary coincidence, the driver of our ambulance recognised Sister O'Brien. She had been a nurse before taking on her new job, and had once taken care of Veronica in Dr Debois' clinic. As a result of this fortunate encounter, the ambulance headed for Malines.

Every time Sister O'Brien regained consciousness for a moment, she murmured the same words: "Thank you, thank you." We could feel that these words expressed all her supernatural acceptance of her suffering. When she regained full consciousness, Sister O'Brien could remember nothing about the accident; her last memory was of the prayer we had recited: "My Mother, my Trust..."

Dr Debois kept her in his clinic for about three weeks, then prescribed two months of complete rest, with no visitors; he insisted that no one should be informed of her whereabouts. The accident had been mentioned in the newspapers, so there were almost fifteen visitors each day at the clinic: priests, religious, brothers, and legionaries arrived from every corner of Belgium; there were also half a dozen French priests and some legionaries from France, including Brother Tual and Brother Levet...

Before returning to Paris, I went to take a look at the car in the garage. What a mess! It was nothing but a heap of scrap metal, and the steering-wheel that Sister O'Brien had held in her hands was twisted completely out of shape. We had had a very close call. The policemen who came to investigate the accident told us that accidents on that spot were always fatal. Our lives had hung by a thread, but the thread was in the hands of the Holy Virgin Mary and she held it safely.

On a tree near the spot where the accident occurred, there is a little shrine to Our Lady; we are planning to go there one day, on a pilgrimage of thanksgiving. *Deo gratias!*

This event marked the end of Veronica's roving legionary activities; it was the turning-point which led her to other tasks and new horizons.

A letter from Frank Duff

This letter from Frank Duff, dated January 3, 1959, illustrates the wave of emotion, sympathy and prayers which followed the accident.

I must admit that we were frightened when we received the telegram from Brother Bihin telling us of the accident. Later that evening, we received another telegram, which we opened in a state of panic, fearing the worst.

The photograph of the wreckage suggests that the two cars collided with such violence that everyone could have been killed. I think that we must believe that there was a miraculous intervention in favour of our important legionaries.

Indirectly, this accident is something of a blessing for Sister O'Brien; it will give her the rest which she needed so much. She will have time and space for prayer and reflection. I am sure that her rest, her prayers and her thoughts will have many important results for the good of the Legion and of the Church.

Please tell her of the immense relief with which all of us here in Dublin learned that her condition was progressing well. Tell her that a wave of sympathy enveloped her the moment we heard the news, and that countless prayers were said for her.

I look forward to writing to her personally in the near future.

Frank Duff's words proved to be astonishingly prophetic: the Council was just around the corner, and new horizons were indeed about to open. Veronica's apostolic commitment would find expression at the level of the Church as a whole.

After the accident, Cardinal Marella, who was then nuncio in Paris, wrote to me: "Truly Miss O'Brien has experienced a miracle, and it will be good for her to take time to rest and get well. I have already written to her directly at the clinic."

A crossroads

As a result of the accident, Veronica was unable to leave Brussels for several weeks, and she was obliged to live a quieter life thereafter. She rented a flat in rue de Suisse, planning to settle there with Yvette and two other legionaries from Paris.

The problem of her future apostolate presented itself once again, this time in new terms. Should she continue to introduce the Legion throughout Europe? Or should she rather choose a closer and more direct collaboration with the auxiliary bishop I was at the time?

Veronica went to Rome to present her problem of "concrete apostolic vocation" to an archbishop whom she knew — Mgr Van Lierde, Vicar General of the Vatican City. In a spirit of faith, she asked him to hear her confession in the Basilica, "as close as possible to St Peter's tomb", so that his answer might be that of the very first apostle and "fisher of men".

The advice he gave her was very definite:

"You must love the Church more than the Legion! There is no better way for you to serve the Church today than by placing yourself at the service of Mgr Suenens, auxiliary bishop of Malines."

A few weeks later, Veronica went to Lourdes on a pilgrimage of thanksgiving for her recovery. In front of the grotto, she ran into her friend Fr Philippe OP. She asked him whether he supported the advice she had received concerning the orientation of her life; his answer was exactly the same as Mgr Van Lierde's. Veronica saw in this a double response from heaven: that of Mary in Lourdes and that of Peter in Rome. She decided to settle in Brussels.

Our collaboration, which had begun on a part-time basis as early as 1948, took on its full scope in 1959. It has been the great spiritual grace of my life.

For Veronica, this was the beginning of a new "walk on water". At this stage, we could not foresee that I would be appointed archbishop and then cardinal; nothing foreshadowed the greater mission which would be entrusted to me and which would allow me to serve the Church on a universal level.

Thus Veronica put into practice the prayer by Cardinal Newman, which she had once written out on the back of a holy card to give to me. These words express every nuance of the decision she made, in faith, at the crossroads where new horizons were opening for us both:

Thy way, not mine, O Lord;
Choose out the path for me.
I dare not choose my lot,
I would not if I might;
Choose thou for me, my God,
So shall I walk aright.

A gift to the Focolari

Although Veronica's change of orientation meant that she would be settling in Brussels, she still had full responsibility for the house in rue Boileau.

She tried to donate it to some religious congregation, since the Legion does not allow communities within its structure. She turned first to Fr Degryse, who was at the time Superior General of the Congregation of the Missionaries of Scheut. She knew him well; he had promoted our initiatives in formation to the apostolate among religious congregations in Belgium. For a time, the house was placed at the disposal of the Sisters of the women's branch of his Congregation, who often went to Paris to attend courses. They cared for the last surviving member of the Oeuvre des grands malades, Sr Louise, Countess Boudet, who died in 1969.

The time then came to find a permanent solution for the building. Veronica's first thought was to hand it over graciously to the Congregation of St Clotilde in Paris, in memory of her past. They were touched by her offer but, due to their reduced numbers, were unable to accept it.

Then Veronica had a spiritual experience similar to the one which, long ago, had led her to go to Paris and look for the

Oeuvre des mourants. During the night of December 31, 1970 – the feast of Mary, Mother of God – the word *focolari* rang in her ears with a mysterious insistence. She was not familiar with this word; but she felt that this was a supernatural inspiration to do with the building in rue Boileau.

Early on the morning of January 1 she came to ask me what the word *focolari* meant; she was convinced that it contained a suggestion from the Lord. I was familiar with the Focolari movement, and had authorised its establishment in my diocese; I had been struck by the fervour of its members, and by their ideal of unity. Without any hesitation, I encouraged Veronica to pursue this inspiration.

That same day, we made contact with the Focolari by telephone. After a long search, we finally reached the person in charge of the French branch of the movement; she communicated the offer to Chiara Lubich, the foundress, who agreed to take the house for three years, on a trial basis. The experiment was very successful, and resulted in a formal settlement.

On December 8, 1974 – a Marian date which we chose deliberately – a great gathering was organised at 41 rue Boileau. Chiara wanted to be there, to express her gratitude in person. This is the speech she gave, as it was reprinted in *Nouvelle Cité:* *

Your Eminence, and dearest Veronica:

On behalf of all those who are gathered here today – who include most of the members of the Focolari movement in France – I welcome you on this day, this memorable day in the history of our movement; a day rich in Christian fellowship, and above all rich in gratitude. Today, every word, every gesture, every song has one purpose: to express our deep and sincere gratitude – to God first and foremost; to Mary; to you, Mgr Suenens; and to you, Veronica.

For the past three years, this gratitude has lived in our

---

* February 1975, pp.5-7

hearts; today, we express it openly and wholeheartedly. A dream — your dream — has come true, and a prayer — our prayer — has been fulfilled.

I still remember how it all began. It was October 1970. In Rome, those in our movement who were responsible for the French region were discussing their burning desire for a house, a "cradle" in Paris; this had become essential to the movement in France. They spoke of this need with such conviction that I came to share their concern, as did others at the main office.

But what could we do? Where could we find the means to create a Mariapolis centre — even the beginnings of one — for the formation of the various existing branches of the institute? Only God, our Father in heaven, could answer our questions. But he does not ask us to look for houses; he asks us to seek his kingdom, and tells us that the rest will be given to us over and above. That meeting ended with an urgent prayer, in which we asked God not only to increase the number of people involved in the movement in France, but also not to leave them homeless.

A few months went by. Then came the meeting with Veronica, and her moving story. She told us that on January 1, 1971, she had had an inspiration, and that the Cardinal had given it his full support; as a result, she offered to give this building to the Focolari movement, also known as the Institute of Mary.

We all know that two other institutes, both of which served the Church, have preceded us in these buildings. What can we say to Cardinal Suenens and to Veronica? We must promise them that we will not neglect God's gift; we must assure them that it is our intention, with God's help, to make it increase and bear fruit as much as possible.

My own experience of living next to the Mariapolis centre in Rome leads me to dream of a similar centre here. In

Rome, thousands of people are always passing through the centre, and going on to every corner of Europe, and even beyond, inflamed with Christ's charity. I dream that something similar may develop here, for the good of Christians in France; for the development of ecumenism; for a deeper understanding of Mary, Mother of the Church; for co-operation in bringing about the concrete realisation of Vatican II in every aspect of Christian life; and, in a very special way, to bring back to God those who have drifted away.

Does God want this? God wants it.

To you, my dear ones who share my ideal, I entrust the realisation of these words – through action, but above all through our characteristic unity.

Then Cardinal Suenens and Veronica will know with certainty that their gift will not have been in vain.

This describes only the official side of the transfer. On a more private, spiritual level, Chiara – in accordance with a custom of the Focolari – chose a "word of life" from the Scriptures for each of those in our smaller group. For Veronica, she chose "Mary kept all these memories and pondered them in her heart" (Luke 2:19).

Chiara also gave Veronica a name which was meant to express her own personal vocation. This name was "Grazia". She explained her choice in these words:

because you are a grace for the Church;
because you are a grace for the Cardinal;
because you are a grace for our movement;
because your life is a continuous grace.

17

ON THE SIDELINES OF
THE COUNCIL

1962–1964

My memories of the Council itself make up a large part of
Memories and Hopes. This chapter deals primarily with our
efforts to promote our experiments in formation to apostolate, in
Rome, in the United States, and in other parts of the world.

After the first session

At the end of the first session of the Council, Pope John XXIII
asked me to go to the United States to present his encyclical
Pacem in terris. This gave me the opportunity to make a number
of contacts in that country.

I had agreed to give a series of lectures on the theme "The
apostolic promotion of women religious". Through these lectures
to groups in various cities, I was able to speak to a total of
almost twenty-five thousand nuns.

Meanwhile, Veronica had been officially appointed special consultant to the Institute for Religious Superiors, which was
attached to Notre Dame University in South Bend. Fr Pelton, the
director of the Institute, wrote a little book on apostolic methodology, inspired by Veronica.

The following year, she agreed to give a cycle of lectures paral-
lel to mine. One of these was to be at Fordham University.

One of Veronica's talks has become famous because of its element of surprise. She was discussing adaptations of the religious habit; she suggested that to enhance apostolic effectiveness, habits should be simplified, while still remaining distinctive. Knowing that Americans enjoy a direct approach, she decided to use an amusing device, reminiscent of Fr Martindale's dramatic appearance on stage (see chapter 3). In the middle of her lecture, she suddenly stopped and said to her audience, "A friend of mine is in the next room; she is wearing a simplified religious habit, discreet, casual, but distinctive. Would you like to meet her?"

There was a chorus of "Yes! Yes!" through the hall. Veronica left the room and quickly changed into the outfit that she and her little group used to wear. When she stepped back onto the stage, she did so sideways, so that they would not recognise her immediately. When she finally turned to face her audience, their surprise brought her a burst of applause and general laughter.

In the course of these conferences, Veronica succeeded in winning over an impressive number of young religious to apostolic promotion. She also generally managed to reassure the older nuns, one of whom publicly thanked her in a letter which was published in a magazine. "Thank you," she wrote, "for awakening in us the marvellous grace of discomfort with our own failings".

Paul VI and our experiments in formation to apostolate

My readers will remember that before leaving Rome for the United States, Veronica had written to the Holy Father requesting an audience; in her letter, she had mentioned experiments that were under way in Milan.

At this audience, the Pope welcomed Veronica with particular warmth. When he was Archbishop of Milan, Mgr Montini had made a vigorous appeal to a group of nuns who were especially close to him, urging them towards greater apostolic involvement.

These nuns had reacted enthusiastically to a particularly important speech which he made to them on February 11, 1961; they sent me a French translation of this speech. This text came so close to what we were advocating that I once told the Pope that I was in possession of a very revolutionary statement he had made in the days when he was still Archbishop of Milan. I added that I would be very happy to publish it, if he would personally review it first, as "there might conceivably be a gap between the archbishop of yesterday and the pope of today".

He laughed at this, saying that he trusted me and that I was at liberty to do as I thought best. The original Italian text has since been published by the Paul VI Centre in Brescia.

A Roman villa on Monte Mario

The Council offered us a unique opportunity to promote experiments in apostolic formation and to make contacts with influential Christians, both lay and religious.

Once again, Margie Grace took it upon herself to solve the problem of an appropriate meeting place. She provided us with a spacious villa in Monte Mario, high on the hills above Rome; here we could breathe the fresh air and generously entertain many of those who had gathered in Rome for the Council.

I can still remember the reaction of my Methodist friend Dr Outler, who was one of the observers at the Council; he poked a little fun at me when he saw Villa Miani.

"Oh, oh," he said to me with a smile; "this is not evangelical poverty!"

To which I could only reply: "No, it is only American kindness."

The meetings at the villa involved numerous exchanges of ideas and of experiences. Through the contacts she had made with superiors general in the United States, Veronica managed to have a few nuns sent to Rome, under the direction of Fr Pelton, to help with the organisation of these meetings.

Among the many who took part in the meetings was Frank

Duff; Veronica had invited him to share his apostolic vision. He agreed to speak in French — an unprecedented triumph over his timidity in this respect!

Fr Pelton's team took notes during the meetings, and recorded the presentations which served as starting-points for the discussions. As I look over the report which the nuns prepared for us, I find the names of some of those who came to give us lectures and presentations: Fr Peyton, CSC, Martin Work, President of the International JOC. Raoul Delgrange, International President of Youth Fellowships; Dorothy Day, a convert who was co-founder of the Christian Workers Movement in the United States. In short, a very broad range of views was represented. We breathed an invigorating conciliar atmosphere, and we were free to dream aloud.

Among the names of the nuns who facilitated these meetings, I find that of Mother Mary Thaddée, of the Presentation Sisters; she was to become the first woman religious to be appointed to an important position within the Roman Curia.

I wrote a brief introduction to the final report, which was intended for internal use only.

The proclamation of Mary, Mother of the Church

The third session of the Council ended with Paul VI's proclamation of "Mary, Mother of the Church".

This came as a surprise. I must admit that, like some other bishops, I would have been happier if the Council had been allowed to assume responsibility for this in a conciliar manner — although this is merely a matter of procedure, not one of substance. I imagine that this was the reason for the slight delay before the assembly reacted. In that moment of silence, I saw Veronica standing up and applauding, all alone, in the seats reserved for special guests, anticipating the general applause by a split second.

Immediately after the Council

For Veronica, the atmosphere of the Council was prolonged through a series of trips to various countries, where she went to promote the apostolic initiation of women religious. She travelled to Argentina, Brazil and Mexico, where she spent several weeks at the Cuernavaca centre; in 1965, on the invitation of Mgr Gran, Bishop of Oslo, she went to Norway for the same purpose.

Most of her travels, however, took her to the United States. She participated in a conference which the Diocese of Detroit organised on the fifth anniversary of the publication of *The Nun in the World*. Later, in Steubenville, she took part in a congress of women religious.

By then, she was no longer travelling as she had in the old days in France — with a knapsack on her back, getting from place to place by any means available. Thanks to Margie and Peter Grace, she had more advanced means of transport at her disposal, including aeroplanes and cars — sometimes with a chauffeur, sometimes without.

The car that took leave of its driver

The subject of cars, with and without drivers, brings to mind an incident which could have had serious consequences. Shortly after the event, Veronica sent me a letter:

This morning, I went to the post office. It is about a twenty-minute walk from here, and Margie kindly lends me one of her cars. There are two here — two big huge machines which can hold eleven or twelve people each, plus a dog or two. Every time I borrowed one to go to Mass, I sat at the wheel and felt immensely proud of myself.

Now you must listen to what happened to me, and thank all the angels on my behalf, and let my adventure be a lesson

211

to you as well. Let me say right away that nothing terrible happened!

I parked the car in a side street which sloped down to the ocean; then I went off to the post-office, happily looking forward to all the letters I hoped to find. I came out pressing two letters to my heart.

As I walked toward the place where I had left the car — was I seeing things? Strange things were happening before my very eyes. My car slowly began to move away, with no one inside it, and gently rolled across the street, in the most stately and dignified manner — to the utter amazement of someone who was cautiously approaching in the other direction. Then the car began to pick up speed — and rolled right into a wooden fence around the garden of a nearby house! It finally stopped at the front door.

If you saw the street, you would realise that, according to all the laws of gravity, a car wishing to wander off on its own in this particular spot ought to have rolled right down the hill and straight into the sea; nothing would have stood in the way of its majestic progress as it plunged into the ocean.

Meanwhile, there I was, chasing desperately after the car, and remembering every word of the conversation I had had at breakfast with the Graces on the morning I arrived: they had said that I should not drive in the States, as I do not have an international driver's licence.

A few men came running up — no policemen, thanks be to God. The car was stuck on a piece of wood, and they managed to disentangle it.

I will cut a long story short and simply tell you that Margie found the whole thing extremely funny; we went to the garage, there was not the slightest scratch on the car, and all that remained to be done was to reimburse the owner of the house for his fence.

212

B. IN A CHARISMATIC AND ECUMENICAL PERSPECTIVE

18

OUR DISCOVERY OF
THE CHARISMATIC RENEWAL
1972

On the eve of the Charismatic renewal

To understand the background to this story, we must remember the atmosphere of the times, the post-conciliar mentality, and the various turbulent reactions caused by Vatican II. In 1968, in an attempt to explain some of the implications of Vatican II for the communion of the Churches, I wrote a book called *Co-responsibility in the Church,* in which I stressed the consequences of collegiality. I returned to this theme in an interview entitled "The Unity of the Church in the Perspective of Vatican II", published by *Informations catholiques* on May 15, 1969. My statements were acclaimed by those on the "periphery", but there were also some strong reactions from the "centre".*

Veronica was not directly involved in this controversy. Despite the ever-widening gaps between theologians, she maintained many close personal contacts. She met with Hans Küng, among others, in Brussels and in Switzerland.

In 1970 about a thousand theologians, representing a wide spectrum of viewpoints, met at a congress in Brussels. In other words, before the rift took place, contacts continued, in a spirit of hope, within the hearts of those who had been brought together by the Council. Gradually, however, the storm clouds gathered, as dialogue became increasingly tense and difficult.

---

* See *Memories and Hopes,* pp. 208-229

It was against this background that Veronica was granted an audience with Pope Paul VI.

An important audience

Veronica did not usually put anything in writing about her audiences with the Pope. On this occasion, however, she made an exception; she even wrote about her own feelings before the audience of March 8, 1972.

> My inner disposition: I felt strengthened by the mass which I had just attended.
>
> I did not allow myself to think purposefully about what I was going to say; I was content to be in union with the Blessed Virgin, and, with Her, to "breathe in" the Holy Spirit.
>
> I placed myself in the disposition of Mary, going to the Pope – to Christ in the Pope – with the faith, the humility, the love, the trust, and the immense hope of Mary's heart.
>
> My true purpose was to be like the Magi – to offer the Holy Father, instead of gold, myrrh and incense, all those hearts in Brussels which are at one with my own heart; to offer those hearts, filled with spiritual aspirations, to the Holy Father's blessing.
>
> I only made short invocations: "Look not upon my sins, but on the Face of your Christ", *"Vulnera Tua, merita mea."*
>
> The Pope and I spoke sometimes in French, sometimes in Italian.
>
> The Holy Father looked serious, even worried. He seemed to me to have aged a great deal physically, but his energy and his lucidity were intact, and he welcomed me very warmly.
>
> Our conversation went like this:

THE HOLY FATHER: Come in, come in! We know you well. I know all about your work for the Church; I know of all the good you have done in the Church!

VERONICA: Thank you, thank you, Holy Father!

THE HOLY FATHER: And Cardinal Suenens? I have so much respect for him, so much trust in him. I want him to know that he still has a great role to play in the Church — a very important one! And there is so much he can do in his diocese, that great diocese which has such an impact on the world. I pray for him, I pray so much for him. I have so much hope and so much trust in him.

Then the Holy Father spoke to me about my own vocation. He took my hands and said:

You have a mission to serve unity within the Church. I pray for you, that you may fulfil this mission. You must serve unity in the Church, you must be imbued with it, you must live on it. Is this not what you want?'

"Oh, yes, Holy Father!"

"Oh, that is very good! Very good indeed!"

He added:

"I have a gift for you."

At his request, a dark green satin case was brought to him, and he opened it. I saw a small crucifix of gilded bronze, with two figures at the foot of the cross: not Mary and John, as is customary, but Peter and Paul.

He said to me: "Look carefully at Peter and Paul. You have a mission in the Church; it is to serve Peter and Paul, to serve the unity of the Church. Do you understand? Never forget this."

He repeated this several times before he allowed me to leave.

Mgr Benelli told Veronica that the Pope very seldom gave this particular gift; he generally reserved it for the most important **ecclesiastical authorities.**

After the audience, Veronica wrote a letter to the Pope.

Saturday, March 11, 1972

Most Holy Father;

It is only through the heart of the Blessed Virgin Herself that I can express my immense gratitude for all that you said to me last Wednesday.

I had prepared for this visit in prayer, asking the Holy Spirit to enable me to communicate my spiritual aspirations to you, and especially to help me receive Your Holiness' words — the words of the Vicar of Jesus Christ — with a completely open heart.

The precise 'mission orders' you gave me — to serve the unity of the Church — fill me with joy. I shall never forget them. You may rest assured that they will be fulfilled with equal zeal by me and by all those on whose behalf I came to see you. Yes! henceforth, our sole purpose will be to serve the unity of the Church, each according to his or her different role.

Most Holy Father, accept our infinite gratitude, and be assured of my most filial affection for your person and of my complete devotion to the Church, under the protection of Mary *Mater Ecclesiae.*

Veronica O'Brien

First contacts in the United States

In *Memories and Hopes*, I mentioned that it was Veronica who called my attention to the Charismatic Renewal in the United States. In November 1972, she and Yvette Dubois travelled to several universities where the Renewal was taking shape — in particular to Ann Arbor, Michigan, and South Bend, Indiana. She met with some of the leaders of the movement, and had long conversations with them, especially with Ralph Martin and with the Ranaghans, authors of *As the Spirit Leads Us*, the book which brought the movement to the attention of the Catholic world. Veronica visited some of the early Renewal groups that were being formed, and was delighted by their spontaneity and their spiritual freshness.

Veronica's reaction to spontaneous prayer

For Veronica, it was a great joy to be able to share and express aloud the love of God which filled her heart. She appreciated the free expression of religious feelings; so often, these are repressed on the pretext that this kind of expression is a matter of temperament, and can be rejected with the words "This is not my cup of tea."

Here is what Veronica had to say:

We consider it natural that love and friendship should find expression in outward gestures. But let us admit it: we are terribly complicated when it comes to giving outward expression to our deep religious feelings, before God or in front of others. Our spontaneity is repressed; timidity, human respect, inhibitions and our education – all these condition us to assume a mask of reserve. We have been ossified by formalism and ritualism; we are ready to pray with our souls, but not with our bodies!

Yet this spontaneous prayer, which is intermediary between purely private prayer and liturgical prayer, can be of great help in renewing the spiritual life in the home and in the most diverse types of communities; it brings with it a rediscovery of the true meaning of prayer as a reality which springs from life.

Today, we are awakening to new dimensions of bodily expression and of communication with one another. There is a growing interest, too, in ways of life and prayer that derive from oriental philosophies. Our young people naturally gravitate in this direction; often, they turn away from Christianity, which to them seems stereotyped.

There are numerous testimonies – and to these I must add my own – to the fact that this mode of prayer brings a freedom from spiritually inhibiting bonds, which block our relationships with God and with our fellow Christians. It helps us to find a whole new sense of liberation; it becomes quite natural to us to praise and glorify God with all the means at our disposal, including praying and singing in tongues – to use all the strings of our bow!

For we still have a long way to go if we are to become fully human in our visible behaviour towards God.

Praying "in tongues"

We should note the allusion to prayer "in tongues". Veronica immediately reacted against the pentecostal interpretation, which can still be found in some Catholic groups, and according to which prayer "in tongues" is prayer "in a foreign language". In *A New Pentecost?*, which I wrote in close collaboration with Veronica, I discussed this interpretation at some length, and finally rejected it.

Our American friends from those early days have never forgotten how Veronica once challenged them, in very vigorous terms, during a public debate on this particular issue. She used the debate as a springboard to invite all those present to learn a foreign language so as to take the Gospel to every corner of the earth – her favourite and constant theme! She did this with so much good humour, combined with good theology, that several people in the audience committed themselves there and then to learning a specific foreign language. For Americans, this is particularly praiseworthy, as they often seem to believe that they can travel around the world without needing anything but English.

Veronica convinced one eminent theologian to see this charism in its proper perspective: as a form of spontaneous prayer which unites us with the Spirit, who "prays in us with ineffable groans". It is in this sense that "prayer in tongues" has its proper place and its proper role, and is available to all.

The experience of "baptism in the Spirit"

I asked Veronica what the experience of baptism in the Spirit — which she had received in Ann Arbor — had meant to her; this is how she described it:

> I really and truly do feel that something special happened inside me on that famous evening when Yvette and I were baptised in the Spirit, at Ann Arbor.
>
> The general impression was one of ethereal lightness — as if there was a valve in my soul, and breathing into it made me all light and floating and happy. This in turn means that I see the everyday difficulties of life from a higher level, letting them pass under me, as I float and float on a lovely, bright, safe yet vaporous cloud.
>
> I am nearer to Heaven, and further from the sadnesses of earth. It is a very special kind of balloon travelling: I pull a cord and there I am, going up and up and up, and there has been no forced or disagreeable landing!
>
> My balloon brings me into Heavenland with ease; but it also brings me down to earth easily, at a moment's notice.
>
> *En somme*, I breathe the rarefied atmosphere of the heights with greater ease, so I see everything here below in better perspective.
>
> When I speak of *"là-haut"* — the heights — I mean, of course, *allant chez moi, dans la Ste Famille* [being at home, in the Holy Family], with easy familiarity, with all the angels and saints.
>
> This feeling of spiritual lightness, as opposed to human

heaviness, is what strikes me most at the moment. My soul can skip and run along the hills, like the image Holy Scripture gives us in the Canticle of Canticles – I think it speaks of a deer. Yes! I run and laugh and sing in tongues aloud, with no fear of being heard!

When I open the Bible, it is as if I am seeking some treasure which I am sure to find. From the first moment, I know that I will receive something wonderful.

At such times, I feel that all my reserves of faith are active. It is as if I am about to break down the dams of the supernatural, and waves of faith, of hope and of charity are about to pour out. And often the waves are so powerful that they submerge me, and I feel myself gasping for breath. "Too much, too much." This feeling of being drowned in the lavishness of God's gifts fills my whole being.

I am so grateful to the Renewal, which has brought the Bible back to life for me. I know that the Scriptures will be an increasingly integral part of my life.

Veronica O'Brien

Pentecost, not pentecostalism

Veronica's reaction to the Charismatic Renewal in the United States can be summarised in these words: "We must say 'yes' to the grace of Pentecost, and 'no' to pentecostalism. We must free the immensely precious pearl from its casket; we must believe, with a living and daring faith, that the Holy Spirit is always active in his Church, giving miracles and charisms; we must be ready to receive his surprises."

To this I must add, "and we must do this whatever the cost".

The battle had to be fought on two fronts. The "yes" and the "no" both needed to be said, in spite of the inevitable risk that those on either side would hear only what they wanted to hear.

My personal research resulted in the book *A New Pentecost?* The question mark at the end of the title signified from the outset that there was need for further discernment; the title itself was an invitation to be attentive, and to hear "what the Spirit is saying to the Churches".

Veronica was to play a very important role in the insertion of the Renewal at the heart of the Church; she was instrumental in ensuring that Church authorities would be open and receptive to it.

A daring ecumenical invitation

On one of her trips to the United States, Veronica visited the Episcopalian community in Houston, which was in the vanguard of the Renewal in the Episcopalian world. (Michael Harper has written a detailed history of this community, which deserves to be widely known.) Some years later, I attended a liturgical celebration in this community; I have never seen a more lively Eucharistic celebration, where participation by the faithful is concerned. I also discovered that they had a "charismatic" clinic, entirely at the service of the poor, and a school which the parents themselves had organised along the same principles.

Veronica was invited to give a talk to an ecumenical gathering of pastors. This was most unusual; St Paul's admonitions to women are still held in great respect in these circles, and women are expected to remain silent at assemblies.

Veronica told the gathering of her hopes for an ecumenical future for the Renewal. At the end of the talk, she knelt and asked the assembly to pray over her; finally, she improvised a prayer of her own, and addressed a bold invitation to those assembled, who were deeply moved. "Do not be afraid," she told them, "to go to Rome and pray on the tombs of Peter and Paul. All ecumenical paths lead there."

She added these surprising words: "I see in my mind that one day Cardinal Suenens will welcome the pilgrims of the Charismatic

Renewal to Rome, and will celebrate the Eucharist in St Peter's Basilica, on the occasion of Pentecost."

This prophecy, which she later repeated to me, seemed to me so contrary to Roman custom that I considered it implausible, even impossible. Nevertheless, it was to come true one day, as we shall see, taking its place among the surprises of the "Hidden Hand of God".

VERONICA'S INITIATIVES IN THE SERVICE OF THE RENEWAL

The International Study Commission in Malines

Veronica immediately understood that the Renewal was not a "movement" – a label that is used far too freely in our circles. She realized that it was rather a powerful grace for our time – a breath, a movement of the Holy Spirit, a grace of Pentecost, which could be captured by all the baptised and by every "movement", whatever its name. All her hopes sprang from this awareness.

This grace, however, had to be received in full harmony with the doctrine of the Catholic Church. On this level, some ambiguities remained to be sorted out and dispelled.

Through countless open and fruitful encounters, Veronica endeavoured to free the Catholic Renewal from all ambiguity, making it immune to the temptation – which recurs intermittently through the ages – to gather Christians together, beyond their own Churches, into a kind of super-Church of the Holy Spirit.

In friendly conversations, she pointed out to the main Catholic leaders some of the important points that needed to be clarified – such as, for example, the expression "baptism in the Spirit", which was sometimes taken to mean a kind of "super-Baptism". Above all, she called their attention to the silence that surrounded certain vital aspects of Catholicism: the Eucharist, the sacraments, Mary, the communion of saints. This vagueness was due in part to a lack of doctrinal guidelines; in part to the ever-increasing number of publications of a pentecostal nature; and in part to the speakers — representing a wide range of viewpoints — who were invited to lecture participants in Catholic congresses.

The sheep, left without a shepherd, were being guided by self-styled leaders; there was an urgent need for direct and trusting communication between Rome — the centre of the Church — and Catholic leaders of the Renewal.

At that time, plans were being made for another international congress of these leaders. Geographically, the most appropriate venue for such a meeting would have been Puerto Rico. Veronica managed to convince them to meet at the gates of Rome instead.

Discreetly, she spoke several times with our friend Mgr Benelli, to ensure that the Holy Father's attitude to the Renewal was one of benevolent neutrality, in contrast to the hostile reactions of those around him and in the United States. Mgr Benelli suggested Grottaferrata as a more neutral venue, and Veronica convinced those in charge of the congress to agree to this suggestion. This eliminated the major objection, which was to the idea of holding a charismatic congress in Rome itself.

The congress took place in May 1973, in the convent of the Franciscan Missionaries of Mary, in Grottaferrata.

I kept Pope Paul informed of developments. At the end of one of my letters (which is reproduced in full in *Memories and Hopes*), I mentioned to him that I was planning to attend the congress. At first he responded negatively; later his reaction became more positive. In authorising me to celebrate the Eucharist at the congress, he opened a door for me; given the fact that a eucharistic celebration usually includes a homily, this gave me a certain amount of freedom!

Through Mgr Benelli, Veronica had also obtained the Pope's promise to grant a private audience to about fifteen leaders of the Renewal, to be chosen by us. Our list included, among others, Mgr J. McKinney, the American bishop in charge of the Renewal in the US; Fr de Montléon OP, of France; and Professor Mühlen of Paderborn in Germany.

The audience was scheduled for 11.00 a.m. Even then, we had a moment of panic: at 9.00 a.m., the Vatican informed us that due to the Pope's heavy schedule, the audience would not take place after all. We immediately telephoned our friend Mgr Benelli, and finally we were told that the audience would in fact take place. It was a close call; the Pope's entourage had described the "charismatics" to him as a group of "illuminati", and some of the letters that had been received from the United States were indeed alarming. The audience was an act of faith and hope on the part of Pope Paul, who was touching in his paternal welcome; it was a first step which made possible the great official meeting of Pentecost 1975.

In addition to producing this important step towards bringing charisms and hierarchy into harmony, the Grottaferrata meeting gave rise to an important decision. At Veronica's suggestion, it was decided to set up a commission which would study problems raised by the Renewal, and which would provide doctrinal and cautionary guidelines.

It was agreed that this working group would meet in the Archdiocese of Malines, under my chairmanship, from May 21-26, 1974. It included Carlos Aldunate SJ, of Chile; Salvador Carillo, of Mexico; Ralph Martin and Kevin Ranaghan, of the United States; Albert de Montléon OP, of France; Heribert Mühlen, of Germany; Veronica O'Brien, of Ireland; and Kilian McDonnell OSB, of the United States, who was responsible for drafting the document which the group produced.

A draft of this document was sent for consultation to a number of theologians who were not involved in the Renewal, including Y. Congar, W. Kasper, R. Laurentin, J. Ratzinger, and Hans Küng. In a letter to Veronica, Küng expressed his full agreement: "These guidelines are certainly balanced and theologically sound." Several further documents in the same perspective were later published as part of the *Malines Documents*.

The Pope welcomed the document and was very appreciative of

it; during an audience, he pointed to it, on his desk, and asked me to continue in this direction. He entrusted me with the pastoral mission of watching over the full integration of the Renewal into the Church.

The International Pilgrimage to Rome

Veronica made another important suggestion which was welcomed by the American leaders of the Renewal. She suggested that an international congress should be organised in Rome, not far from the catacombs of St Calistus, and that a "charismatic pilgrimage" should be planned for the Holy Year of 1975. It was a daring idea, considering the strong reservations still held by some members of the Pope's entourage and of the curia. Veronica played a decisive role in abating their fears.

In a letter dated December 23, 1974, Ralph Martin wrote to her:

It appears that the Lord in his providence has prepared you to play a key role in the plan he is unfolding in our time. Thank you so much for your critical help, that allowed the Rome conference to go forward; not only the Rome conference but a major action of God in our time.

19

ROME: PENTECOST 1975
AND FURTHER DEVELOPMENTS

Pentecost 1975

The decisive moment for the acceptance of the Renewal into the Church came in 1975. At Pentecost of that year, ten thousand "charismatics" arrived at St Peter's on a two-day pilgrimage. Catholic leaders from various continents were present, and significant numbers of non-Catholic leaders were invited and came as friends.

The Pope celebrated the pontifical Mass for Pentecost with the customary solemnity. When he entered the Basilica, the Renewal pilgrims started chanting Alleluias, instead of the more traditional "Viva il Papa!" After this, the Mass proceeded as usual until the consecration, when a gentle murmur of spontaneous and astonishingly harmonious chants – in tongues – rose from the crowd of pilgrims; then died away, discreetly, like a wave breaking softly on the shore in a breath of foam. This was the first time that the Renewal manifested itself, in prayer, at the heart of the Church.

The following morning, on Pentecost Monday – which was also the anniversary of the death of Pope John XXIII, who had prayed for "a New Pentecost" – the prophetic words Veronica had spoken in Houston found, for me, their astonishing and moving confirmation. She had predicted that I would "celebrate the Eucharist for members of the Renewal in St Peter's Basilica in Rome, on the occasion of Pentecost"; this became an astonishing reality when the Holy Father asked me to celebrate, in his stead, at the pontifical altar. He offered to join us after the eucharistic celebration and give a homily; this, too, was unprecedented.

Before the Eucharist, the concelebrants — bishops and priests — gathered around me in the sacristy, and prayed over me with extended hands. Then the procession began: about thirty bishops and eight hundred priests — all dressed in red vestments, the liturgical colour for Pentecost — moved towards the altar, up the central nave, our hands raised in prayer, while the pilgrims of the Renewal chanted Alleluias.

The Eucharistic celebration was a harmonious blend of traditional liturgy (accompanied by the choir of St Peter's) and spontaneous prayer. The atmosphere was at once prayerful and relaxed; it felt natural and right — as indeed it is — for the people of God to be celebrating, in jubilation and song, the joy of their faith. It was a true feast.

In my own homily, I pointed out the profound significance of this event. I presented this as a hope, deliberately worded as a paradox:

> May the charismatic Renewal disappear as such, and become a pentecostal grace for the entire Church. To be faithful to its source, the river must flow into the ocean.

As a matter of minor historical interest, I will add that the Holy Father sent two prelates of the pontifical court as observers to the celebration, as a final precaution; Mgr Benelli deliberately chose two of the most conservative. Their report to the Pope was enthusiastic. Fully reassured, the Holy Father left his apartments and joined us in the Basilica. His solemn entrance on the sedia was greeted by wave upon wave of Alleluias.

He gave an important speech, in French, in English and in Spanish. He seemed very relaxed; at the end of the speech, he improvised a few words in Italian, welcoming the charismatic

Renewal into the Church, and describing it as "a chance for the Church and for the world as a whole". He also gave guidelines for discernment, to assist the Renewal in its future development; these took the form of a commentary on St Paul's guidelines to the Corinthians.

Then the Pope walked down the steps from the altar and took both my hands; before I had a chance to introduce the bishops and the six representatives of the congress, he thanked me publicly "in the name of the Lord, for having brought the charismatic Renewal into the heart of the Church". He embraced me, and, in a gesture of paternal affection, placing his hand on my shoulder, he presented me to the crowd, to indicate that he was entrusting the charismatic Renewal to me in a very special way.

Then I introduced to the Pope six leaders from different continents: first Ralph Martin, then Veronica, as I knew that her presence would be reassuring to the Pope.

Mgr Benelli later told me that the Pope had been profoundly moved by this experience. He repeated, word for word, what the Pope had already said to me. I told him that I was surprised to hear the exact words from him; he explained that he had read them in the Pope's *Verbalia*. This is how I learned that the Pope kept a journal in which he wrote down what he had said during private audiences, when he wished to keep a record of his precise words.

On the evening of this memorable Pentecost Monday, we had a friendly meeting at the Columbus Hotel with our non-Catholic guests. They too had been deeply moved by the events. They saw this meeting between the "institutional Church" and the "charismatic Church" as a historical moment for ecumenical dialogue. I heard one of them say, "John XXIII opened a window; Paul VI has just opened the door."

Sr Jeanne d'Arc wrote an important article pointing out the ecumenical significance of this memorable day.*

---

* See *Memories and Hopes*, p. 291.

After Pentecost

Evening came, and morning came, and it was another day altogether.

For the following day, we had planned a meeting between my own small group and those principal leaders of the Renewal who were attached to Ann Arbor. We met at the Christian Brothers. My group included Veronica, Yvette Dubois, Margie Grace, and my secretary, Canon Brieven. The Ann Arbor contingent included Steve Clark, Ralph Martin and Bruce Yocum.

As we shared our reactions to the events of the previous day, we realised that we had interpreted the same events in very different ways. Our American friends saw them as a sign of the Church's recognition of charisms — in particular of the prophetic charism, on which we felt they placed too much emphasis. Bruce Yocum has written a book on the subject; I will mention him again, in connection with a very curious prophecy.

For us, on the other hand, the significance of the events lay primarily in the aspect of "integration" of the Renewal into the heart of the visible liturgical and sacramental Church. We came to the realisation that these two understandings were far from harmonious. The discussion became intense and painful; that night we sat down to our evening meal together, but in silence, to avoid more arguments. We agreed that we would each spend ten minutes putting into writing what we felt in our hearts to be our options for the future. I no longer have the piece of paper on which I wrote my own feelings, but I know it was filled with the darkest pessimism. I have, however, found Veronica's, in which, yet again, she opted to hope against all hope.

Finally, we decided to meet again the following morning, in St Peter's Basilica, to pray together and to place the future in the Lord's hands.

As she prayed, that night, Veronica felt inspired by the Lord to invite our American friends, Steve Clark — our main opponent — and Ralph Martin, to come to Brussels for two or three years.

231

This would give us the opportunity to continue the dialogue on the institutional Church and the charismatic Church, and to try to bring the two together; at that point, the outcome of these efforts was far from decided.

Fortunately, the ten thousand pilgrims were in no way a part of all this tension; they felt themselves to be joyfully and unproblematically at the heart of the Church.

We met the following morning, as we had planned. We would have liked to pray together near St Peter's tomb, but the crowd of tourists forced us to seek refuge in a side chapel, slightly out of the way — the chapel of the Archangel Michael. Passing tourists were intrigued by our strange little group, kneeling there with a cardinal in the middle. Wilfried, my secretary, was in charge of keeping the curious away — no doubt they thought that a wedding was being celebrated!

It was here that Veronica invited Steve Clark and Ralph Martin to come to Brussels to continue our theological work. They agreed in principle; however, they needed confirmation from the Committee in Ann Arbor. This was later granted, and they eventually moved to Brussels.

We parted in a climate of hope. I rushed to the audience hall, where the Holy Father had convened all the cardinals in Rome for a noon meeting. I was in time, but only just. As I entered, the cardinals mistook me for the Pope; much to my consternation, they all rose to their feet to greet me! I hope that those who may have found my late arrival somewhat cavalier will look upon it more kindly now that they know the extenuating circumstances!

The memorable Pentecost congress was the result of Veronica's initiative and mediation, in close collaboration with Mgr Benelli. It ended on a positive note. A letter from Steve Clark officially expressed the gratitude of the directing body of the charismatic Renewal in the United States:

Dear Veronica:

God's peace be with you.

At our recent Service Committee meeting we all felt that a note of appreciation to you on behalf of the committee for your involvement in the International Congress was long overdue. We are grateful for the assistance you offered at so many points during the planning, and for your many efforts on our behalf.

Indeed, had it not been for your initial suggestion and your subsequent persistence, there might not have been a congress in Rome this year. Looking back at the events preceding the congress and the congress itself, we can only marvel at the work God did among us. Thank you for placing a vision before us and working with us for its fulfilment.

Sincerely yours in Christ,
Stephen B. Clark
Chairman

A letter from the Holy Father

In 1975, Veronica celebrated her seventieth birthday. The Pope, informed of the date, sent her a photograph inscribed with these words:

To Veronica O'Brien, on the occasion of her seventieth birthday. We pray that the Lord may give her light, strength and love, so that she may continue in the service of Christ's Church with unfailing generosity and fidelity. We send her our cordial apostolic benediction.

From the Vatican, August 16, 1975
Paul VI

Veronica responded to this thoughtful gesture in the following words:

October 30, 1975

Most Holy Father,
The kind wishes and paternal blessings which you so thoughtfully sent me, on the occasion of my seventieth birthday, have brought me tremendous encouragement, and I thank you with all my heart.

For me, this blessing has a particularly profound message from the Lord, because of the task which He is unexpectedly entrusting to me.

I have to admit that at my age, after so many years of apostolic wanderings, I was expecting to 'retire' to contemplative life. The Lord, however, has decided otherwise; He has somehow plunged me into the charismatic Renewal which is spreading to the people of God throughout every continent. Is this not extraordinary?

My previous vocation in the Church leads me to feel that I have a very special mission to accomplish in the charismatic Renewal, to ensure that two important focal points of the Church's life will not be blurred under the pretext of "ecumenical charity". These focal points are Mary and Peter.

This blurring is what I have tried to avoid, in particular in dealing with the Ann Arbor (USA) leaders, Ralph Martin and Steve Clark. It seems that this message has been fully accepted; the most recent evidence of this is the fact that I have been invited to be part of the international coordinating team, as a "special consultant".

Holy Father, I am convinced that the blessing you have kindly sent me has first alighted on these two men who have been chosen by the Lord to be pioneers of the great breath of the Holy Spirit; your blessing, Most Holy Father, has touched them as they await the day, which they hope is not far off, when you will grant them the grace of receiving them to bless them personally.

I shall cherish the words of your apostolic blessing; in this last stage of my life, I shall endeavour to fulfil them concretely, more and more, with all my heart and soul, despite my weaknesses and my failings. I know that this blessing gives me special grace and a special strength — that of Jesus Christ, our Saviour and Lord.

Thank you once again, Your Holiness, from the depths of my heart, for your kind and thoughtful gesture.

Please accept my respectful and filial affection.

Veronica O'Brien

The complementarity of charisms

As we have seen, Veronica's relationship with Paul VI played a significant role in the acceptance of the "pentecostal" Renewal by the hierarchy of the Church. Her role is, in a way, an illustration of the two aspects of the Church, which is at once visible reality, institutional and sacramental, and invisible reality — a receptive welcome to the workings of the Holy Spirit.

All egalitarian claims which tend towards functional equality underestimate the true role of women. If we compare Mary's role with Peter's, we come closer to the true perspective. In a speech to a group of French women religious, Pope John Paul II made the same point clearly:

"The Church, in the hierarchical sense, is led by the successors of the apostles, and therefore by men. In the charismatic sense, it is certainly true to say that women lead the Church just as much — perhaps even more...".

For his part, Cardinal Ratzinger, in a book with a thought-provoking title — *Marie, première Eglise (Mary, the First Church)* —

wrote the following passage, which takes this concept a step further:

> The Church needs the Marian mystery; indeed, the Church is herself Marian mystery.... Wherever the Church is still viewed in a masculine, structural and institutional perspective, the very nature of the Church has disappeared. The Church is not an organisational structure, but the organic body of Christ.
>
> Such an approach is rich in implications.

THE AMERICAN LEADERS' STAY IN BRUSSELS

Ralph Martin and Steve Clark

Some time later, we attended a farewell ceremony in the United States, in honour of Ralph Martin and his family, who were leaving for Belgium, the central authorities in Ann Arbor having given their authorisation.

Ralph Martin spent four years in Brussels, where he edited the newsletter of ICCRO — the International Catholic Charismatic Renewal Office — which he had founded; his office was established in my residence.

Ralph asked Veronica to be a special consultant to ICCRO; our dialogue therefore continued on a weekly basis. We usually met on Mondays.

In the morning, we discussed underlying theological problems with Steve Clark and Ralph Martin. I had invited Kilian McDonnell OSB (an American theologian, director of the Ecumenical Institute in Collegeville, and author of the first Malines Document), and Professor Jan Van der Veken of the Univeristy of Louvain, to join our side in the debate. Fr Kilian, who was on the same wavelength as we were, was unable to participate for health reasons. He still plays an important role in ecumenical dialogue with the

Pentecostals; he has recently published, in collaboration with George T. Montague, a seminal study entitled *Christian Initiation on Baptism in the Holy Spirit.** In this book, he sheds light on the history of pastoral work during the first eight centuries; this will be of great help, I hope, in the in-depth renewal of our pastoral of the Sacrament of Confirmation.

The Malines Documents were a result of these morning discussions, where we compared our theological points of view.

In the afternoon, Veronica continued the conversation, on a more strictly religious and spiritual level, with Ralph Martin, who has always been very close to her.

Ralph's eldest son, John, attended the European School in Brussels. We have affectionate memories of his refreshing directness. One of his teachers once asked the class, as part of a language exercise, to answer the question: "Why are you here in Brussels?" Most of the children's answers were quite predictable: "Because my father is ambassador to Brussels," or "Because my father is the local Toyota agent." John's answer was beautifully candid: "Because God told my father to come to Brussels."

We discussed theology, ecclesiology, exegesis — although we did not always reach a common understanding. Malines Document No.2, in particular, gives a sense of our discussions; these were sometimes difficult, but always took place in a climate of friendship and prayer.

One of the charisms we talked about was the gift of prophecy. A revealing incident connected with this issue took place at a later date. It happened in the Hotel Alicorni in Rome, where the American and the European charismatic groups had gathered during a synod. One of the Ann Arbor leaders, Bruce Yocum, author of a book about the gift of prophecy, came to me in my hotel room, accompanied by Ralph Martin and Steve Clark. In the strictest confidence, he told me that he had received "a prophetic message" announcing Veronica's imminent death.

They were very surprised by my reaction: I calmly suggested,

---

* Published by The Liturgical Press, Collegeville, Minnesota, 1991.

"Let's all go and tell Veronica about this prophecy." We went and knocked at her door, and I repeated to her the message they had given me.

I shall never forget their amazement when they saw Veronica's reaction: she was jubilant; she burst into a joyful Magnificat , and even began to dance across the hotel room.

All of this happened about twenty years ago!

Strangely enough, Bruce Yocum was back a few years later, with another announcement of Veronica's imminent death; once more, events fortunately gave him the lie.

I mention this episode not only to illustrate Veronica's joy in the face of death, but also to point out how careful we must be in these matters, where discernment is absolutely essential and the risk of mistakes particularly great.

There was, in fact, still a great deal of discernment to be done. Our work continued in the best of atmospheres.

Mgr Benelli also participated, as a friend, in this dialogue; he had become Archbishop of Florence and, in 1977, Cardinal. During the Roman Synod of October 1977, we met with him at the Christian Brothers. He listened attentively and benevolently to the testimonies about the Renewal in every part of the world. We recorded his final reactions:

I am very impressed, and I thank you for each one of your testimonies.

The Renewal brings great hope: communities are showing that it is possible to live in love for one another.

But it is not only the communities which impress me: there is also a great momentum which you have generated and spread throughout the world, and which is a source of hope.

We do not yet know where the Spirit is leading us; gradually, we shall come to see more clearly. But we can already see in the Renewal a hope for the Church.

Steve Clark's stay in Brussels came to an end in May 1978, after three years; Ralph Martin stayed for four years, and Gerry Rauch for five. As a result of their stay, a charismatic community called "Jerusalem" was born in Brussels; today it has about four hundred members.

Special consultant to ICCRO

In Ann Arbor, Ralph Martin had started the ICCRO newsletter, which was a source of information and communication. He directed its publication from Brussels; when he left, the job was handed over to Fr Tom Forrest CSSR.

Ralph Martin had asked Veronica to be special consultant to ICCRO, and she took this role very seriously. She suggested that the international charismatic congress, which was organised by ICCRO, should be held in Dublin, in the heart of Ireland, rather than in the United States, as had initially been planned. This suggestion was adopted, and the congress took place in Dublin from June 12-19, 1978. This was Veronica's way of offering her native land a chance to seize the Renewal which Pope Paul had described as "an opportunity for the Church".

Veronica's most significant contribution, however, was her suggestion to transfer ICCRO to Rome, where it would be at the heart of the Church. This suggestion was accepted, after some discussion. This allowed ICCRO to take full advantage of the support and the guidelines which would give the Renewal security and ecclesial integration.

Veronica also suggested to Fr Tom Forrest that a world retreat for priests should be organised in Rome, so that they might experience the spiritual richness of the Renewal. She also felt that such a retreat would give the Roman authorities an opportunity to see for themselves the tremendous revitalising potential of the Renewal. Her suggestion was adopted; in the end, however, this second aspect was not given sufficient prominence, as a result of various influences. However, the event itself, which brought six thousand priests together to renew before the Pope their commitment to the priesthood, deserves to be mentioned.

On the last evening of the retreat, Tom Forrest sent Veronica a telegram to say "Thank you".

A second world retreat was held in Rome in 1990. Due to health reasons, I was unable to give the final conference as had been planned. Instead, I sent each of the participants a booklet entitled *Spiritual Journey*.

The twenty-fifth anniversary of the Renewal

As I write, the twenty-fifth anniversary of the birth of the Catholic Renewal is being celebrated in Pittsburgh. I have just received a letter dated June 8, 1992, from Ralph Martin, the principal promoter of the Catholic Renewal in the United States, on behalf of the congress. In a spirit of communion and of thanksgiving, I include it here.

Dear Cardinal Suenens;

Gathered here to celebrate the twenty-fifth anniversary of the Catholic Charismatic Renewal in Pittsburgh, we have all been deeply touched by the video message you have sent us. We have also been very moved by a video retrospective which reminded us of some of the great moments and brought out the services you have rendered to the Church and to us all during all these years.

On behalf of all our brothers and sisters in North America, I thank you again for all that you have done for us and I congratulate you on the occasion of this twenty-fifth anniversary of the Catholic Charismatic Renewal which continues to grow more and more deeply into the heart of the Church. It is here that we find the great love of the Immaculate Heart of Mary and of the Sacred Heart of Jesus.

I know how much Veronica took part with you in all of this past, and naturally we include her in our feelings of gratitude and our very best wishes.

20

ECUMENICAL ENCOUNTERS
1975–1980

An Ecumenical Pilgrimage to Jerusalem
(26 May – 4 June 1977)

Our preoccupation with ecumenical *rapprochement* expressed itself through a variety of contacts. In *Memories and Hopes* I mentioned the pilgrimage of thanksgiving which I undertook in honour of the fiftieth anniversary of my ordination to the priesthood.* Here let me fill in a few additional details.

I was accompanied on this pilgrimage by a number of non-Catholic companions, representing several Churches. They included: Larry Christenson, minister and Lutheran theologian; Dom Basham, a well-known preacher in Pentecostal circles, and author of many books; Derek Prince, Free Church preacher; Charles Simpson, Baptist minister; Ern Baxter, Free Church preacher; Bob Mumford, Presbyterian minister; and Tom Smail, theologian and Anglican minister, who was working in a London parish.

We gathered in Malines; after a brief stop in Rome, we went on to Assisi, and from there to Jerusalem.

Rome

In Rome, we attended a public audience, at which the Holy Father had a special message for us:

---

* p. 313.

Perhaps you remember that our predecessor, Leo XIII, asked that during this novena, as we prepare for Pentecost, we pray specially to the Holy Spirit for unity among Christians. We therefore invite you, dear friends, to pray, with all of the disciples of our Lord Jesus, for this gift of unity in truth and in charity.

The entire Church is called to pray to the Holy Spirit. It is He who allows us to receive and to put into practice the word of God, the deposit of faith entrusted to the apostles and to their successors.

We invoke on you, and on all your brothers here present, the light and the strength of the Holy Spirit, the One who guides us to the Truth, as revealed by Christ.

Jerusalem

For me, the high point of the trip was our celebration of Pentecost Sunday at the Cenacle in Jerusalem. On that day, I renewed the promises I had made at the time of my ordination to the priesthood, and of my consecration as bishop; and there in the Cenacle, I praised the Lord greatly for the considerable graces he has bestowed on me.

This ceremony brought us all together, Catholics and Protestants. We were all filled with the need to express, in some way, the union of our hearts and of our souls. Through meaningful and moving gestures — exchanging kisses of peace, and asking one another for forgiveness — we expressed the burning desire in each of our hearts to be builders of unity at the heart of the still painfully-divided Church.

As I knelt at the foot of the altar, the members of the group came to pray over me, with chants, words from the Scriptures, and spontaneous prayers. This was one of the most intense moments of the ceremony.

Our ecumenical group remained together in the Holy Land for several days. Then my own private group — which included

243

Veronica, Yvette, Margie, Fr Lebeau SJ and Tom Smail — left for Nazareth. Here, at the end of a eucharistic celebration, we had a surprise encounter: fifteen or so pilgrims who had been present during my mass suddenly ran up to us, with cries of joy and friendship. They were the active members of a legionary group from Turkey — a group which Veronica had founded twenty-two years earlier, and which was still active in its apostolate. We had a great fraternal celebration.

ON THE OUTSKIRTS OF ROMAN SYNODS

The context

Pope Paul, looking ahead beyond the Council, had instituted the synod, a body intended to ensure co-operation between the pope and the bishops of the world. The synod was to meet in Rome, on a regular basis; it was to include delegates of the episcopal conferences.

Veronica saw in this a providential and compelling opportunity to promote fusion between the hierarchical Church and the charismatic Church, and to attempt to eliminate some of the fears and prejudices which prevailed within the Roman Curia.

She invited a number of international Catholic Renewal leaders to go to Rome during each synod. They were divided into two groups, one English-speaking and the other French-speaking; as the synod lasted a month, each group remained in Rome for two weeks. During the early post-conciliar years, Veronica organised these groups herself.

Their schedule included eucharistic celebrations which were quite traditional in style, but enlivened by a breath of the Renewal. This was intended to give members of the Curia, who were invited to come and celebrate with us, a glimpse of the true face of the Renewal.

Most importantly, Veronica also organised two weekly sessions of prayer and information, alternating between French and English. These were held in the Jesuit generalate, in Borgo Santo Spirito; the superior general, Fr Arrupe, not only gave us the use of a room, but sometimes participated in our meetings. My particular role was to invite the cardinals and bishops who were participating in the synod. This was not an easy task: the meetings at the Borgo were held at 8.00 p.m., and we were all usually exhausted by the end of a day at the synod. Nevertheless, whether through courtesy or curiosity, quite a few came to join us.

Pope Paul, and later Pope John Paul II, expressed their gratitude for the prayerful presence of these "charismatic" groups on the outskirts of the synod. Pope Paul sent each participant a souvenir of his pontificate; Pope John Paul invited each language group in turn to attend his private Mass.

To add a final touch to the picture, I will mention that our friend Mgr Benelli — who was substitute at the Secretariat of State — often joined us, incognito, for a quiet meal, late in the evening, after the day's last working session with the Holy Father.

A meeting with Vincent Synan

Veronica met Vincent Synan, General Secretary of the Pentecostal Holiness Churches, in this context. He was in Rome, with a group of Pentecostals, for ecumenical dialogue with the Roman Secretariat for Christian Unity.

He and the members of his group had been invited to our evenings at the Jesuit generalate. At the end of the ordinary prayer meeting, after the periods of witnessing and sharing, he and Veronica went out for a stroll along the Borgo Santo Spirito. She suggested that they should go and pray at the nearby church; at that late hour, however, it was closed, so she invited him to pray with her on the church steps, in front of the closed doors. Given the circumstances, this was a very symbolic act.

They then talked in the street late into the night. I will let Vincent Synan describe the conversation and give his impressions in his own words; I quote from an article of his that was published in *The Spirit and the World* in September 1987.

He begins by introducing Veronica to his readers as "an Irish lady who is a very important person, whom the Lord is using in a very great way in the worldwide Catholic Charismatic Renewal." He then goes on: "Since my family name is Irish, O'Synan, Veronica and I had a lot of fun talking about being Irish."

The article then turns to the substance of their conversation, and to his proposal to celebrate Pentecost together each year. I published his concrete suggestions in Malines Document No.2, which deals with ecumenism.

Here are a few points from his proposal which I feel deserve particular attention:

1. That around the world, Pentecost Sunday be designated as a day for ecumenical celebration by people of all Churches. That this be a "birthday celebration" for the birthday of the Church in which the coming of the Holy Spirit is recalled and emphasised.
2. That the ecumenical week in January has not had the impact that was desired, and that Pentecost Sunday is easier to remember and plan for. It is one of the three great feastdays of the Church and should rank with Christmas and Easter as an important celebration for Christian people.
3. That the celebrations be held in the afternoons or evenings so that the people could attend their own services in the morning and come together in a central place later in the day. There would be no Eucharist in the celebration, thus avoiding problems connected with intercommunion.

4. Pentecost day celebrations would arise from the common people of the cities of the world. They would not occur where local vision and leadership were not adequate. But where possible, great Pentecost Sunday celebrations would create the interest and enthusiasm for others in neighbouring cities. In time the whole Christian world could be enriched annually as believers from all denominations gathered on Pentecost Sunday to proclaim that "Jesus is Lord" in the power of the Holy Spirit.

5. These celebrations would be an opportunity to share a common witness to the Church and the world about the outpouring of the Holy Spirit "upon all flesh" in these days. The infectious joy and power of the Holy Spirit would then flow back into the churches to bless them.

6. Coming from these celebrations would be a new level of unity between the Christian Churches in response to Jesus' prayer "that they all may be one, even as my Father and I are One". The unity of the Spirit must be demonstrated before any kind of structural unity can be contemplated. Being together at one time and one place in unity (as in the Upper Room) would go far to heal the divisions which have fractured the Body of Christ for centuries. This witness to Christian unity would be one of the prime fruits of such a celebration.

7. The cause of evangelism would be strengthened from such united witnesses occurring around the world. Our unity in Christ through the Holy Spirit would be a sign to the non-Christian world — "that they might believe!"

This suggestion aims to unite all Christians in a common prophetic witness; at the same time, it anticipates the fulfilment of our ecumenical hope. The charismatic Renewal, which is already reuniting Christians of so many denominations, could well carry out this proposal as an initial experiment, which could then be extended universally and received by all Christians, whether or not they are involved in the Renewal.

Christians would thus be returning to the path of their common history, which descends to them from the time when "all with one accord devoted themselves to prayer, together with several women, including Mary, the mother of Jesus..." (Acts 1:14).

The idea has spread since our meeting in Rome, and there have been many common prayer meetings organised in the United States. I was asked to introduce them on American television with an introductory prayer, which was transmitted so as to be heard simultaneously in the various places where Christians had gathered for this purpose.

To stress the ecumenical aspect, Vincent Synan invited me to join him in Oklahoma City, which I did.

The Templetons

The Templeton Prize, which was once awarded to me, exists thanks to the initiative of a generous American businessman, John Templeton, who founded it to support all efforts "to stimulate the knowledge and the love of God, and service to God on a grand scale, throughout the world". The prize is completely non-denominational, and the jury is composed of Christians of various denominations, Jews, Moslems, Hindus and others.

John Templeton had come to see me in Brussels. We met again in London, when I received the prize; he invited me, Veronica and Margie Grace to visit him in the Bahamas. And so, during one of our trips to the United States, we went to visit him.

The aeroplane deposited us in a world that seemed unreal. Mr and Mrs Templeton met us at the airport; they took us to their home in a Rolls-Royce on very high wheels, which, I imagine, must have been worth its weight in gold.

The island on which they live is very strange – a tiny island, with its own private police force; a sort of enclave reserved for a super-élite of top business people. Fishing boats and yachts are anchored off-shore, and flowers bloom everywhere; it feels much like a smaller version of Monaco. From this island, Mr Templeton telephones his financial decisions to all the world's great business capitals.

Our conversation immediately turned to religious problems. Mr Templeton is Presbyterian, his wife is a Christian Scientist, and both are deeply concerned with helping the world of today to rediscover the values, or at least the religious dimension, of the Gospel.

Mr Templeton was remarkably open and receptive to any suggestion which coincided with the objectives of his Foundation. Veronica took the opportunity to suggest Chiara Lubich, founder of the Focolari movement, as a possible candidate for the Templeton Prize. It was, in fact, awarded to her in 1978. Encouraged by this result, Veronica later suggested Frank Duff, founder of the Legion of Mary. John Templeton travelled to London to meet Frank Duff; but Frank Duff's death, in 1980, put an end to his candidacy.

The ecumenical society of the Blessed Virgin Mary

In *Memories and Hopes*, I described my meeting with the founder of the Ecumenical Society of the Blessed Virgin Mary,* Martin Gillet; he came to Malines on the occasion of the fortieth anniversary of the end of the Malines Conversations (which, between 1921 and 1925, brought together Cardinal Mercier and a group of Catholic and Anglican theologians).

Later, Veronica and I tried to set up a branch of this society in Belgium. After a few meetings, which brought together Catholics, Orthodox and Protestants, we had to abandon the experiment; we were unable to create the desired atmosphere, or to go beyond the polemical exegetic arguments raised by some of the Protestants.

Our final effort in this direction was to invite a few people to the Marian Ecumenical Congress in London in September 1979.

---

* See p.240.

With the help of a generous friend, we were able to pay travel expenses for four people from Belgium and six from France; among these were two Protestant pastors, one of whom, Pastor Roberts, we had met on several previous occasions.

Cardinal Hume opened the Congress. Martin Gillet, founder of the Society, was present, even though he was paralysed and extremely weak and knew that he was near death; for all of us, he personified that grain of wheat dying in the earth so that the harvest may grow.

The speeches by various Protestant participants at the Congress converged in stressing that the first generation of reformed was much closer to Catholic positions than subsequent generations have been; this corresponded to what von Allmen had told me long before. A brilliant presentation by Professor Ross Mackenzie on Calvin, and another by Professor Dauwe, also from the University of Virginia's faculty of theology, were on a similar note. Later, I met these two scholars again, this time in the United States; we prayed together, in a spirit of hope.

In later years, Martin Gillet twice called me to his bedside when he was sick – once in London, once in Oxford. He wanted to read me his memoirs (which he was still able to dictate), in particular those passages which dealt with our early meetings. He died in 1985. His ashes rest in Walsingham, a Marian centre which is famous in England and which is shared by Catholics and Anglicans; during a conference there, I blessed his ashes, which have been walled into one side of the small chapel.

Let us pray that ecumenical dialogue, which began around Mary, will some day bring us back together around "the Child and his Mother", who are indissolubly united.

The two wings of an aeroplane

The mention of Mary's name has reminded me of an important moment during a Renewal Congress which took place in the stadium of Notre Dame University, in Indiana, USA, in June 1973. I alluded to this particular congress in *Memories and Hopes**; here is a more detailed account of the "Marian incident" which caused so much turmoil among the organisers.

Because of their bonds of friendship with some of the Pentecostal guests, the organisers tended to play down Mary's place and role, for fear of offending the Protestants. This was a cheap form of ecumenism, which I later attempted to define and discuss in Malines Document No. 2. So as not to offend anyone, the organisers of the Congress had asked me to give a simple personal witness rather than an official closing speech. I felt that I could not accept the organisers' neutrality — most of the people in the stadium that day were Catholic — but as I stood up to speak, I did not know how to cross the "sound barrier" to Mary.

In the middle of my speech, a powerful aeroplane flew over the stadium. The noise it made forced me to stop in mid-sentence; as the sound died away, I concluded my improvised speech with these words:

"My friends, look at that aeroplane; it has a message for us. It needs two wings to keep its balance and fly. The same is true of the Renewal: it has a powerful motor in the Holy Spirit, but to keep its balance in flight, it needs two wings; Mary is one, and Peter the other."

The audience greeted these words with a long ovation.

The incident has not been forgotten; from time to time, echoes of it still reach me today. As a glimmer of hope for the future of ecumenism, I include, in this record of the workings of the "Hidden Hand of God", an article and its covering letter which were sent to me from the US in 1987. The article informed me of the existence of a Marian ecumenical group; the author sent it to me to remind me of the Notre Dame incident.[†] This is what he wrote:

Your speech at the stadium greatly influenced the develop-

---

* See, p.273

† The article appeared in *The Spirit and the World*, September 1987.

ment of an ecumenical ministry, which is aimed at bringing our reformed brethren to an appreciation of Mary's
role, and which I believe to be prophetic.

To illustrate his point, he described a retreat which a Catholic
priest gave for about forty Protestant pastors; this priest simply
asked them to "let Christ live in them, and to love Mary with
Christ's heart". That is precisely the key to our own perspective.

We Catholics do not point out often enough that it is Jesus,
alive in us, who leads us straight to his mother; she is the one
whom he loved most here on earth, whom he sanctified through
thirty years of intimacy, and whom he glorifies in the apotheosis
of the Assumption as "the eschatological icon of his Church".

As I was finishing this chapter, I received another letter from
the US; it is dated March 11, 1992, and is from Walter Matthews,
president of the national conference organised in the United
States on the occasion of the twenty-fifth anniversary of the
Renewal. He ends his letter with these words, which refer to the
aeroplane which flew over the stadium at Notre Dame:

I regret that I have never had the privilege of meeting you,
but your words in the Notre Dame Stadium in 1973, about
the two wings of the airplane – Peter and Mary – have for
years echoed in my ears, along with the hopes you
expressed so persuasively in *A New Pentecost?*

21

THE WORK OF DISCERNMENT

A grace for the whole Church

In a letter dated January 11, 1982, Pope John Paul II wished me "a new year of fruitful service to the Church, with the powerful help of the Lord, and springing from your long experience in the discernment of spirits."

I must admit that in all matters involving "the discernment of spirits", my task has been greatly simplified by Veronica's constant collaboration. Her unfailing doctrinal correctness, vitalised by her extraordinary spiritual experience, has helped me to distinguish the authentic presence of the Spirit and of his charisms from the deviations and excesses encountered along the way.

The first mistake that had to be avoided was that of including the Renewal in the category of "movements". The Renewal is not a "movement" in the usual sociological sense: it has neither founder nor statutes; it is not homogeneous; it includes a wide range of manifestations.

It is a flow of grace, a renewing breath of the Holy Spirit, intended for all the members of the Church — lay people, religious, priests, and bishops. It is a challenge to us all.

One does not "become part of" the Renewal; rather, the Renewal becomes a part of us, provided we accept the grace that it offers.

The word "charismatic" also lends itself to misunderstandings. If we place too much emphasis on the role of charisms, however real these may be, we run the risk of forgetting:

- that the first gift of the Holy Spirit is the Holy Spirit;
- that the first sign of his active presence is an increase of the theological virtues — faith, hope and charity;
- that "ordinary" charisms are numerous and precious;
- that "extraordinary" charisms are, as the term indicates, exceptional — they are not necessarily permanent, and they require careful discernment;
- that the Holy Spirit is the Spirit of the Father and of the Son, and that he always leads us to the heart of the Blessed Trinity;
- that the term "charismatic" has in itself no exclusive meaning; the entire Church is charismatic; all Christians are charismatic, by virtue of baptism and confirmation, whether they are aware of it or not.

A document for Mgr Benelli

Together, Veronica and I prepared a series of draft guidelines, which we called guidelines for accompaniment, for Mgr Benelli's personal use. We also asked Mgr Benelli to meet, in Florence, those of the American Renewal leaders who were closest to us. All of this took place on a completely informal basis.

Here is the letter Veronica wrote to Mgr Benelli concerning these guidelines:

Saturday, March 1, 1975

There is someone leaving for Rome tomorrow morning, someone involved in the Renewal, and so I will have this envelope delivered to you by hand. It contains several documents; the proposed Guidelines are the most important; they were truly written with faith, love of the Church, and love of souls.

As you shall see, there is a great deal of strong criticism, and strong insistence on the need for changes. We have dared to go into all the details, making suggestions to the various authorities — even to the Holy Father.

I have given the best of myself, and I have truly submerged myself in the Holy Spirit, to do this.

More and more, I feel within myself the prophetic words and the advice given to me by the Holy Father, exactly two years ago, I think: "Your mission is to promote unity between Peter and Paul." This "Paul", as you see, can have various meanings; at the moment it appears to mean those in charge in South Bend and Ann Arbor.

Cardinal Suenens feels that it would be useful if he could give this document to some of his confrères, here and there, and in particular to fellow bishops in Belgium. Perhaps when they see that the Cardinal is not taken in by appearances, they will be more receptive to his suggestions and to the paths which he believes he can take.

Our feeling that the work we are doing is particularly important — that God wants us to do it today and not a day later — has been reinforced by a telephone call I received yesterday from Margie. She told me that a small number of the original companions of the early days (former leaders in South Bend and in Ann Arbor, who are no longer there) are preparing a book, a sort of catalogue of complaints, full of strong criticism of the movement as it exists today in these two places. Their purpose is to ensure that the Holy Father and the authorities in Rome see this book before the pilgrimage, to make sure that we are not welcomed too warmly.

The Cardinal will hear all the details from Fr Kilian, and he will faithfully share all the information with you as soon as he returns from the United States, where he will be spending a couple of weeks, beginning next Tuesday.

From what I can gather, the whole matter hinges essentially around a psychological conflict with the leaders in these two places. However, it would not be surprising if there were in fact some truth in it; we must remember that their "covenant",* which is a very serious and deep alliance, comprising all sorts of demanding personal commitments, involves 1,400 people in Ann Arbor, and almost 600 in South Bend. Difficulties of this sort inevitably happen in every movement.

In any case, all of this leads us to believe that our criticism, which we hope is constructive in every way, will prove especially useful. Kilian prepared the first draft of this document, after talking with me; apart from that, however, all of the work came from the heart and the spirit of your poor Veronica — with every word checked, of course, by the Cardinal. I am telling you all of this simply because I am sure that you want to know the exact truth.

You can imagine how eagerly I will wait to hear your reactions, and to find out how and with whom you will be able to make use of this; and also, to hear whether you think it would be appropriate for the Cardinal to use it with his confrères, as I mentioned above.

An unlikely meeting at the Holy Office

Our work did not consist only of written communications; we also initiated meetings and direct personal exchanges, aimed at resolving misunderstandings and eliminating prejudices.

I had spoken a number of times with Mgr Hamer — now Cardinal Hamer — who was at the time assessor at the Holy Office, and with his assistant Mgr William Levada, the American prelate in charge of relations with the United States. He was very much on our wavelength, and became our friend. Today, he is Archbishop of Portland. At the request of Mgr Jadot, the Holy See's apostolic delegate to the United States, I had also contacted

---

* This is an agreement among the various communities.

a certain number of American bishops in Washington who were particularly involved with the Renewal.

Veronica, for her part, took the initiative of arranging a meeting, in Rome, between representatives of the Holy Office and the main American leaders, Ralph Martin, Steve Clark and Kevin Ranaghan. Because of our friendship with the American leaders, she took part in the meeting to make them feel more comfortable at the Holy Office. The Holy Office was represented by five members, and the meeting was chaired by Mgr Hamer. My secretary, Canon Brieven, was there to represent me. It was indeed an unlikely gathering!

I have before me a detailed report of this meeting, which took place on October 18, 1977.

Mgr Hamer opened the proceedings with a reading from chapter 13 of the Letter of St Paul to the Corinthians, which deals with the charisms of the Holy Spirit. Then he read the letter in which I had suggested the meeting; I had previously discussed with him the three major points that needed to be addressed.

The first of these points had to do with a handbook entitled *The Life in the Spirit Seminars*, which was being used as an instruction book for a seven-week course of preparation for baptism in the Spirit. This handbook lacked the necessary sacramental and ecclesial rooting. Since then, a Catholic edition of the handbook has been produced; in some countries, other introductory texts have also been published.

The second point concerned the true nature of ecumenism, which must respect the identity of each faith.

The third point dealt with the internal structure of the groups and with their relationship to the bishops.

The conversation lasted over two hours. It took place in English and French, in a very friendly atmosphere.

It then remained to put the necessary clarifications into writing. This is where our work of discernment took place, in the form of the Malines Documents*.

---

* See *Memories and Hopes*, p.276

An amazing charism of discernment

I have always admired Veronica's doctrinal and stylistic perspicacity in editing a text. She has not only a gift for spotting any typographical errors that might have escaped the eye of the most meticulous proof-reader, but also a gift for pointing out anything that is imprecise or unclear in the text.

I still have a vivid memory of one of our early working meetings, many years ago. Veronica was visiting Malines; she had just arrived in the house where I lived with my mother, around the corner from the Archbishop's house, when I was informed that Cardinal Van Roey wanted to see me. To keep my visitor occupied while I was gone, I handed her a packet of proofs. They were the proofs of a *Code of Family Ethics*, which had been drafted by an international group of sociologists and moralists, under the Cardinal's chairmanship. The Cardinal had been asked to write a preface to the Code, and he wanted me to read the proofs very carefully, as an extra precaution, to be sure that he could lend his authority to every word. I had not yet started reading it; I asked Veronica to take a look at it while I was gone, simply to keep her occupied while I went to see the Cardinal. When I came back, she had read several of the most sensitive pages, and she pointed out to me some phrases and expressions which, in her opinion, needed to be corrected, elucidated, or worded more carefully.

On the following day, I took the manuscript back to the Cardinal and suggested these amendments to him; he immediately agreed to them, and thanked me for reading the text with such care!

Over the years, I have had many opportunities to appreciate Veronica's perspicacity and the sureness of her eye. Today, at the age of eighty-seven, she places this charism of discernment and lucidity – which is still very active – at the service of the FIAT publications.

C. THE EVANGELICAL ASPECT

22

A FADING PAST

IRELAND

FRANK DUFF

His apostolic charism

The first memories which Veronica and I share are of Ireland and Frank Duff. Had it not been for him, we would have had no common history.

It is only appropriate that in writing of Frank Duff I should emphasise the charismatic perspective; although — for reasons I explained elsewhere* — he kept his distance from the "movement". Frank Duff, more than anyone else, received the charism of the lay apostolate and put it to concrete use on a worldwide scale. He reminded us all that souls are like torches, setting one another on fire. His message and his example are still relevant today.

Veronica once said, "Frank Duff belongs to the future, not to the past."

The relevance of his message

Nobody in heaven gives interviews; but if, just for once, Frank Duff could give us some advice on evangelisation for today and tomorrow, I believe that this is what he might say to us:

The struggle must continue, until all Christians are convinced that they must be apostles by virtue of the baptism they have received; this is a vital duty of which we must constantly remind one another, whatever obstacles we may encounter.

---

* See *Memories and Hopes*, pp. 315-316.

We must announce the Gospel, in word and in deed, everywhere and at all times; this means that we must be in a permanent state of "apostolicity".

We must dare to believe that the impossible can be divided into possible fractions; we must dare to walk on deep waters.

We must encourage and favour the direct approach, through personal contact and living witness.

The laity must assume responsibility, but in direct symbiosis with priests, who have an essential role to play in interpreting the thinking of the Church and in providing moral guidance.

Christianity cannot be lived in solitude; we must form living cells of Christians who commit themselves to regular meetings, in order to pray together and give each other support in their task of evangelisation.

The apostolate is a redemptive mystery, and souls are bought at the highest price.

I once thought I could hear Frank Duff speaking through the voice of Cardinal Danneels, who has never hidden his admiration for this promoter of the ordinary Christian apostolate for ordinary people – in other words, all of us. In July 1991, Cardinal Danneels gave a homily in Beauraing; the main part of this homily was summarised as follows in an issue of *Koinonia* (no. 5, May 1992):

> When you speak of God, just say whatever comes to your mind; don't look for complicated words, and in particular, don't try to find gimmicks to convince people; simply be yourself, and allow the name of Jesus to rise to your lips. If you only know three words of the Gospels, just say those three words!
>
> Begin by speaking directly about Jesus, then about St Paul, and about Jesus crucified. Do not look for those things in the Gospels which you think might please your listener.... Tell the truth about Jesus.... Speak about his

poverty, his purity of heart, his passion.... Do not water down the message, do not try to make it reasonable – it isn't reasonable.

Never say "I am weak, I am a poor speaker, I have no talent, I can barely string two sentences together; and I am a sinner, I am so weak and so poor that I do not deserve to preach Jesus." For it is precisely because you are weak, because you are a sinner, because you have no talent, because you are not gifted for mission, that you will succeed. If you were strong, eloquent and competent, sinless and learned in theology, you might easily assume, when others listened to you, that you were the one who was converting them; and the Lord will never allow this to happen. He wants it to be clear that, as St Paul said, it is never you who convert others; they are converted by the power of His Word. When I am weak, says St Paul, then am I strong.

The miracle of mission is in the fact that simple people open their mouths. You have nothing else to worry about – not what comes before, nor what comes after; only the moment when your lips part. If you do this a few times in your lives, if you let your mouths open, the Lord will take care of the rest.

The question of a beatification

In any process for beatification, the most important thing to emphasise is the miracle of the life itself. I am thinking in particular of Edel Quinn, the Legion of Mary delegate to Africa who died in 1944. I wrote a biography of her, entitling it *A Heroine of the Apostolate*;* her missionary life, despite her serious illness, shows superhuman spiritual strength.

Frank Duff worked for the Department of Finance in Dublin. In 1921 he founded the Legion of Mary, a lay apostolic organisation – the first of its kind – which today is active in more than

---

* See *Memories and Hopes*, pp. 47-48.

two thousand dioceses throughout the world. If this were not remarkable enough in itself, one has only to read the extraordinary story of his direct religious apostolate in a disreputable neighbourhood of Dublin. He tells this story personally, minimising his own role as much as possible, in an astonishing book called *Miracles on Tap*, subtitled *The Incredible Transformation of Dublin's Bentley Place*.

Will the cause for the beatification of Frank Duff be introduced one day? I cannot say. During the Council, I pleaded – in vain – for a complete revision of the existing procedure in these matters, and I welcomed American journalist Kenneth Woodward's attempts to bring about such a revision through his well-informed book, *Making Saints*.*

I believe that the approach must be completely re-examined, from beginning to end. The first step must be to eliminate the requirement of a miracle which must be authenticated by a medical panel before the cause can even be officially introduced. Pope John XXIII complained about this requirement; in the case of one saint – St Gregory Barbarigo of Bergamo – he cheerfully waived it.

As a joke, but a pointed one, I sometimes say to my audiences: "My friends, you must try to become saints, but don't even try to become canonised saints: it is far too complicated and chancy!"

It would not be appropriate for me to give an opinion concerning the question of the beatification of Frank Duff. However, I am quite prepared to appropriate a statement that Mgr Jacques Leclerc once made about Fr Lebbe (the famous Belgian missionary to China, who braved sea and wind to encourage the appointment of native bishops), whose biography he wrote. "I don't know," he said, "whether or not Fr Lebbe will one day be canonised; it is up to the Holy Church to make that decision, with the inspiration of the Holy Spirit. Having studied saints all my life, however, I can say that Fr Lebbe was such stuff as saints are made of."

---

* Published by Schuster, New York, 1990, and mentioned in *Memories and Hopes*, p. 144.

FRANCE

The list of those who shared our paths here on earth, and who have now moved on to the fullness of life in the peace of the Lord, grows longer day by day. These memoirs would be incomplete were I not to mention a few more names.

In the world of the Charismatic Renewal — which, in recent years, has been our world — a few names from the Emmanuel Community have particular significance: Pierre Goursat, Danielle Proux, and Bernard Michaut.

PIERRE GOURSAT — 1914 — MARCH 25, 1991

I first met Pierre at Ann Arbor, in the United States. He had gone there, as I had, to hear what the Holy Spirit might perhaps be saying to the Churches over there.

How can I describe Pierre Goursat? He was as unexpected and undefinable as his famous *Péniche*, the houseboat which was moored at Neuilly, on the shore of the Seine, and in which he lived and worked until his death. Beneath his ordinary, almost banal, exterior was a vibrant and concretely creative personality, enlivened by the intense spirituality which was his life and his strength.

In some ways, he was not unlike Frank Duff, the founder of the Legion of Mary, to which Pierre belonged for some time. He had the same unfailing assiduity in prayer, expressed above all in adoration; the same devotion to Mary, which led him directly to the Heart of Jesus; the same modesty, which made him disappear in a crowd; the same zeal for evangelisation, aimed at one and all, regardless of social class; the same love for the Church, to which he submitted in filial devotion; the same sense of humour, which relaxed those around him and helped him to communicate his message. And like Frank Duff, he was very attached to his bicycle, which he used almost until the end of his life. That is how I will always remember him: in Paray-le-Monial, on his bicycle.

The Emmanuel Community, which he inspired, is based on his own three-word motto: "Adoration, Compassion, Evangelisation".

Eucharistic adoration, as Pierre experienced it, was a living lesson of faith in prayer.

Compassion embraces the vast gamut of human misery. The centre for AIDS patients which has opened in Paris — and which Pierre inspired — is a concrete example of this.

The concern for evangelisation must be embodied in our lives and on a worldwide scale.

Essentially, Pierre was a man who was faithful to the Church as it is today, while remaining open to the urgent needs of tomorrow and to the necessity for adjustments.

No one who knew Pierre will ever forget the playful sense of humour which was such an essential part of him. Earlier in this book, I mentioned his comments on Veronica's letter to Mr Ogino, in Tokyo. Another example, in the same vein: he had invited Veronica to speak to the leaders of the Emmanuel Community; knowing full well that she would undoubtedly urge the community to bold apostolic ventures, Pierre called out to the audience, just as Veronica was about to start speaking: "Fasten your seat-belts!"

Your own seat-belt has been unfastened, dear Pierre, and you have flown away; but you will never cease to promote vocations to the priesthood, and to inspire the "new evangelisation". And you will feel particularly comfortable, up there, with a few slightly bohemian saints who were there before you!

DANIELLE PROUX: 1943 — DECEMBER 3, 1983

On our visits to Le Rocher, near Nice, we often spent time with Danielle and Claude Proux and their household, in the Aix-en-Provence community of Les Genêts.

Danielle, who was gravely ill, gave a wonderful example of serenity and courage in the face of severe trials. On the eve of her death, I wrote her a farewell letter, in which I spoke to her in

266

the language of faith. At the end of her funeral – a religious ceremony filled with Easter joy – copies of this letter were distributed to all those who attended.

My dear Danielle,

...I would like to say to you: a happy and holy feast of Easter!

It is the path Jesus followed to his Father which is for each of us the ultimate feast and the path to follow; and this path is at once shining truth and eternal life. You are going into life, into beauty, into infinite tenderness. In God, you will be, more than ever, loving mother and caring wife. Your vocation here on earth, God's dream in you, will reach its complete fulfilment. You will enter into the joy of God, the joy that is God, the joy that absorbs every tear.

Now more than ever, have courage, and trust in the fatherly love of God, who calls you by name.

Have courage, and trust in the brotherly love of Jesus, who brings you to live in his brotherhood.

Have courage, and trust in the Holy Spirit, who comes to flood you with his grace and his power, concealed in the shadows of suffering, of darkness, of temporary separation.

Have courage, and trust in Mary, your Mother, faithfully invoked in each Hail Mary, to be present at the hour when, for each one of us, Easter will be fulfilled.

With your family, with all the members of your brotherhood, with all those whom you have helped to know and love the Lord, we share with all our hearts in your pain, in your silence, in your peace.

I thank you for the past; and may the joy of God be poured upon you for all time!

In His name, with all of the Church in union with you, I send you my loving blessing.

L.J.Cardinal Suenens

BERNARD MICHAUT: 1920 — FEBRUARY 22, 1992

I have recently learned of the death of another dear friend: Bernard Michaut has just died in Paray-le-Monial.

He was our friend in France and in Belgium. He was constant and faithful in the service of the Lord; his faith was simple and unfaltering, and he lived in complete forgetfulness of self.

His wife Marcelle wrote to us describing the last moments of his life. She told us that Bernard had invited those around him to be very prayerful as he prepared to meet the Lord; he said to them, "Let us be silent and live Jesus' passion with him."

A few weeks ago, we went to pray on Bernard's tomb; it is in Paray-le-Monial, not far from that of Pierre Goursat. With Marcelle, we thanked the Lord for his life, for the strength of his faith, and for his constancy in the midst of trials. He makes me think of Nathaniel in the Gospel, of whom Jesus said, "Behold, a man in whom there is no guile!" He was the kind of Christian who is beloved of God.

May he rest in the peace and the joy of the Lord!

23

PAST INITIATIVES
FOR THE FAMILY

The Louvain international symposium

On Veronica's suggestion, and with the assistance of her sister, Dr Kitty Owler, I decided to organise a meeting of doctors, specialists in sexuality, and moralists, at the University of Louvain. I hoped to institute a yearly international symposium on research on birth control methods compatible with Christian ethics.

Many of those invited responded to the invitation and regularly participated in the symposium; they came from various European countries, and from the US.

The authorities in Rome were aware of our purpose. Fr de Rietmatten, the Swiss theologian who was in charge of family matters at the curia, participated in a few of the meetings, and remained in contact with us. Pope Paul VI chose some of the participants – doctors and moralists – to be members of his enlarged pontifical commission.*

For a few years, I presided over the meetings of this symposium. My book *Love and Control* was a direct offshoot of these meetings.

Marriage Encounter

At about this time, as another of our joint initiatives in the area of family life, we introduced Marriage Encounter to Belgium. This is a movement whose purpose is to bring about greater

---

* See *Memories and Hopes*, p. 144.

unity within couples by fostering deep psychological and spiritual harmony.

Margie Grace had introduced us to some of the movement's leaders, including Fr Gallagher, in the United States. Veronica and Yvette participated in one of their weekends and found it extremely interesting. A few months later, on Long Island, I took part in a similar experience; as participants must work in pairs, I teamed up with Guido Heyrbaut, a young vicar from Brussels. For me, this was a very unusual situation; I had carefully concealed my identity (only the directors of the course knew who I was), and so I was able to observe human psychology at work in a spontaneous and uninhibited way. I, too, found the experience an interesting one.

As a result, we invited Fr Gallagher and his team to come to Brussels to organise a model weekend. This took place, in English, in a convent in Brussels; the experiment was very successful, and the movement got under way.

Love and Truth

As a result of this initiative, and along the same lines, a new organisation was born in France: it is called Amour et Vérité – Love and Truth – and is associated with the Emmanuel Community in Paris. In its own way, it responds to the same issues as Marriage Encounter, and has the same purpose: to strengthen conjugal love by deepening it in the light of the Gospels and of human psychology. This organisation now has branches in various other countries.

Love – a word which has lost its meaning

This was the title of a booklet which I wrote some time ago, as a reaction to an official brochure distributed in France; this official brochure was intended to initiate people to "love" – a "love" that was antithetical to the Christian understanding of love. Since then, authentic love has been further debased and profaned. Now, more than ever, evangelisation calls us to denounce the misuse of this word, and the ambiguities that surround it.

A Chinese sage was once asked what he would do if he were to become master of the world. He answered: "I would give the meanings back to words."

This would be a great service to humanity; distortions in language wreak imperceptible but incalculable damage. Cars are not the only things that need to be regularly checked and serviced; if we are not very careful, our language becomes the vehicle which, unbeknownst to us, can carry contaminated goods. When the words that are distorted are key words which touch the very foundations of human life – and, for Christians, the very roots of faith – the duty to react becomes an imperative.

For Christians, love is a sacred reality, which has its source in the very heart of God, who is love, and who created man and woman in his image.

Christians have an obligation to call moral disorder – in plain language, sin – by its true name. We cannot accept language which attempts to disguise moral error beneath camouflaging labels.

A famous general once said: "Words are the battles of today; the right words are the battles we win, the wrong words are the battles we lose." Every verbal compromise is in itself a capitulation.

The word "love" is lost ground, and it will be difficult to win it back. No other word has been so abused. Magazines and newspapers are full of it; on the radio, there are "love" songs, day and night, on every wavelength; television, films, videos, all provide endless "love" scenes; advertisements link this image of "love" to the most diverse products.

This stunted version of "love" is used to excuse anything and everything, and is presented as its own justification. It is a veil which is used to cover up all manner of moral turpitude; an alibi used to conceal misconduct, adultery, lust, and shameless behaviour.

My desire to enhance the value of love, as seen through the eyes of faith, once motivated me to write a message to two of our young friends, on the eve of their wedding. This was written in an aeroplane — literally between heaven and earth.

A HOME WHERE TWO LOVES MEET

Look down at a city from an aeroplane.
There is nothing like an aeroplane to help us see people and
  things in their proper perspective,
in their true dimension.
Look down and ask yourself:
what is the meaning of each of these houses,
the secret of each little apartment?

What is a house?
It is a shelter for a home.
The shelter may be poor or luxurious;
the reality within is always the same:
a home.

What is a home?
It is where two loves meet;
a man and a woman
who met one day.
Their meeting was the result of a thousand chance events,
mysterious coincidences which we call Providence.
This man and this woman exchanged a few simple words:
"I love you."
For there are no other words;
and they are the same in every language.

The poor and the rich have spoken them, in the same voice.
For once, there is equality here on earth.

Why this particular meeting?
Who can tell?
A man will find reasons;
because he likes to think he is reasonable,
he will invent reasons for loving
and he will repeat them to himself
and to his friends, if they will listen.
But his friends will only half believe him;
and they will be wise.
A woman will not try to explain:
she loves because she loves, and that is that.
Her love will be less tentative because it is not built
on a logic made of reasons which can be argued.

From these two loves a home is born.
A home is a hearth where two flames have become one
and no wind must ever blow it out.
There comes a day when this single flame
gives birth to another flame,
and then another.
A home is a like a grotto in Lourdes
filled with so many tiny candles
gathered around the large one which protects them.

This flame is what we call love,
and each candle is a reserve of love.
This flame is the image of God;
for God is Love.
And anything real that ever happens
in one of these houses which glimmer in the night
touches the life of this flame.

The Hidden Hand of God

Man was made only for this,
and so was woman,
and so are their children
and the children of their children.

They must keep God's Love in fragile vessels.
And the only way to keep it,
the only secret,
is to spread it all around.

Whoever wants to keep love – as one keeps one's soul –
must lose it,
lose it in other souls,
who will live by this gift
for time and for eternity.
Love never dies,
for God never dies,
and it is God who loves
in every human heart.

24

FIAT IN GOD'S WORLD TODAY
1981–1992

The birth and growth of FIAT

Because of her age, Veronica can no longer personally "take the Gospel to the far corners of the earth"; but she can still fulfil the same objective, through the projects which she initiates and encourages. She likes to remind us of the wonderful new technologies available to us – such as the fax, which allows us to transmit messages instantly to the other side of the earth. "We must love God," she says, "not only with our hearts, but with all of our imaginations." The FIAT initiatives reflect this attitude.

The acronym itself – FIAT – indicates immediately that the spiritual perspective of these initiatives focuses on the very heart of the mystery of the Incarnation, fruit of Mary's "Yes" to the action of the Holy Spirit.

The goal of FIAT projects is to increase the intensity of Christians' spiritual life, and thus of their apostolic life, especially in the context of the family.

The first of these initiatives springs from Veronica's continued concern and care for the upper echelons of society, which do not fit into the framework or the categories of organised Catholic action. At first, Veronica experimented, here and there, with what she called "l'apostolat des salons" – the drawing-room apostolate. In chapter 10, I described the first of these experiments, where she faced the unexpected with great courage. Later, she conceived a more elaborate and diversified plan to give shape to this type of apostolate.

In a spirit of faith, Veronica decided to request the Pope's blessing for her project; she asked him for an audience.

An audience with Pope John Paul II – 1979

Pope John Paul was familiar with Veronica's legionary activities in France, and in particular with her work with the Polish community during the War. At an audience, he had asked both the Cardinal of Armagh and Frank Duff for news of Veronica; earlier, he had invited her to lunch with me and four of the leaders of the Renewal. His doors, therefore, were already open to her, and her request was easily granted.

During the private audience – at which I was present – she told him of her apostolic dream. She showed him a drawing, a visual representation of her trinitarian approach, which is now on the back of the FIAT medal. She explained that the trinitarian mystery must be lived in its paternal dimension, in particular by the Christian leaders in society; in its fraternal dimension in Jesus Christ, especially through commitment to service to the poor – and then Veronica began to speak of the spiritual dimension, to be lived under the breath of the Holy Spirit, at work in the Renewal; but the Holy Father, who was listening very attentively, interrupted her with a smile and, pointing at her, said, "The Holy Spirit – that's you!"

At the end of the audience, she requested a word of guidance from him; he said to her, very solemnly, "Continue, continue."

Then, without transition and much to our surprise, he added: "Go to Holland!"

This unexpected direction, which had no connection with our conversation – and even less with Veronica's nationality – had many consequences. One of its unexpected results was our contact with the Foundation of the Witnesses of God's Love, instituted by

Piet and Trude Derksen. This foundation has provided valuable support for various FIAT initiatives.

FIAT'S first steps

The little group known as FIAT — Family International Apostolic Team — was born in Paray-le-Monial, during a Renewal retreat.

It included several young couples, who had asked to pray together that they might receive Baptism in the Spirit. This intimate ceremony took place in the Carmelite chapel which still exists in Paray-le-Monial. I gave a homily, in which I quoted these words from Scripture: "Old people will have dreams and the young will have visions."

Some time later, I received a message from the original group; these lines recall their early hopes and point to future paths.

Paray-le-Monial, July 16, 1984

FIAT

"The old have dreams and the young have visions."
So many dreams are barely sketched,
So many dreams are beginning to take shape,
So many dreams have already come true.

Thank you for having dreamed them
and for having made them real,
Thus giving us
a more solid grounding,
a greater openness,
greater hope with which to face the future.

Our visions are very ordinary —
and yet, in spite of that, they are extraordinary;
for, more than ever, we see

the hand of God on each one of us,
on our families,
on our countries,
on our world.

Yes, we set forth in life
armed with trust in the wonders of God.

Thank you for all that you stand for,
for all that you have given us
of time, of love, of wisdom, of joy,
of prayer, of trust, of humour.

In Ea,
Your little FIAT
(which, please God, will be very big someday).

The cenacle retreats

Through a "chance" encounter with Fr Jean Meeûs SJ, FIAT
came into contact with a small association called "The
Annunciation", which organises retreats in a spirit of pentecostal
Renewal. The purpose of these retreats is to form Christians *ad
intra* and *ad extra*, in the double perspective of inner life and
apostolate, and to multiply evangelical cells.

The FIAT publications

A wide field of literary apostolate has recently opened to us. This
is a particularly urgent field of activity, especially as the fall of
communist regimes in the East favours this spiritual apostolate
of Christian *ressourcement*. We are attempting to spread new
and ancient writings, in various languages; these can be an aid to
in-depth revitalisation.

The Marian year and the nativity of Mary

The Marian year was a good opportunity to call attention to the feast of the Nativity of Mary. I decided to emphasise its importance in a brief article:

The Congregation for Divine Worship, in Rome, has provided a series of wise and practical suggestions for making the Marian year a fruitful time within local churches. In a document entitled *Orientamenti e Proposte per l'Anno Mariano*, the Congregation calls attention to four Marian feasts which deserve to play a more significant role in popular devotion. The Feast of the Nativity of Mary, which we celebrate on September 8 is mentioned as one of those which need to be given greater prominence.

I feel that at present, Christian believers do not give sufficient importance to the Nativity of Mary. The feast is hardly noticed at all – perhaps because it appears as part of the ordinary liturgy of the week; perhaps because it is eclipsed by other feasts which have been given a more prominent place.

This Marian year provides us with a unique opportunity to give the proper emphasis to the feast of the Birth of our Mother in Heaven, and to celebrate it with the splendour it deserves, on September 8 of this year and of the years to come.

Mary's birth must be emphasised in the light of faith, in particular because it is related to the unique grace of the Immaculate Conception, which situates, in a special way, the coming into this world of the one who was to become the Mother of our Saviour.

Why should we not associate ourselves more closely with this jubilation? Mary's birth is a prelude and a preface to the mystery of salvation; let us joyfully celebrate the

Birth of our Mother. At a time when Mother's Day is
becoming increasingly popular throughout the world, we
Christians are called to give new prominence – especially
in our homes – to the Birth of the one who was to make
possible the Birth of the Redeemer.

In so doing, we do not forget for an instant that Jesus
alone is the Saviour of the world; but how can we not celebrate with gratitude the mystery that is a prelude and a
preface to his Birth?

Listen to St John Damascene expressing his joy:

"Come all, joyfully, to celebrate the Birth of the joy of
the whole world! Today, from earthly nature, a heaven has
been formed above the earth. Today is the beginning of
salvation for all the world."

An icon for Mary's nativity

The Feast of the Nativity of Mary is an important one in the history of the Legion of Mary, which was born in Dublin at the first
vespers of the Nativity in 1921. As soon as the Legion was established in France, Veronica encouraged the legionaries to celebrate
this feast. A hymn for this day, inspired by Veronica, was written
at the time; more recently, the melody has been beautifully and
very successfully rearranged by a member of the Emmanuel
Community.

For a long time, Veronica hoped that the Church would give
greater prominence to the feast of Mary's Nativity. To prepare
the souls of the faithful for this day, she asked one of the Poor
Clare Sisters in Nice, Sr Thérèse Michel (who died in 1991), to
paint a picture of the Nativity of Mary being celebrated in glory
in heaven. Veronica specified every detail with great care. The
painting is marvellously delicate and prayerful. At the moment,
the icon is travelling around the world; it is a form of visual evangelisation.

I have written a spiritual commentary on the icon; it can be summarised as follows. The painting shows us the Feast of the Nativity of Mary as seen from two different angles: on the one hand, seen from heaven, it leads us into God's plan for the salvation of the world; on the other, seen from earth, it holds the freshness of dawn and of early morning.

From a heavenly perspective

This is a trinitarian feast, for it is the first moment which prepares the covenant between heaven and earth. Mary is the privileged daughter of the Father, who prepares her for her destiny. She is the one who, at the Annunciation, will respond with the decisive "Yes" to the coming of the Holy Spirit. She is the future Mother of the Word of God, who will make his home in her.

In the painting, the Trinity dominates the scene: the Father, with open hands, gives us the Virgin who will give birth to his Son; the Son appears as the radiant morning star; the Holy Spirit, the rainbow of the covenant, is a bridge linking heaven and earth and overshadowing Mary. The angels and saints are present, sketched in discreetly, in attitudes of contemplation and thanksgiving. St Joachim and St Anne thank God for the child who has filled them with joy and sealed their love.

This is the meaning of the picture; it invites us to broaden the horizons of our faith, and helps us to enter into its hidden depths. Our Christian vision is often too narrow, too earthbound. We do not understand clearly enough that Christianity is an alliance between heaven and earth, which is sealed in Jesus Christ "born of the Holy Spirit and of Mary".

From an earthly perspective

How can we give more concrete significance and warmth to the feast of Mary's Nativity? We celebrate this feast formally on

September 8 but very inadequately in the context of our Christian lives.

Christian families should prepare for the feast and celebrate it in their homes. A painting or icon of the Nativity of Mary might be placed in the "prayer corner" which so often graces today's Christian homes. Joyful singing should invite one and all to rejoice and to welcome Mary as a smile from heaven.

The Feast of Mary's Nativity is a feast of hope for the renewal of the Church. It marks the beginning of the Holy Trinity's plan for the salvation and happiness of humanity. This liturgical date should be particularly dear to us on this account.

As Cardinal Decourtray recently said, "The Church must rediscover its youth by rediscovering its Mother."

In celebrating the birth of Mary, we transpose our feelings of filial gratitude – which have inspired the increasingly popular institution of Mothers' Day – on to the supernatural level.

> In the eyes of faith,
> Mary is the Mother of all humankind,
> Mary is the Mother of all mothers,
> Mary is the Mother of the Church,
> now and for all time.

A letter to the Holy Father

Motivated by this desire to give greater importance to this feast, both in the life of the Church and in the lives of Christian families, I wrote to the Holy Father, on August 19, 1988, to inform him of our initiative and to obtain his support.

> Most Holy Father;
>
> At the end of the Marian year, you stated that "The time to lift up our eyes to Mary never comes to an end," and

you called on Christians to prepare for the new millennium with Mary.

In this spirit, and with a view to promoting the Feast of the Nativity of Mary (which is celebrated on September 8), our little FIAT group has taken the initiative of distributing a picture and a prayer which might encourage Christians to celebrate the birthday of the "Mother of all mothers" in their homes.

I take the liberty of enclosing a copy of the prayer, which is being translated into a number of languages — including, of course, Polish. I hope that you will read it with joy. This is our way of thanking you for the encouragement you have given to Marian devotion, which we endeavour to promote within the Renewal in the Holy Spirit.

We pray for you, Most Holy Father, that the Lord may guide you on all the paths of the world, and open before you those doors which are still closed; and that Mary may be for you, more than ever, *Vita, dulcedo et spes tua.*

Receive, Most Holy Father, my devotion and filial respect.

L.J. Cardinal Suenens

In his answer, the Holy Father welcomed our initiative and warmly congratulated the FIAT group.

To His Eminence Cardinal Leo Jozef Suenens,
former Archbishop of Malines-Brussels

I thank you for your letter of August 19 and congratulate you with joy on the welcome initiative which your Eminence has undertaken, with the FIAT group, in order to help Christian homes and believers in many countries to prolong the spirit and the good effects of the 1987-1988 Marian Year, in particular through the fervent celebration of the Nativity of the Virgin Mary "who brought to the world the hope and the dawn of salvation".

May the Most Holy Mother of Christ the Redeemer assist you in your apostolic work!

I bless you with all my heart.

From the Vatican, October 5, 1988

Johannes Paulus II

FIAT — In the service of the family and of love

In February 1991, Veronica was asked about the purpose of FIAT. Her answer, which was published in *The Newsletter*, goes straight to the point:

In my heart, I could hear only one word: the word love.

The ultimate goal of FIAT is love — to be love, to make love known, to accept being loved. God's plan is love; God himself is nothing but love.

We must never dissociate nature from grace. Look at a small child, only a few weeks old; he watches his mother and smiles at the sound of her voice. He is already expressing joy and love. Every human being dreams of loving and of being loved.

We must love those around us, in obedience to the greatest commandment of all: "Love one another, as I have loved you." And then we will experience in our hearts a growing joy. Jesus said to us, "If you follow me, I shall give you joy that no one can ever take from you." This word of the Lord is true, and we can experience its truth every day.

All of creation was created for joy, for love.

But at the beginning, all of this love was distorted by sin; and today, because the word love has become synonymous with sin, this dream of authentic love is possible only if we allow God's love to live within us. This means that we must struggle against the caricatures of love which Satan spreads throughout the world; we must reinstate the true meaning of the word love, and teach others what love means. Let us do all we can to make love known.

FIAT's vocation is to make love known; this means to be capable of loving as God himself loves, with all that this implies. We must teach everyone to be God's lovers.

FIAT's battle cry is LOVE.

The FIAT Rosary

Here we enter into a supernatural world which does not depend on our own initiatives; only the future will reveal its meaning for our world.

In 1984, during the night between September 7 and 8 — the feast of the Nativity of Mary — Veronica had an extraordinary spiritual experience. She described it to me, the following day, in these words:

During the night before the Nativity of Mary, I was saddened by the thought that although Mother's Day is becoming more and more popular, the birthday of Mary, Mother of all mothers, would not be celebrated in Christian homes.

In my prayers, I said to the Lord:

"Jesus, tomorrow is the feast of the Nativity of your Mother. Every child in the world gives his mother a present for her birthday. What will you give your Mother, Jesus?"

And suddenly, as in a spiritual flash of light, I saw in my mind an image of a small, reduced rosary, and I thought I heard the Lord say to me:

"Here is my birthday present to my Mother; it will help her to make me known to the very ends of the earth. Make it known all over the world."

When Veronica told me of this experience, she added that in her heart, Mary cannot be separated from the Holy Spirit, and that this little rosary should be introduced by a prayer to the Holy Spirit. To Veronica, this was an integral part of her vision. Together, we composed the prayer to the Holy Spirit which precedes the recitation of the Rosary.

Most Holy Spirit,
Help us to relive, in union with Mary,
the joyful, sorrowful and glorious mysteries of Jesus.
Amen.

Grant that we may be
inspired by the faith of our Baptism,
nourished by the Eucharist,
renewed in the grace of Pentecost,
so that we may live,
in word and in deed,
always and everywhere,
as faithful witnesses to Christ
and to the love of His Divine Heart.
Amen.

I later wrote a booklet introducing this new rosary: *The FIAT Prayer and Rosary.** I described the special aspects and characteristics of this rosary from the various perspectives of the family, the Church, ecumenism, and evangelisation.

FIAT has received letters from over one hundred countries, in every continent, requesting rosaries. A newsletter is published from time to time, in French, Dutch, English and Spanish; it con-

---

* Published by FIAT

tains moving testimonies, particularly from families. There are now FIAT centres in the United States and in Ireland.*

Reactions

On the morning after Veronica's vision, one of our closest collaborators, Fr Jean Meeûs SJ (whose pastoral activities have taken on international dimensions), came to visit Veronica. She told him of the night's event; he listened, much moved, and told her solemnly, "This is a message from above."

Veronica decided to submit this vision to the official ecclesial authorities — in this case, my successor, Cardinal Danneels — at once. In the following words, written on December 8, 1984, Cardinal Danneels encouraged the spreading of the FIAT rosary:

> May this little rosary find its way into many homes, so that they may become cenacles of apostles, gathered around the Virgin Mary to receive the Spirit of Pentecost.

Some time later, during an audience, I told the Pope about this grace. I offered him a rosary, saying: "Holy Father, we are doing things backwards today. Usually, you hand out rosary beads to your visitors, but this is a rather special case: your visitor has come to bring you rosary beads."

Frank Duff and the FIAT medal

The FIAT rosary begins with a medal representing the Holy Spirit overshadowing Mary. This symbol can be inserted, if one wishes, into the heart of any traditional rosary, where the branches meet. This idea is a response to a suggestion which Frank Duff made to me almost half a century ago; I quote from his letter:

---

* The international centre of Friends of FIAT, and of FIAT initiatives, is in Belgium. Roger Matthys and his family co-ordinate FIAT activities from their home at Gravenplein 9, B - 9940 Ertvelde, Belgium.

The manner in which the Rosary is recited is important, and it is indeed providential that the Legion is in the habit of beginning the recitation with an invocation and a prayer addressed to the Holy Spirit.

I think it would be appropriate for the medal linking the three parts of the rosary to have, on one side, a symbolic representation of the Holy Spirit.

He asked me to write an article suggesting this; now — after some delay — I have fulfilled his request.

D. IN SPIRITUAL COMMUNION

25

A FEW PAGES ON SPIRITUALITY

A brief introduction

In earlier chapters, I outlined a few of the more important aspects of Veronica's apostolic life. Now it seems appropriate to give my readers at least a glimpse of her profound spiritual life, through excerpts from some of her letters and writings, going back over the years. A more complete collection of her letters and memoirs will be published at a later date; this will include testimonies from various sources. For now, to give my readers a foretaste, I have selected, from fifty years' worth of correspondence, a few excerpts and isolated thoughts.

My own memoirs have been set largely in the contexts of the institutional Church and of the apostolic Church. In some ways, a collection of Veronica's writings would provide the third panel of this triptych: the context of the charismatic Church.

This is in no way a well-organised or structured chapter. I have chosen, arbitrarily, two headings which shed some light on a life lived in the mystery of God and in Marian communion; my approach stems from this double perspective.

1. In the Mystery of God

A. God is Trinitarian Love

O blessed Trinity

O blessed Trinity — those three words are music to my heart and to my soul! I yearn to be, in each of the persons of the Holy

Trinity, their mutual love, their mutual admiration, each one's gratitude to the other two — to offer eternal love to eternal gratitude and to eternal wisdom. Some day, will you give me a whole lesson on the Holy Trinity?

Union in Trinity

What union in the Trinity; and what activity in that silence!

In constant communion with the Holy Trinity

Do not be afraid; you can do several things at once. If you are faithful to grace, you will never know the meaning of a minute's rest, for you will be haunted by the value of each single minute, and by all the good that can be accomplished in sixty seconds.

The secret is to keep — at the very core of one's will, of one's heart, of one's spirit — a profound and loving silence of adoration of the Holy Trinity; and constantly to throw more fuel on the fire of your love, through the humble and simple use of ejaculatory prayers.

From time to time, stop whatever you are doing to recite one of those burning acts of union; for instance, repeat very slowly, "In the name of the Father, of the Son, and of the Holy Spirit." What a wonderful prayer this is! It gives you the strength of a giant, and lets you undertake herculean tasks.

Never set aside Fr de Caussade's little book, *Abandonment to Divine Providence*, for too long. I know of no other book in the world that is more powerful in helping us to communicate with the divine will in the present moment.

Trinitarian love

I find it so normal, so instinctive to adore Jesus in the Blessed Sacrament; but always and everywhere I adore him with reference to the Holy Trinity.

I believe I could never dissociate the Son from the Father, just as I cannot separate the Mother from the Son.

I am with my Father, in the arms of my Mother.

When I say Mary, she says Jesus, and Jesus says Father. These key words point to a Christocentrism which is wholly oriented towards God the Father.

For me, Love never means "two"; it always means "three or more". But in the end, this "more" is always reduced to one Trinity.

Lord, teach me to love!

B. God is Love

God loves me

I feel a great desire to give more time to spiritual reading, to read about God — Father, Son and Holy Spirit.

At the moment I am reading a book by Fr Plus, as a bride-to-be might read the letters of her future bridegroom: each line is intoxicating; I feel I can almost touch the weight of God's love.

"God loves me" — these three words contain all time and all eternity. Will you explain to me, some day, the meaning and the richness of these words? Who is "God", really, and what does "love" mean? And who is this "me"? This may sound like a paradox, but I am happy to belong to the category and the family of great sinners, to be able to glimpse the meaning of "sin", and in some way to be sin. Sin creates such a special relationship between us and Jesus. When I recognise myself as "sin", I am truly myself: it is this very "I" — solitary, empty, tired — who brings Jesus down from heaven to take me in his hands, in his arms, like a small, suffering child.

I feel crushed by grace: it is awful to be loved by a God, and to take this love to men. I give endless talks — all of them excellent — and *Theology* and *Edel Quinn** are selling like hot cakes. At night, around midnight, in bed, I plunge into these pages, to find

---

* Two books by Cardinal Suenens.

life in their words; despite my exhaustion, I always find that I have enough strength to enter into each line, to taste all the nectar contained in each word. It is intoxicating. My God, my God, have mercy on me: my sins are a great consolation to me!

I cannot even imagine what it would be to love someone outside God, on the margins of God. It is so obvious to me that I was made for God alone – that I belong to him and yearn for him. And he loves me, with a wonderfully inventive love; he comes to me with countless signs – and above all, in the Eucharist.

Imagine, just for one moment, what would happen if God were to take back his love – in other words, himself – from my life. I would cease to exist; it would be death – a state of putrid corruption, where every vice would triumph in me, and Satan would be master.

Just as there is only one God, there is only one love. It is He who draws us to himself, using all of creation to this end. Is it not marvellous to think that each tiny thing that comes from his hands has a vocation? Every thing is but an instrument, created in order to bring us into communion with God and with his love. Fr de Caussade says this beautifully in *Abandonment to Divine Providence.**

A jealous God

Day by day, I see more clearly that love is passionately jealous and will suffer no rivals.

Every creature – even the holiest and the most detached – is an enemy to the soul, for our poor human hearts are so deeply attached to earthly things that they cling with extraordinary ease to all that is created.

To live God and God alone, you must have your dagger always at hand. *Noli me tangere.* We must be equally on guard whether a saint or a sinner approaches us.

These words of caution must be always on our lips, especially with respect to any kind of work, any worries, joys, or sorrows – to

---

* This book is now available from FIAT.

all that belongs to this world; for all things must be part of the Holy of Holies, who wants love for himself alone.

One God in heaven and on earth

The concept underlying all of *Theology of the Apostolate* is that action is only a form of prayer, and that normally prayer can only be completely fulfilled in action.

Essentially, it all comes down to the one great commandment: you must love. How is love manifested? On what does it feed? How does it grow and become fruitful?

Once again, we have to admire the wonderful unity of God's design. There is, in fact, only one commandment, only one person to love – God.

There is not one God in heaven, and another God in the Eucharist, or in our hearts, or in our neighbours. No, there is only one Lord, one God alone; and we must love him and serve him with every heartbeat.

To bring about this unity, however, we must recognise him, both in the men and women we meet, and in the bread and wine.

There is only one love, and God is love.

The Lord has enveloped me in the warmth of his love; he has stretched out to me his strong arms, and welcomed me, after my long journey in darkness and in cold, alone on perilous roads.

Love is blind

You know the saying – love is blind. Well, God, who is love, must be very blind indeed! I imagine that he must use all sorts of devices to escape from his own justice and turn a blind eye to our "merits"!

It is easier to know God than to know human beings

Only God can know me to the very depths of my ignoble self.

295

The Hidden Hand of God

The greatness of man lies in the fact that no created intelligence can understand him or know him to his innermost core. In a way, it is almost easier to know God than to know man; there are no surprises in God, and we need only accept the fact that he is. Whereas human beings are not... so many things. That is why they are so exhausting! God, on the other hand, is restful; he is peace. Our mother, the holy Church, addresses a marvellous farewell wish to her children when they begin their long journey to eternity: rest in peace!

To know God is everything: we need no longer struggle to know ourselves, for our selves will be lost in him. What rest, what peace!

It would be so good to hear a homily on this very simple theme: "May he rest in peace — *requiescat in pace.*"

I am not afraid of God, if he knows everything

In one of your letters, you wrote such consoling words; you told me that you have found, in my poor self, something resembling honesty and transparence.

I would so like to understand better and better this simple word: truth. For me, the word "truth" is synonymous with the word "faith", for faith alone enables us to see the true meanings of things — allows us to see the ultimate origin of things, in the thought and the will of God.

There is such depth in the words which I once copied down from a book you lent me: "I am not afraid of God, if he knows everything." This is so restful; it gives me such joy, such security; for I am in God, and he is in me, and he allows me to share in his understanding of men and of all things."

God alone: not God and something else
(from a letter to a fellow worker)

Let yourself be guided gently by Providence — do not force the hand of our Queen; it may be that she wants you to be in Paris during the tragic days ahead. You will know her will by completely abdicating your own, and placing yourself in a holy indifference to all the details which are so unimportant – place, date, and so forth.

Be very watchful, and do not let your soul be filled with the desire to have news of all those whom you love here. We must love silence very much, and create it all around us. God alone – these words are such beautiful music to the soul! But if we seek God and something else, however holy it may be, straight away there is discord, and false notes disrupt the divine harmony.

You must see the hand of our Queen in all of these refusals and disappointments. 'Give me whatever draws me closer to you' – let these words be on your lips in all your dealings with others."

Always give thanks

I believe that my gentle Queen is going to use me to serve her once again: I feel the pressure, and I know I shall soon be on deep waters once more. And I am happy, all day long, pushing the past away and looking only to the future.

Deo gratias, with every heartbeat, for everything; for the chair I sit on, and for every single thing, and for all things. I would like to die in a moment of thanksgiving, murmuring "thank you, thank you". We thank you for what you are, because you are God, love, unity, Trinity; and because you are so understanding. And what a gift those words are: "If God knows everything, then I am not afraid." And I am so sure of his loving mercy. Do you not love those words, too? There is something so beautiful in this confession addressed to Someone who loves and understands.

The responsibility for the fault remains, but it is all imbued with the certainty that he understands and redeems all.

How is it possible to live without faith? I must get back into the habit of repeating, thousands of times, "Lord, increase my faith."

Will "Thank you!" be your watchword too?
In Ea, and that is all.

Human love, the image of God's love
(from a letter to a couple)

I cannot help being overcome by a wave of adoration. The Lord
has come down from heaven to bring love to the world; how
great is his success, every time a couple discovers this gift and
he is incarnated in them! Their love is union and Trinity.

The world around them may be in turmoil, but God's purpose
is accomplished: love is born again, and this is a triumph over
atheism and materialism.

All love is an outpouring of the Holy Spirit; but most lovers
ignore him. How surprised they will be to discover, in heaven,
that God came down upon them, united them, became flesh in
them and through them — that God is love.

I believe in one Love

How wonderful it is to know that God is love, and that he can be
and do nothing but love. Love is food and drink, life and breath,
a person and a way of being. I believe in one God — which is to
say, in one Love.

2. IN MARIAN COMMUNION

Mary in God's plan

To understand Mary's role and place in Veronica's spiritual life,
we must keep in mind that Veronica's constant desire to welcome
Mary stems not from a personal choice dictated by sentimental
preferences, but from simple obedience to God's plan. We must
welcome Mary because she is God's gift to us, because God has
willed her to exist for the good and the joy of humankind.

Some years ago, I wrote, in dialogue with Veronica, a book entitled *Mary the Mother of God*;* here I will reproduce an excerpt
which expresses the views that Veronica has repeated so frequently and insistently.

True devotion to Mary comes not from below, but from
above; it has its source in faith, not in sentiment. It is, first
of all, adherence to God, and acceptance of his plan. It is
integral to the single-mindedness of our intention with
respect to God. For Christian rectitude begins with a voluntary adherence to the plan willed by God; with a decision to
be on God's side as he traces the trajectory of his grace as
he sees fit. God has chosen to associate Mary with his work
of salvation. Through her, he gave his Son to the world.
This "order" is unchangeable: God does not withdraw his
gifts. Mary's maternal mediation is for all time, for it is part
of God's design.

Christ always did his Father's will. With immense love, he
entered the world in the way chosen for him by the Father.
We, as his disciples, must not hesitate to share his feelings
for Mary. Since it is God who chose her for his son and for
us, we do not need to choose her, but only to receive her as
our Mother. Her beauty and her goodness attract us; we
feel the need to turn to her; but we must be happy to yield
to God's will, above all through obedience.

This is the supreme reason for our devotion to Mary. It is
not for us to set limits to divine action, or to dispense with
the mediators whom he has freely chosen for us. It is God's
nature to love us with a love that is lavish in its abundance,
and to glorify his creatures by making them his instruments. In God there is room for every lavish excess; it is
only we who set limits and restrictions. Our filial devotion
to Mary is simply an act of thanksgiving for the lavishness
of God's love, of which she is the living and abiding proof.

* Faith and Facts Books, London, Burns & Oates, 1963.

It would be a serious mistake to consider Marian devotion a pointless excess which interferes with our worship of God. Such devotion is not a superfluous refinement, or a concession to imagination or to popular sensibility, or a cut-price means of salvation. It is, for us all, with no distinction, an integral part of God's plan for salvation.

Mary is God's law, but she is also his gift. This expression of divine will conceals a mystery of love; for Mary is the greatest of God's graces. Jesus said to the Samaritan woman: "If you only knew what God is offering!" That offering includes the gift of Mary; the mystery of the Son encloses that of his Mother. We must not hesitate to accept, from the hands of God, the one who is thus offered to us. To each one of us, God repeats the Angel's words to Joseph: "Do not be afraid to take Mary to yourself; what she has conceived is of the Holy Spirit." We must humbly receive this gift from the Almighty; we must welcome, with an open soul, all of God's love invested in Mary for her joy and for ours. All we need to know is what God willed for her, and for us through her. St Paul said that every Christian receives grace "in the measure of Christ's gift." What is the measure of Mary's grace? This is all we need to know, so that we may love her as God has loved her.

Veronica once wrote to me, continuing this train of thought:

We must turn to Mary, in the first place, not because she is good, but in obedience to God's plan — and also through compassion for God's holiness. Our prayers are not pure: our musical notes grate on the ears of the Father, the musician par excellence. We must let him hear the voice of the Immaculate, the only success story of human nature.

Mary has not lost her role of giving Christ to humankind. This role remains unaltered for all time; it is a truth which we must retain in our hearts. Mary is continuously giving birth to Jesus, in our hearts, through the power of the Holy Spirit. And it is the Holy Spirit who can unite us with Mary, so that, with her, we may live the life of Jesus.

Mystical union with Mary

A theologian's opinion

Accounts of Marian mystical experience can be found throughout religious literature, but in general these are not widely known. *La Vie d'union à Marie*, by Fr E. Neubert, a Marian theologian, includes several chapters on this subject. Fr Neubert analyses the way in which Mary leads faithful souls from a cold worship of the Blessed Trinity to a living devotion to the three divine persons.

> For souls blessed with the gift of Mary's presence, a new and powerful factor comes into play: an awareness of Mary's action within them leads such souls to experience the veneration, the tenderness, and the trust in Mary's heart. Loving Jesus with Mary's heart, these souls speak with her heart to the Father and to the Spirit. In a way, they are Mary speaking to the Father, confiding in the Father, praying to the Father, loving the Father, glorifying the Father; they are Mary contemplating, loving, honouring, and praying to the Holy Spirit.
>
> These souls, in union with their Mother, feel themselves to be all love; they perceive, much more clearly, how the relationships that bind together the three Persons are three loves that actually make up one single love.

To illustrate his thought, the author uses a personal testimony, but respects his witness's anonymity. In fact, these lines came from Veronica, whom he knew at one time. She had written to him:

> In my soul, I feel that I am Mary of Gratitude. I never cease to give thanks to the Holy Trinity for what it has done for Mary: to the Father, for creating her for his Son; to the Son, for accepting her as his mother; to the Holy Spirit, for taking her for his bride. Each time I say "In the name of the Father...," I must do so slowly, with veneration; for it is Mary, in me, saluting the Holy Trinity. I busy myself with external matters, I pay attention to conversations, but inwardly I remain close to Mary and to the Holy Trinity.*

Veronica's point of view

On April 5, 1948 — the Feast of the Annunciation — Veronica wrote the following letter to Canon Cordier:

> ...Still, I must tell you that I sincerely believe I yearn for the Lord a little more every day.
>
> He torments me incessantly; I feel that I shall only be at peace when I am at home, for all time, in Mary, happily lost deep within her Immaculate Heart. Then the Good Lord, the terrible Good Lord, seeking me and finding Mary first, will forget me completely — so great will be his Heart's delight at finding her! And then I can be at rest.
>
> But when I have the misfortune to step out of this holy tabernacle, even for a moment, it is so terrible! The Lord, good though he is, is relentless in the immensity of his love, and I feel crushed beneath its weight! Then those words of prayer, "Have mercy on me!" take on a different meaning. They mean "Draw back and leave me. Do not show yourself to me; for when you do, I see myself in your light, and the sight tortures me."

---

* *La Vie d'union à Marie*, Alsacia, Paris, 1954, p. 303.

But in Mary, through Mary, we can see the holiness, the divinity of God; she tempers and softens, as it were, the devouring fire which is the love of God in love with his poor little creature.

Also, curiously, when we are in Mary we never see ourselves. We are far too busy looking at all that she is doing in Heaven; we forget our selves. Oh! how restful that is!

Veronica explains her experience of this union
(excerpts from various letters to me)

I hope that our gentle Queen will allow you to live in her, in a wonderful way, during this holy time of Advent which is approaching.

Every word in your breviary will open wider and more beautiful horizons to you.

I am terribly luke-warm these days, but I make up for it as best I can by offering the Blessed Trinity my own Mother's heart, which is so pure and so passionately loving. Yes, she is all mine, and all that she has belongs to me. That is why I am not worried by my misery, or by my sins, or by how lukewarm I have become.

In union with Mary, we shall always be in a state of Deo gratias, and of *Domine non sum dignus* [Lord, I am not worthy]. A simple, profound and peaceful "thank you" contains a world of things. That is why I aspire to be the Blessed Virgin's "thank you" here on earth.

I imagine that she must be pleased with my poor efforts to thank the Father and the Son and the Holy Spirit for all that They have done in her and through her.

Being one with the Blessed Virgin

There has been a gradual change in my relationship with

the Blessed Virgin. She is no longer outside me, by my side; instead of loving her with all my strength, instead of praying to her, instead of offering her beauty and her perfection to the Holy Trinity, I feel that I am somehow one with her. She seems to be in me and I in her. We are united in a single being wholly turned towards Jesus, towards the Holy Spirit, towards the Holy Trinity.

I seldom think of her nowadays; but I am always very consciously with her, in the same orientation towards God and towards all that is of God in heaven and on earth.

Allowing Mary to empty us of our selves

To speak to souls in Mary means seeing, in each person who listens to me, not merely a listener, but "my child"; it means being convinced that the instrument of grace which will touch these people is not human eloquence, but the extent of my maternal love for each one.

The principle and the secret are always the same: action is fruitful when Mary empties us of our selves to make room for God. We must be Mary, so that Jesus may be at ease within us, so that he may act through us.

The Lord is happy to come and live in a soul which is established in Mary, for He is truly at home only in her.

Reflect on each word of the following passage by Fr Olier about Mary:

"The least share in Mary, the smallest participation in her grace, is a treasure far more precious than all that the seraphim and other angels and saints will ever say to God. There is nothing in heaven or on earth that can come close to that life, to that admirable inner world where every adoration, every praise, every love of the Church, of men, and of angels can be found; it is a thousand times more than all that all the creatures will ever give him. Such is the eminence of her grace and of her holiness.

"This is why we make more progress in increasing the glory of God, the good of the Church, and our own perfection through union with Mary than through any of the other methods or practices available."

Read these golden words by Fr Olier, and choose the path to holiness which you shall make your own: there can be no hesitation. Eternity will not be long enough to thank all those who have made known to us, and helped us to experience, this humble and hidden secret which is a path through which we may be filled, at every moment, with an overabundance of divine grace.

It seems to me that the whole secret is in the *nunc*, the "now" – the present moment – in the way that I feel somehow one with Mary. I too am "full of grace", so full that I can give and give without being impoverished; and this is because at every instant, all of her fullness becomes mine, if I so wish. And then the wonderful thing happens, in that second when I "become Mary" to such an extent that God, captivated by my beauty, murmurs: "This is my beloved daughter, with whom I am well pleased." And he gives himself to me, so completely that with him I can do anything, enriching all those whom I love with his gifts and his graces.

The fruits of union with Mary

How kind and gentle is our beloved Mother Mary; how generously she rewards us, in her dealings with us, for the smallest gesture of trust!

She has the courage to lead us along the path to Calvary; often she does not give us a single word of comfort or encouragement along the way; but if we show some good will and courage, how quick she is to lift the veil and allow us to glimpse the reasons and the purpose of what is happening!

After one has been at her school for some time, the supernatural world comes so near! At times, it becomes so luminous that I am tempted to believe that I have lost all my faith; for I see God's hand clearly in the smallest events of daily life.

Mary's humility

I can say calmly that I am humble, and I do not blush with shame; and yet I know that humility is the summit of perfection.

But nowadays, in these modern times, we know that there is little merit in reaching a summit: we can land up there easily, carried gently by an aeroplane. And this is exactly what has happened to me! Our Lady of the Air — the title may seem strange, but it is a true one — comes down to fetch you, in the valley where you are, and carries you off to her kingdom. All we have to do is be there, at the appointed time and place — preferably with as little baggage as possible.

Contrition and union with Mary

When I say to Mary "All I have is yours," I am offering her above all my faults, which are the only things that really belong to me personally. The Holy Virgin takes them and makes them her own; then, in a way, for a moment at least, I am immaculate.

When I am in union with Mary, I have the feeling that the Most Holy Virgin blames herself for my faults, whose number and malice she sees infinitely better than I can.

My contrition becomes the contrition of the Blessed Virgin — which is so much more perfect, because Mary's love is so much greater! What offends God is not the seriousness of the fault itself; it is the extent of the soul's unfaithfulness to a love which is infinite. It is in Mary that we experience the greatest sorrow for the least imperfection.

Here is an easy analogy: when a baby dirties the carpet, its mother is aware of damage which the child does not even suspect, and she offers her husband her own contrition!

Deliver us from evil

Increasingly, our gentle Queen fills my soul with a fear, a real dread of sin, especially of those little sins of thought which can so easily be overlooked. I probably commit several hundred each day; and they interfere with communion with the supernatural, and are an obstacle to the flow of grace in great waves over my soul, and, from there, to other souls.

As time goes by, I find that the final request of the Lord's Prayer reaches deeper and deeper within me. Deliver us from evil — yes, oh, yes, Jesus, Jesus: deliver me from evil! Evil is the only real obstacle in the world; and suffering of any kind is first and foremost a short cut to the Calvary where we all must die one day.

I am overwhelmed with gratitude to the One who has delivered me from so much harm.

Do you ever thank Him, with an overflowing heart, for all the sins you have not committed?

Mary and the Rosary

When I recite the Rosary, "in" and "with" Mary, she takes my prayer and transforms it. I am like the needle on a turning record: the needle is sharp and nasty — that's me; yet when it is plugged into Mary and in union with her, it is she who sings like a prima donna on the record of our Rosary.

The Rosary must be a communion with the concrete action of the Holy Spirit in each mystery.

307

The Hidden Hand of God

In union with Mary

I always speak as if the audience were hearing these things for the first time ever, and as if I were to die immediately afterwards. My maternal love for each person in my audience is the instrument of grace. Each listener is my child.

I tremble with joy when I see that our gentle Queen still uses me as she has in the past.

"Look not on my sins, but on the faith of your Church" — and your Church is, first of all, Mary.

"Lord, have mercy on me" — this is my constant prayer.

A few random thoughts, from various letters

Mary, Mother of God

The greater a reality is, the fewer words are needed to express it. Mary is the Mother of God — that is enough; the rest is silence.

I dazzle God by offering the Father to the Son, the Son to the Father, in Mary.

Depending on the Holy Spirit

In Mary, we must live in dependence on the Holy Spirit. When I speak, I am careful to remain in contact with her.

Mary and the Scriptures

We must offer God Mary's understanding of the Scriptures, without worrying about fully grasping every meaning; God enlightens in his own time.

Mary, the ultimate Mother

Our own mothers are only wet-nurses in comparison with Mary's motherhood. Mary has never lost her role.

Grace is not in the words you speak, but in your goodness, your union with Mary, your "motherhood". It is in Mary's womb that the Word became flesh.

Your soul is my business

People will say to you: "Mind your own business." Your answer is: "Precisely; your soul is my business."

Mary's humility

There are two kinds of humility. One is St Vincent de Paul's humility; he says, "I have done nothing." The other is Mary's humility; she says, "The Lord has done great things in me."

26

NATURE AND GRACE IN SYMBIOSIS

Inner life: In communion with God

Veronica lives simultaneously in the supernatural world and in the natural world. For her, there is no visible dividing line between the two: she is supernaturally natural and naturally supernatural, and there is no transition from the one to the other. This is the very opposite of a surface overlay of "supernatural plating".

To those who know Veronica well, this is the most striking thing about her: nature and grace are in full harmony within her, in vital unity to a rare extent. This is a key to understanding her life.

The secret of her intense apostolic activity lies above all in obedience to God, in attentiveness to his word, in communion with his will. For many years, Veronica has slept little and fitfully; she spends hours each night in prayer, listening to God – countless hours of prayerful reflection and of reading the Bible. Every book of her bible, from Genesis to the Apocalypse, is heavily underlined.

Now and then, an inner word arises within her and motivates her to initiate some project. If the initiative is an important one, she submits it to religious authorities to be authenticated.

Each day, she is nourished by the word of God which the Missal offers us. She often shares this word with others before beginning a conversation, even on the telephone.

Veronica is a contemplative living in the heart of the world; she feels perfectly at home in contemplative religious houses.

She lives in intimate familiarity with the saints in heaven, and very specially with St Paul; she conscientiously honours the saint of the day as prescribed by the Missal. She has introduced her friends and their families to her practice of choosing a "saint of the year", at random, to be each person's special protector; she asks each person to read the life of that saint, over the year, and to pray to him or her every day.

Veronica once pointed out to me, with great joy, a speech which Pope John Paul II gave to the Carmelites in Lisieux; he expressed beautifully the relevance and the youthfulness of saints.

"The saints," said the Pope, "never really get old.... They never lapse into obsolescence. They remain forever witnesses to the youthfulness of the Church. They never become characters from the past, men and women of yesterday; on the contrary, they are always the men and women of tomorrow, the men and women of the evangelic future of humanity and of the Church, witnesses to future worlds."*

Outwardly: In a state of mission

The rhythm of Veronica's apostolic work

Veronica's rhythm of work is unusually intense; she makes as many demands on herself as on those who work with her. She is aware of this — and has been for quite a while: in a letter dated August 15, 1949, she describes a so-called "holiday" which she took in a convent in Nice. I had spent a few days there with her and Sister Deslondes, president of the Legion in France, to prepare a document to be sent to Rome. Veronica ended her letter with these words:

Raymonde left on Saturday, *Monseigneur* left on Sunday. Apparently I have lost none of my ability to exhaust people; I think they were both delighted to leave me and get a little rest in Nevers and Malines.

---

* From a speech made on June 1, 1980, quoted in *Ce que croyait Elisabeth de la Trinité*, by Fr Jean Romy.

The rhythm at which she works is practically superhuman; only a supernatural input of energy can explain it. St Paul's words spring to mind: "They think we are dead, and yet we live."

In a letter written in 1950, Veronica tried to explain her gift of strength:

> I myself am the first to be amazed at the amount of nervous energy which is in me, and which overflows so abundantly the whole day long.
>
> I sometimes wonder if it is not some sort of supernatural strength, a manifestation of the gift of strength which Confirmation conferred on me.
>
> I very, very often pray for this special gift: "O, Holy Spirit, give me strength, give me strength." And I can almost feel my soul drinking in great draughts of energy and strength; for — would you believe it? — I am constantly being beaten flat to the ground, into the most profound and total weakness.
>
> Physically, I am continually in a state of overpowering fatigue; but prayer, Holy Mass, Communion, and very specially the Sacrament of Reconciliation, have a definite energising effect on me.
>
> My thirst for absolution returns more and more insistently; I am constantly on the alert, ready to receive this sacrament as often as I can — and that may mean several times a week!
>
> Do you ever receive an "extra" absolution, a very special one? You must have so many opportunities to see a priest.... Think of the effect on the whole Church; be more ambitious to enrich yourself, by every means in your power, every single day.

A similar comment on this combination of weakness and strength appears in a letter to Canon Cordier, dated September 20, 1946:

We must go not only to the limits of our strength, but beyond them; and we must do so every day, until Providence itself stops us.

Do you remember the picture of Our Lady of Abandonment, with the angels offering a chalice and a crown of thorns? Well, they are here, handing them to me; and now – now or never – I must smile and say thank you.

I think that when the heart is heavy with anguish and the horizon is very very dark, we do have some right to speak of Divine Love, of prayer, of trust, of abandonment, of thanksgiving...

The Sacred Face of our gentle Saviour is constantly before my eyes; and it seems to me that little by little, my soul begins to put on His sacred features.

Help me quickly to be at ease with suffering, for if I am not, our gentle Mother will not have the courage to continue. She will feel that she must give me a few sweets, instead of pieces of the true Cross.

In March 1950 Veronica wrote to me:

It is wonderful to be able to tell you that I am drained of all strength and all vitality, and to know that you will not believe me. The words "Just for today" are all that save me ("One day at a time; your grace is all I need").

Through Veronica, I have come to understand that "God is new each morning". We are too quick to assume that he is somewhere in the distant past; we forget that he is creating us at this very moment, that He causes the water of eternal life to spring forth before our very eyes, in all its newness and freshness.

I have often encouraged her – in vain – to take some time off. She lives St Paul's words literally: "Christ's charity is pressing us onward."

Many years ago, I wrote to Yvette Dubois about this:

> What a torrent of light our dear Veronica is; but how does
> she live? Perhaps one of these days the Lord will have to
> grant her the gift of at least trilocation; the gift of speak-
> ing in tongues; and a few other gifts...

I wrote this at least thirty years ago — well before the Charismatic
Renewal!

In another letter, this one to Veronica, I asked her to be gentle
to herself:

> Won't you be surprised when you get to Heaven and the
> angels say to you: "Sit down! It's time to rest!"
>
> How will you resist the desire to go to St Joseph and do
> something nice for him? — say a few kind words to him
> about those innkeepers in Bethlehem who would not let
> him in; or to St Dominic, to apologise for having forgotten
> for so long that he was Spanish; or to St Teresa, to ask her
> where exactly in Avila her convent was; or to St Ignatius,
> to ask him for precise details about the siege of Pamplona;
> or to St Patrick, to thank him for giving Ireland a faith as
> solid as the cliffs of Dover; or to Edel Quinn, to congratu-
> late her, with a hearty handshake, for managing to die so
> quickly, in spite of everything...
>
> And how will you ever resist the desire to smile and say
> a kind word to all those directors of institutes who refused
> to help you? And who will blush so deeply, when they see
> you, that Our Lady will cover them with her blue mantle
> as you go by, to keep you from noticing the colour rising
> in their faces!
>
> No, I really do not think you will ever be able to adjust.
> The only reassuring thing is that you will be in the king-
> dom of pure speed — of lightning thoughts, instantly exe-

cuted; of wishes fulfilled the moment they are formed. *Dixit et facta sunt* – no sooner said than done.

I wish you the most improbable thing: a little bit of rest.

I hope you will resolve to look up the word "holiday" in the dictionary – that would be an excellent resolution for you. We are all available to give you orally any additional information you may require as to the precise meaning of the word, with which you are evidently unacquainted. Perhaps you would understand it better if you looked it up in an English dictionary, since "holiday" means "holy day" – a day that is holy and must be sanctified. It does not have the implication that it does in French – the idea of doing nothing. Perhaps you could try to come up with some mixture of the English and French meanings!

One of our FIAT friends recently wrote to her:

I know that your physical strength is not what it used to be; but until your last breath, you will always have enough to light fires all around you.

Her directness in apostolic formation

Veronica leads her companions into apostolic action in a manner that is at once virile and maternal. Her obvious love gives her the audacity to disturb inertia, laziness and fear of obstacles. She likes to give the example of the Irish pony who answers marvellously to his master's whip, provided he knows that the master loves him.

One of her early collaborators once described her own reactions to "this force that does not crush, but rather expands":

Sister O'Brien is always on the alert to discover the will of God, and she is quick to focus our attention on things that we might otherwise have allowed to slip...

She is so simple that she can introduce the life of "union with Mary" to a passing beggar just as easily as to a very holy friend. With her, the one essential is trust: one must be able to let go of everything, as one lets go of a balloon.

She is direct, and her aim is straight and sure. Yvette Dubois once put it beautifully: "When she hurls a stone and it hits you hard, she knows just why she is doing it" — it is because she loves souls and she knows they will put these stones to good use. The extraordinary thing is that the stones she hurls never knock you out; on the contrary, they enlighten you and give you new energy — always provided that you receive them properly. Sister O'Brien never leaves things unfinished, no matter how painful this is; she searches, and searches again, until light is shed. You should see how willing she is to begin again and again with each soul, each time as if it were the first time.

This clear-sightedness, this direct way of thinking, this way she has of "hurling stones", are combined with great delicacy, gentleness and deep sensitivity. She can be very unsettling: each of these aspects could in itself make a rich personality, but in her they all come together, and the result is quite extraordinary. One should not pass her by and miss this grace.

A letter from Veronica to one of her co-workers provides an example of this directness:

> As I told you so "cruelly", there are many things that you lack. My greatest reproach to you is that you have been content to be good — not holy; they are not the same thing.

Veronica's sense of humour

Veronica has a startling and unique sense of humour. It is not

English humour, which relies so heavily on understatement; nor is it French humour, which likes to play with words and create epigrams. Veronica's humour is full of surprises; it has the daring to say aloud what others think but do not say. This fresh sense of humour has left many an audience in stitches, has overcome objections, has made old-fashioned bishops smile despite themselves, and has brought tears of laughter to the eyes of non-committal listeners.

Humour and humility are not far apart. In Veronica they have found a meeting point.

A few more excerpts

In a letter to Mme Roche, in Nevers, Veronica thanked her for her hospitality and then went on to discuss flying saucers, which at the time were on everyone's mind:

> I have yet to see a single flying saucer, despite my great desire to see one. No doubt I do not lift up my eyes to heaven often enough! But I am determined to be more vigilant in future. At any rate, I am quite ready to fly off on the first available one, to go and organise a little praesidium of the Legion of Mary among the Martians.

From another letter:

> So here I am in Madrid.
> To keep my sanity, I went out and bought myself an Agatha Christie: *Murder on the Links*. I shall bury myself in it before I go to sleep. A few gunshots and dagger thrusts here and there, two or three dead bodies at my feet — no doubt I shall be fresh and bright in the morning, and my day will suddenly seem quite easy and simple. Thank you, Agatha Christie: you have saved many generations of readers by plunging them headfirst into your

tragedies, which make our own seem insignificant by comparison.

She ended her letter with the words:

Heaven will be such a delightful place: rest, rest, rest. Meanwhile, however...

From Greece, she sent this letter to her little niece:

My dear Georgina;

Your aunt Lulu is writing to ask you to give your little brother a big kiss from her. She would also like you to write to her very soon, to tell her when the christening will take place. I don't know his name yet!

And find me a photograph of yourself, because I cannot imagine what you are like nowadays. I know that you have a nose, a mouth, and two eyes, but I would like to know what they all look like together on your face.

I work very hard trying to get people to love Jesus — people who do not know him at all. You can help me by being very very good today, and being very holy when you say your prayers.

Yesterday we had an earthquake here — your father will tell you what that means. All the walls and the furniture shook a little.

A telephone conversation

Veronica is very close to her youngest sister, Ruth. Although Ruth lives in France, they have not seen each other for a long time, but they often communicate by telephone:

RUTH: I will gladly come and see you in Paris when I have

a chance, but on one condition.
VERONICA: What is it?
RUTH: That you won't be too holy.
VERONICA: That's an easy thing to promise; too much of anything is always too much, and so it can't be good.... I'll just be holy.

Laughter from Ruth. Veronica added:

Besides, I am very obedient in these matters. The other day, just as I was going to see the doctor for a check-up, the Cardinal said to me: "And will you please talk to the doctor about your health, not about the Holy Trinity." Well, I was very obedient: I never said one word about the Holy Trinity. I only talked about the Eucharist.

If people only knew...

Veronica, hearing that people had used the word "holiness" in speaking of her, once said to me:

"Do you know what I was reminded of, when I heard about this? My final examination in education, at London University. After I had passed it, when I had my degree in my hand, I said to myself, "If this is what it means to be a university graduate, well, it's really no great thing – if only people knew!" And if holiness is what people say I have... well, it's not worth making a big fuss about!"

Post scriptum

When I had finished writing this chapter, I took up the Letters of St Paul, for my spiritual reading, and discovered a line which I had never noticed before. Writing to the Colossians, St Paul says: "Let your speech always be gracious, seasoned with salt, so that you may know how you ought to answer every one."

319

So St Paul has made humour respectable; and here again, Veronica can claim to draw her inspiration from him!

Leo Moulin gave a good definition of humour when he called it "an exquisite way of relativising oneself." Here is one last example of this sort of humour.

A few months ago, as I was working on this book, I said to Veronica:

> You once said to me, "Please never write anything about me — or if you do, make sure you include a complete list of my sins!" Well, now I am about to put you on the spot. I am writing pages and pages about you, despite your request; how can you explain the fact that you are letting me go ahead without protesting?
>
> "Oh," she said, "when I said no to any articles about me, I still existed; now, I no longer exist."

This liberating answer leaves me free to proceed, somewhat in the vein of Chateaubriand writing his *Mémoires d'outre-tombe*.

27

ON THE THRESHOLD OF ETERNITY

Like Anne at the Temple

Veronica feels that because of her advanced age, the time has come for her to give up the active apostolate, and to enter into the last phase of her life, following the example of St Anne: scripture tells us that from the age of eighty-four, Anne never left the Temple in Jerusalem (Luke 2:36-37).

In a letter dated February 2, 1983, Veronica wrote to Danielle Proux that she planned to follow Anne's example; she felt called

... never to travel far from the Temple,
to remain in the Temple,
and never to leave the Temple.

There, in the Temple, Anne invites me to seize every opportunity to praise God, to speak of Jesus the liberator of humankind — to give Jesus to the world. Inspired by the Holy Spirit, and blessed by the Cardinal, I am entering the Temple; and, lost in the Immaculate and Sorrowful Heart of Mary, I hope by the grace of God never to leave it again. And then, one day, I shall wake up in the Temple of Temples: the Holy Trinity! Amen, Alleluia, in Ea always.

Divine Providence fulfilled her wish in a manner as gracious as it was unexpected: friends of FIAT provided the ideal place for such a retreat, giving her the use of their country house.

Veronica has turned this house into her apostolic convent; here, with Yvette, she is living out the last years of her life.

The rhythm of Veronica's life is structured around private and communal prayer. Elisabeth Leseur once said, "A soul that uplifts itself uplifts the world." Veronica is a living illustration of these words: even her prayers continue to be universal and apostolic.

At the entrance to the chapel in her house, there are two paintings: Teresa of Avila is on one side, John of the Cross on the other.

With God, who gives joy to our youth

Veronica's life continues to be amazingly joyful, with a joy that springs from a deep inner source. In the course of her life, she has been spared neither physical nor moral suffering; but her spiritual gladness breaks through every barrier. She once said to me, at the entrance to the chapel, where she was going for the Adoration of the Blessed Sacrament:

"I am going to my Bridegroom; with him, I am twenty years old!"

Her joy is nourished primarily by long hours of meditation on the readings for the daily mass. On a piece of paper, she has noted every occurrence of the word "joy" in the year's liturgies. From her I learned that the word "joy" appears 580 times, and the word "love" 970 times. Her missal is the fountain of youth in which she refreshes herself daily.

In union with Mary's Magnificat

Veronica sings her thanks to God with Mary's lips and Mary's heart, in union with her in heaven. She once thought she heard the Lord inviting her to join in his mother's Magnificat, "the song to which the heavens listen in deep silence." Every half hour, she sings a chant which she herself composed, expressing Mary's thanks to the Trinity; those around her sometimes join in:

O thank you, my Father,
O thank you, my Son,
O thank you, my most Holy Spouse
For making us all one!

Once Veronica thought she heard the Lord say to her, "If you do only this well, in all the day, your day will have been a good one."

A yearning for Heaven

Veronica's spiritual life is marked by a charismatic gift which is quite unusual in our western tradition, though more common in the oriental tradition: the gift of tears.

I have never seen Veronica shed tears about herself, on account of some personal grief. They were always tears of emotion at the thought of the presence of God, who is already so near; an emotion that is intensified by her yearning for heaven. By suffering and going beyond the suffering, she lives concretely the words which Francis de Sales spoke and which Pope John XXIII made his own: "I am like a bird singing in a thorn bush."

Occasionally she has let fall a few words that revealed how close God is to her. "It is difficult to stay in this world," she once said to me; "the invisible is so near, so tangible, and the waiting is so painful."

At regular intervals, she sings:

Nearer to you, my God,
Nearer to you,
Every moment, every instant,
Nearer to you.
I want to give my voice,
I want to dance my joy!
Nearer to you, my God,
Nearer to you.

For Veronica, God is the shortest path between any two human beings. Like St Paul, she aspires to leave this world; but, like him, she is prevented by charity from asking God to hasten the hour.

One day, struggling to hold back the tears, she said to me: "I don't know how I am still alive; I am three-quarters in heaven."

She likes to talk, with enthusiasm and humour, about the little footstool she hopes to receive in heaven; from this vantage point, she believes she will be able to admire the saints in paradise from a respectful distance, and share in their joy. We all believe that the Lord has prepared for her, not a little footstool, but a place of honour in the front row; but we are far too polite to contradict her.

Here is something Veronica wrote to thank some friends for being so understanding about her yearning for heaven. The title is her own, as is the style:

Thank you, thank you, thank you

Blessed are you who understand
   that my gaze is turned towards the Promised land,
That I'm only "half here" and can almost see
   Jesus and Mary beckoning me!

A bit more ready
   to fight the good fight
With my files and my papers,
   till they all are set right.

A little more leisure to sit and dream
   of Heaven, and angels, and things unseen.
A little bit nearer that wonderful day
   when Jesus will call me "HOME" to stay.

Yes, blessed are you for letting me go,
and making me feel that it should be so.
Jesus is with you; Jesus is with me
and we all are "ONE" in the Trinity.

A pilgrimage of thanksgiving – June 1989

Since our first meeting in Lourdes in 1948, an International Centre of the Legion of Mary has been established in Lourdes, on Veronica's initiative. In accordance with her wishes, this Centre is both a meeting-place for legionaries, who come to Lourdes on pilgrimages from all over the world, and an apostolic centre for individual pilgrims and passing tourists. Legionaries in Belgium gladly raised some of the necessary funds. The original building – which has since been extended – was a gift from a hotel owner, Mme Colomer Soubirous, a relative of St Bernadette. The house has been placed in the competent hands of Mme Getten, one of Veronica's first collaborators. According to an article in the Legion's newsletter, Dublin considers this house to be "one of the major success stories of the Legion in France". For our part, I may add, we saw in this success a smile from St Bernadette.

Veronica and I had decided that before departing for heaven, we would go to Lourdes on a pilgrimage of thanksgiving. As I have mentioned, it was in Lourdes that the spiritual alliance which we have lived for almost half a century began.

Veronica and Yvette reserved rooms in the convent of the Assumption, which looks out on the Grotto; this allowed them to have a quiet and solitary retreat, without mingling with the other pilgrims.

I stayed in the house of the Chaplains. My programme for the retreat included a daily visit to the Grotto, in the late afternoon. On the eve of our departure, the heat was so intense that I decided to go in the late morning instead. At first, I mingled with the crowd of pilgrims and sick people in front of the Grotto; but almost immediately, some Belgian pilgrims recognised me and came to talk to me, very nicely, asking me to bless their rosaries, and so forth. I decided to move on and pray quietly, trying to preserve the anonymity I had hoped for. This proved to be impossible; I had to change places three times, moving from one part of the square to another. When, after these three attempts, I was approached by a charming pilgrim who told me that in Brussels he goes to the same barber as I do, and that he always inquires about my health, I decided that it was pointless to keep moving around; I left the square and headed for a shady spot where I could pray in solitude.

This is how I came to be sitting alone on a quiet little path, behind the Grotto, which leads uphill to the chaplains' house. At last I was alone and in the shade. I prayed for a long time, with my eyes closed and my FIAT rosary in my hand. When at last I opened my eyes, I automatically glanced at a person who had also come to pray on this shady path, only a few steps away from me. It was Veronica. She had decided, contrary to her initial intention, to come and pray near the Grotto; her search for a shady spot had brought her to the very same path. We were both amazed!

Together, we went to thank Our Lady of Lourdes; in the Grotto, close to the spring, an empty bench gave us a chance to sit down and sing, in the silence of our hearts, our jubilee Magnificat.

For us, this "coincidence" was a smile from Our Lady, a delicate attention which was both humorous and unexpected. It provided me with an opportunity, in that privileged place, to thank the Lord for all that went into weaving the patterns of my life — and in particular for that greatest surprise of them all which had its beginning in Lourdes in 1948. Thanks to that meeting, almost half a century ago, I discovered Mary's maternity, always at work, in the one who for me has been her most transparent image. She has helped me to experience the full alliance between the hierarchical Church and the charismatic Church in symbiosis.

The secret action of our infinitely loving Father

As I glance back over my past, I feel that I have no choice but to believe in the "Hidden Hand of God", at work in my life; in his attentive, loving, unfailing presence through the joys and the sorrows.

Jesus said: "If you believe, you shall see the glory of God." God keeps his word. Faith is a magnifying glass which helps us to see and to discover God, secretly and anonymously at work, in the chance events of human life.

In God, the incredible is true.

Gabriel Marcel has said that "Human life is like a sentence: its meaning is only clear after the last word has been spoken."

In the Advent liturgy, we recite this moving antiphon, which is at the very heart of our hope and of our faith:

> O Wisdom,
> You fill the universe
> And hold all things together
> In a strong yet gentle manner.

Towards the last stage

My goodbye letter to the people of my diocese included the following passage, which I would like to quote here, as a conclusion to this chapter.

> For me, the future is filled with the light of anticipation of the final encounter with the Lord.
>
> A few days ago, a stranger came up to me at the door of the Cathedral and asked me: "Should we be afraid of death?" I replied, "No. We are all going towards the Father's house; we are expected there, and so are all those whom we have known and loved here on earth. It is the supreme rendezvous; go to it with joy."

327

The Christians of the early Church awaited with impatience the glorious return of the Master. They were mistaken with regard to the time; but they were not mistaken in their intense feeling of expectation. This Advent is an integral part of all Christian life.

On her deathbed, St Teresa of Avila cried out: "Lord, it is time for us to meet." Only God knows when the hour of the encounter is to be. As for me, I am content to know that the choice of the moment will be dictated by God's mercy, which is always loving and attentive. Beyond death — that paschal transition — the God who awaits us is an infinitely loving Father, who comes to meet his child with arms open wide. In him, with Mary our Mother, in the communion of the angels and saints, we shall know a joy, a tenderness and a youthfulness that go beyond our wildest hopes.

28

THE HOLY SPIRIT, IN WHOM I REST MY HOPE

The future of humanity is in the hands of those who will know how to give future generations reasons to live and reasons to hope.

Gaudium et spes

As I look to the future, I cannot avoid stressing the role of the Holy Spirit in the Church of tomorrow. He is always "the life-giving Spirit," in the fullest meaning of the words. This is the idea I would like to emphasise by way of farewell.

The Holy Spirit in the Holy Church

The Creed speaks of the Church as "one, holy, catholic and apostolic". Of these four attributes, the most ancient is holiness; the Church is described as "holy" in the earliest versions of the Creed. It is likely that the earliest wording was: "I believe in the Holy Spirit, present in the Holy Church."* The holiness of the Church thus appears as the first gift of the Spirit. Our ancestors in the faith spoke of "Our Mother the Holy Church" for a reason – these words are not mere pious literature.

We believe in the spiritual motherhood of the Church, who brings us into life and into holiness. The Church of our faith is not simply the gathering, the sum of those who, whether individually or in community, claim to be followers of Christ. The Church has an existence, a substance, which precedes and goes

---

* See *Je crois à l'Esprit-Saint dans la sainte Eglise pour la résurrection de la chair*, by Pierre Nautin, Editions du Cerf, Paris, 1977.

beyond the conscious adhesion of believers to Jesus Christ and to the particular community to which they belong. She is both the community which we build together – "the Church is us" – and the matrix which carries us, the mothering community which brings us into the life of God, in Christ and through the Spirit.

The Church of our faith was born holy. Her holiness is not made up of the sum of the saints to whom she gives birth; it is her own holiness – the holiness of Christ and of his Spirit in her – which bears fruit in us. The saints are not admirable in themselves; it is God and God alone who is to be admired in the saints.

In this sense, the Church is a mediator of the holiness of God. She is a mother who gives birth to saints, who allow themselves to be fashioned and formed by her. Properly speaking, we do not need to "become" saints; rather we need to remain saints, and to grow in the initial holiness which we receive at baptism.

The Holy Spirit at the heart of the new evangelisation and of ecumenism

It is a recurrent temptation to think of the renewal of the Church in institutional terms – in terms of reorganisation, of readjustment of external forms, of a reform of structures – much as one would in dealing with human institutions. But although we are able to build canals and install pipelines, we are not able to make a spring gush forth.

Pope John XXIII did not deny the need for certain reforms; but he went to the very heart of the matter, to the source of living water, when he called on Christians to welcome God's gift so that a new Pentecost might be fulfilled in the Church. The Church is always in need of being refounded, at the very spot where she was founded: in the Upper Room, in the foundational experience which was the first Pentecost.

The renewal that we can expect from an actualisation of

Pentecost is not primarily an external renewal; rather it is a renewal at the very source — in the freedom we give to God to "Christianise" us, in depth, through his Spirit. All our ecumenical hopes of a return to visible unity for all Christians lie in this kind of renewal.

* * *

Let my final lines be a prayer of hope:

> Lord, give us
> eyes with which to see,
> hearts with which to love,
> and your breath to breathe.
>
> WHEN WE ASK FOR EYES TO SEE,
> we are asking you to give us your eyes,
> so that we may see the world,
> those around us and their history,
> and our own history,
> as you see them.
> Grant us the gift of corresponding to your thought,
> day by day and hour by hour.
> May we become, little by little,
> what you have created us to be.
> Let us adopt your point of view,
> your perspective.
> Make us amenable to your Word
> which enlightens and transforms all life.
>
> GIVE US HEARTS WITH WHICH TO LOVE —
> hearts of flesh, not hearts of stone —
> so that we may love God and our fellow human beings.
> Give us your own heart
> so that we may love truly, forgetting our selves.

331

We need to have your heart grafted into us
in place of our own hearts,
which beat so inadequately when others are at stake.
Let it be you, Lord,
loving through us.
Give us your heart to love the Father;
give us your heart to love Mary, our Mother;
give us your heart to love your brothers and sisters,
who are also our brothers and sisters –
those who live all around us on the earth,
and who sometimes press on us from all sides,
whether they know it or not.

AND GIVE US YOUR BREATH
so that we will not lose our breath along the way;
so that we may move forwards into tomorrow
without looking back, without measuring the effort.
Give us breath
so that we may live up to all that people –
and therefore you –
expect of us.
Give us breath to hope again,
as though life had just begun this very morning;
to hope against every wind and every tide
because of your presence and your promise.
We carry within ourselves all the suffering of humankind,
but also all its hopes.
Give us breath;
or rather give us your breath –
the Holy Spirit whom you sent to us from the Father,
the Spirit who blows wherever he wishes,
in gusts or in gales,
or as a gentle breeze,
when you invite us to follow your inspirations

and to act out our prayer
so that the Church of today
may be a witness to the world;
and so that the world may recognise Christians
by the serene light in their eyes,
by the warmth of their hearts,
and by that unflinching optimism
which flows from the hidden and unchanging spring
of their joyful hope.
Amen.

Index